Advance praise for Shrewdunnit

A wonderful collection by a gifted and thoughtful writer: a delight both to dip into and reread for insight and enjoyment…
Jonathan Elphick, author of *Birds: The Art of Ornithology*

A wide-ranging, warm-hearted and generous love-letter to wild things, near and far, Shrewdunnit *is a delightful and beguiling collection in the great tradition of local naturalists. It is alive with the mysteries that surround us, while showing us how nature is something cherishable and very close to home.*
Helen Mcdonald, author of *H is for Hawk*

A delightful diary of 'everyday Britain', seen through the eyes of one of our most perceptive nature writers.
Stephen Moss, author of *The Great British Year*

Conor's stories are gently beguiling, strikingly original. They speak from his heart to our souls and carry the profound wisdom of a thoughtful and perceptive observer.
Derek Niemann, author of *Birds in a Cage*

Shrewdunnit *is a delightful read, wonderfully crafted by a writer and naturalist at the top of his game. Conor Jameson takes us through the seasons in his own inimitable way, introducing us to an array of wild characters, at home and abroad. This is a lovely book, something to dip into at leisure or, as I did, to read cover to cover in just a few days. It's a must have for anyone with a passion for the countryside and an appreciation of great writing.*
Iolo Williams, author of *Wild About the Wild*

Conor is a man who hears cuckoos breathing. That should tell you all you need to know about this book. For most people, hearing that bird's unforgettable spring call would be thrill enough, but Conor's unquenchable curiosity is satisfied only by getting closer, seeing more and understanding better than your average wildlife enthusiast. And in Shrewdunnit, we reap the rewards. Like a magpie, Conor has collected an assortment of stories that sparkle with insight, imagination and affection. Nothing escapes his all-seeing eyes, whether it's in his garden (which is a veritable hotbed of murder, sex and violence), Kings Cross station or a park in Berlin. It's almost as if the wildlife chooses to reveal itself to Conor's appreciative gaze. Adventurous water shrews, troubled common lizards, neurotic blackbirds and devil-may-care stoats all put on private performances for him. And through his stories, we are privileged to share them.

Sophie Stafford, former editor of BBC Wildlife Magazine

Conor Mark Jameson is one of those people who, if they didn't exist, would have to be invented by SOMEONE in a world which so desperately needs his profound knowledge, his wise and amusing observations and his tireless campaigning on behalf of the natural world. In Shrewdunnit, Conor has written a book of great charm and variety – from day-to-day observations of common species throughout the year to the defence of vultures and the beleaguered migrating birds of Cyprus, from Conor's own English garden to his work in New Zealand, the Seychelles, Italy, Berlin and Cyprus, he involves us delightfully with his thoughts on a dazzling array of subjects and species while making the case powerfully for the importance of the preservation and restoration of an astonishing catalogue of species and habitats. Equally delightfully, the book is scattered with excellent advice on gardening, hedge planting, creating ponds and providing everything necessary to attract and look after birds – including how to turn an old football into a robin's nest. More than this though, the book gives an awe-inspiring insight into the work done by those who like Conor, work for organizations such as the RSPB – you cannot read it without a sense of gratitude.

Esther Woolfson, author of Field Notes from a Hidden City

Conor Mark Jameson

Conor Mark Jameson has written for the *Guardian, BBC Wildlife,* the *Ecologist, New Statesman, Africa Geographic, NZ Wilderness, British Birds, Birdwatch* and *Birdwatching* magazines and has been a scriptwriter for the BBC Natural History Unit. He is a columnist and feature writer for the RSPB magazine, and has worked in conservation for 20 years, in the UK and abroad. He was born in Uganda to Irish parents, brought up in Scotland, and now lives in England, in a village an hour north of London. His first book, *Silent Spring Revisited,* was published in 2012 and his second, *Looking for the Goshawk,* in 2013, both by Bloomsbury.

He is a recent recipient of a Roger Deakin Award from the Society of Authors. When not campaigning for a better, safer planet, and writing sketches such as those you find here, he tries to find time to tinker with shrubs, and look for goshawks in a variety of habitats.

Shrewdunnit

The Nature Files

Conor Mark Jameson

PELAGIC PUBLISHING

Shrewdunnit: The Nature Files

Published by Pelagic Publishing
www.pelagicpublishing.com
PO Box 725, Exeter, EX1 9QU, UK

978-1-907807-76-3 (Hbk)
978-1-907807-75-6 (Pbk)
978-1-907807-77-0 (ePub)
978-1-907807-78-7 (Mobi)

British Library Cataloguing in Publication Data
A catalogue record for this book is available from the British Library.

Jacket artwork by Delphine Lebourgeois
www.delphinelebourgeois.com

This one's for Mum

Contents

Preface

Recently, I found a rare gem of a book in the Royal Society for the Protection of Birds (RSPB) library. It's called *The Vertebrate Fauna of Bedfordshire*, by J. Steele-Elliott. It was published in 1901, and just 150 copies were printed, which may say something about the niche this precious little record occupied then. This copy is number 77, issued and signed over to Howard Saunders, Esq. (who may have later donated it to the library) by the author himself. 'Bedfordshire in the hands of the Zoologist has received less attention than almost any other county,' it notes in the preface.

The book is full of revealing old records of species found here then, some of them long gone. I love that corncrakes – or land rails, as they were then known – disturbed the author's sleep as he camped by the River Great Ouse here at my village. 'I was kept awake a considerable time by one so vociferous, that it caused me to seek an interview; it was found perched on top of a tall hawthorn hedge, to which, much to my disgust, after being disturbed it soon after returned.'

He may not have guessed that a century later the land rail would be unknown not only in the village but in the county, and indeed virtually all of mainland Britain. Had he done so, he might have been more forgiving of its antisocial, nocturnal raspings.

Tis like a fancy every where
A sort of living doubt
We know tis something but it ne'er
Will blab the secret out.

John Clare, from *The Landrail*

Steele-Elliott, needless to say, had the best of intentions with his book. 'In conclusion,' he writes, 'let me hope that in making these notes public they may promote a further interest in the study of Natural History within the county, and if possible to kindle the flame of such knowledge...'

I feel I'm carrying that sputtering flame now, a hundred years or more later. Mr Steele-Elliott is one of the guiding spirits through this journal, along with W.H. Hudson, John Clare, Rachel Carson and others. I will be comparing notes with these luminaries and others as I go along.

Today, this part of the village is essentially just one long street, off the A1 (the Great North Road of Roman times), with houses from many periods lining it on both sides, punctuated with working farms, and laced with mature trees. It's separated from the church end of the village, close to the junction of the rivers, by the A1. We have woodland, parkland, sheep, cows, horses, chickens, ponds, old walls, churches, pubs that are now houses, ditto blacksmiths and tanneries, crops, scruffy pastures, hedgerows and spinneys.

The house I live in is semi-detached, the last before the open fields. It has generous garden space, front and rear. Beyond, there are a few more farms and then the railway. The station was closed, as many stations were, in the 1960s. There is a level crossing which takes the walker or cyclist across the tracks to a fork in the road, both leading to more farms and dead ends to vehicular traffic. There are then bridleways, and the disused airfield, a secret place in World War II, used back then for flying spies and supplies to the Low Countries in the dead of night. Beyond that is the greensand ridge – our local uplands – whereon the RSPB has its headquarters at The Lodge, Sandy.

This book is about everyday, lowland Britain, and forms a record of some of the things I've done in my garden and on mostly short – but some longer – trips that involve wild nature, and captures some of my thoughts about them. I hope the reader can connect with some of the things I describe, and can enjoy a similar connection with nature in everyday life – if this isn't the case already – wherever they are.

CMJ
Bedfordshire
Spring 2014

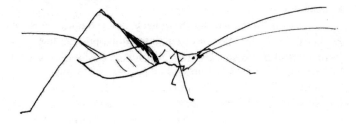

Acknowledgements

I am sure that hundreds of friends and colleagues have shared in or contributed in some way to the files in *Shrewdunnit*. These are just a few, and I thank you all.

Carry Akroyd, Cliff Andrews, Umberto Albarella, Brigid Allen, Elizabeth Allen, Rainer Altenkamp, Guy Anderson, Sue Ansell, Mark Avery, John Barrett, Neil Barton, Richard Bashford, Alfredo Begazo, Chris Bettles, Dorothy Bettles, Mont Bettles, Tim Birkhead, Lynn Blackadder, Richard Bodmer, Chris Bowden, Rachel Bristol, Richard Bradbury, John Brown, Catherine Buchanan, Peter Buchanan, Abi Bunker, Dan Burnstone, Carles Carboneras, Pete Carroll, Clare Chadderton, Chipangura Chirara, Dan Clark, Paulina Clark, Mark Cocker, Paula Cocozza, Martin Collinson, Dominic Crawford Collins, Jason Cowley, Rob Cunningham, Steve Dakin, Ian Dawson, Paul Donald, Euan Dunn, Tommy Durcan, Mark Eaton, Jonathan Elphick, Aniol Esteban, Sara Evans, John Fanshawe, James Fair, Andre Farrar, Viktar Fenchuk, Rob Field, Graeme Gibson, Gillian Gilbert, Stephen Gosling, Jenny Green, Richard Gregory, Emma Griffiths, Mark Gurney, Rachel Hammond, Sandra Hanks, Martin Harper, Sheena Harvey, Katya Hauptlorenz, Malcolm Henderson, Alison Hibberd, Richard Hines, Ben Hoare, Deirdre Hume, Rob Hume, Robert Hume, Lizzie Infield, Richard James, Kathleen Jameson, Kevin Jameson, Shelley Jofre, Lynne Myfanwy Jones, Rosamund Kidman Cox, Andrew Kitchiner, Marcus Kohler, Giles Knight, Clive Knott, Lars Lachmann, Rob Lambert, John Lammie, Clark Lawrence, Richard Lawrence, Linda Lear, Christopher Lever, Ceri Levy, Toni Llobet, Vladimir Malashevich, Mick Marquiss, Stephen Mason, Nigel Massen, Teresa McCormack, Bob McGowan, Duncan McNiven, Gary Melville, Jeanie Messenger, Suzy Mills, Alec Milne, Patrick Minne, Heather Mitchell, Allison Moorhead, Isabel Moorhead, Stephen Moss, Ian Newton, Tom Newman, Derek Niemann, Barry Nightingale, Ben Norman, Stacia Novy, Martin Oake, Old Frank, Val Osborne, John O'Sullivan, Kieron Palmer,

David Payne, Adar Pelah, David Pennington, Juliet Pennington, Giovanna Pisano, Rebecca Porter, Richard Porter, Amanda Proud, Eric Pyle, Sarah Richards, Roger Riddington, Ian Robertson, Norrie Russell, Cinthya Rynaby, Chris Rollie, Steve Rowland, Norbert Schaffer, Nirmal Jivan Shah, Edith Shaw, Innes Sim, Martin Sreeves, Robin Standring, Rowena Staff, Sophie Stafford, Lucy Stenbeck, Sue Steptoe, Jim Stevenson, Caroline Stroud, Dan Sturdy, Sylvia Sullivan, Jose Tavares, Nat Taylor, Russell Thomson, Martin Todd, Ralph Underhill, Alan Vaughan, Jo-Anne Vaughan, Terence Vel, Pat Vesey, Ray Badger Walker, Patrick Walsh, Joshua Wambugu, Mark Ward, Alice Ward-Francis, Bobby White, Ellen Williams, Graham Wilton-Jones, Marie Winn, Richard Winspear, Sam Wollaston, Derek Yalden, Matthew A. Young.

Thanks also to *BBC Wildlife* magazine, *Birds* magazine (now *Nature's Home*), *Birdwatch*, *Birdwatching*, the *Guardian*, *New Statesman*, the *Ecologist*, *British Birds*.

To the Whitbread family and Southill estate staff for kind permission to repeat the historic 50-year nesting survey.

And thanks especially to Sara, for all your love and support, again.

Foreword

What I like about Conor and his books is his obvious liking for people, and his determination to enjoy their company and their knowledge, be they the people next door, local farmers, writers, artists, or high-ranking scientists. You only have to look at the names – and the number of them – in his acknowledgements.

Being with Conor – out and about or in the office – keeps you on your mettle. He asks a lot of questions, seeks whatever he can winkle out that might be of use or interest to him. But he always gives you more in return. An hour outside, or a few minutes chatting over coffee, is usually enough to get you thinking for days.

Conor also pays homage to many past authors, the sort of writers and naturalists that others too easily forget: there have been many great communicators before, and I'm delighted that Conor is inspired by them, and quick to say so.

His observations often concern wild creatures that are fast disappearing, but he rarely admits to being depressed: he remains determinedly upbeat and optimistic, in the main. And he writes a good deal about conservation successes, too, and the people who can take credit for them. But most of all he writes about his own place in the scheme of things – the way he creates a new hedge, or a pond, how he engages with local people, how he finds things out, learns to identify what he sees and then goes on to find out that bit more – that important bit more, beyond mere naming of the animals, farther than most of us generally go. And, as you will see when you read this book, he just writes supremely well, so often crafting a phrase, a sentence, or a passage, that makes the reader think 'I wish I could write like that'. I wish I could.

Conor's is a rare talent, one that seems so simple, but that he works on long and hard to perfect. This new book is a joy, and we can all feel grateful that he has given us the opportunity to benefit from his wisdom and his delight in the natural world around him.

Rob Hume

Introduction

As I'm sitting down to write this, the sky is cloudless on the May Day bank holiday weekend. I'm aching satisfactorily from a day in the garden yesterday, dawn till dusk attending to odd jobs and ongoing maintenance. I can see badger scat on the grass below, beyond the bird bath and the clump of cowslips. The ash trees are sending out their buds in the front hedge. Wisteria flowers graze the windowsill in front of me, their petals pecked in places by birds. The pair of house sparrows probably responsible are mating in the hedgerow, close to the rusty tin pot in which they are both building a nest; although the receptacle was intended for robins.

Author Jay Griffiths is on the radio, talking about the issues around modern-day Western children's disconnection from nature and wildness. Looking across the road beyond the hedge to the play area opposite, I become aware that the bird chasing flies among the molehills and dandelions is a yellow wagtail. I reach for the binoculars and watch it more closely, to admire its slender, lemon-coloured head and tapering body and its flicking tail. Another returning migrant has made it back. I heard the first of them calling overhead a couple of days ago, and am pleased to get a closer look at this one, which has stopped off for a replenishing snack.

Yesterday, on a short bike ride, I flushed a turtle dove near the disused airfield, back to one of its few remaining haunts in the county. I was thrilled, relieved and surprised to see it. I also got a rare view of not just one but two nightingales that I surprised near the spinney, which has been a traditional site for them, just along the road. I can hear them from bed, though for some reason I couldn't hear any song from them last night in the hours before dawn and before the blackbirds and the robins started up.

Beyond the play area is a huge field growing grass, with a pheasant's head and neck just visible within it. To the right of that is a crop of oilseed rape, already a blanket of custard yellow, mirroring the wagtail and the dandelions, on an industrial scale. The bird scarer bangs out its regular salvo warning to the woodpigeons, and none take off in response. Rooks commute to and from their colony in roadside oaks and poplars to the west, languid against the blue. The occasional swallow races through. The house martins are as yet unaccounted for, missing in action. I'm very conscious of their absence from the avian traffic. A buzzard surges upward, circling higher, wings raised above the horizontal as though in exaltation. I wouldn't have seen that when I first moved here.

This book is about getting back to – and in among – nature, while remaining within sight of suburbia. In my case, this means the twinkling lights of the Fallowfield new-build estate on the southern horizon, which let me know that the small A1-spliced town of Sandy is advancing steadily north across green space towards my tiny village. A bit like the posse that tracked Butch and Sundance, day and night. Only slower. I hope. 'Who *are* those guys…?'

I found the poems in the fields,
and only wrote them down.

John Clare

Southern Solstice

Chapter One

January

A THOUSAND YEARS IN A GARDEN

The name Station Road does not immediately conjure an image of a rural place, but, if it helps, my Station Road has no station nowadays. This was closed to passengers in the 1950s, and to freight a decade or so later. Some stray evening primrose stems and a ground-creeping Boston ivy are remnants of the buildings and garden that once were here.

Station Road follows a line of alluvial soil, which penetrates a sea of blue clay under the open fields around. The alluvium is fertile, workable soil, deep and dark. The clays, meanwhile, are like Plasticine when wet, and hard as Bakelite when dry. My instinct was that our road had been long inhabited, surrounded by scrubby wetlands, long before these had drainage ditches gouged out of them.

I've dug this alluvium many times, but not to the depth I had to reach to meet the building regulations for a new soakaway. I was about halfway to the 1.2 metres required, where the dark soil starts to become paler and more gravelly, when I unearthed an earthenware socket, like the neck of a narrow jar. I might not have thought much more of it, but the depth at which it was lying made me curious.

I later cleaned it, and took photographs. I sent these to the county archaeologist, and awaited a response, expecting little. His email message a day later brought me up short:

> *The pot shard in your photos is a handle from a St Neots ware socketed bowl* [he revealed, with reassuring exactitude]. *It's Saxo-Norman (tenth to twelfth century) in date, but probably post-Conquest rather than earlier. It looks in good condition, not something that's been knocking around, so you may have actually dug into a medieval deposit. There is evidence for Saxon medieval settlements along Station Road, not least the excavated moat in Tempsford Park, so while your find is not unexpected it is interesting and useful evidence that medieval archaeological deposits do survive elsewhere nearby.*

My enthusiasm for history has been re-fired by the find. I took a book called *The Common Stream* by Rowland Parker down from my shelves, to get reacquainted. It is the history of the village of Foxton, not far from here. It could be the story of many villages. The book itself was a chance find for me, in a charity shop in Scotland, back when I still lived there. By further chance I found I had settled in Foxton's vicinity when I arrived in England. It helped me feel a sense of place and belonging. The bowl handle find has helped even more. I love the idea that someone else might have liked living right here, a thousand years ago, and that the charring on their bowl handle is still visible today.

THE HEDGE OF REASON

It's official. The hedge is back in fashion. This is largely thanks to the efforts of conservationists, and the RSPB's backers. We have persuaded most of the population – including those in a position to make a difference – of the value of a good hedgerow for wildlife. They also, in most cases, look nice too.

Wildlife, as a general principle, thrives on the edges of habitats, and hedgerows are often very much like the edges of woods. Without the wood, of course. It's heartening that they are springing up in the farmed countryside again, after years of taxpayer-funded persecution. We might never replace all 118,000 miles of hedge that have disappeared from the British landscape since 1950, the year my house was built, but we can compensate as far as possible.

Having said all that, there are hedges and there are hedges. And I've recently been involved in taking out a hedge. The hedge in question was a monoculture of *Cypress leylandii* in my back garden. I had developed very mixed feelings about it – as mixed as this particular hedgerow was unmixed. When I arrived here, it was already a monotonous green textured wall, really, and an increasingly large one. It ran almost the length of one side of the garden, about 30 yards of it in all. It was higher than the optimal height for these things – around seven feet – and formed a solid boundary between our house and next door.

According to the previous owner, its primary purpose was as a barrier. He'd planted it basically to assert the privacy of his domain, much as had been widely done in the eighteenth and nineteenth centuries through the enclosure of common land. There's often politics, as well as wildlife, in a hedgerow.

The meaning of gardens has changed over time. These may have been small holdings and drying greens for the war generation, social spaces for the exchange of local gossip and root vegetables, but this was now the 1980s. Private ownership had arrived. Shrub roses were replacing vegetable plots, twirly washing lines were being planted, and regiments of cypress were supplanting rows of carrot.

By the time I arrived, the green wall was resolutely up. The hedge had already reached a difficult age. Cypress trees are just that – trees. They are straining every resinous fibre to be 100 feet tall, and quickly.

My feelings about what was now my hedge, and my responsibility to control, were mixed because, while I wrestled and teetered twice-yearly with vintage shears on an even more vintage step-ladder (with 'Alfie', the name of a former owner, lovingly carved into it) to keep it in check, I recognised its shelter-giving properties, both for me and for nesting birds, notably blackbirds, dunnocks and greenfinches. And although not exactly a tapestry of wildlife interest, it certainly offered a significant degree of privacy. I could sit on my side of it in a deckchair in underpants if I wanted to, in splendid solitude, at any time of year.

But somehow this wasn't enough. From my garden seat I could – and often did – daydream that instead I was gazing upon a different kind of hedge. In my mind's eye I envisioned a flourishing parade of hawthorn, blackthorn, holly, beech, wild privet, yew, elm, wild pear, gorse, hazel, maple, hornbeam (was I being greedy, do you think?) and guilder rose, laced with dog rose and honeysuckle, wild flowers woven into its base, with here and there a gangly ash sapling protruding skywards from the tangle. A bit like the one I had had the foresight to plant in the front garden as soon as I arrived here, for example. It needs management too, but it rewards me with its ever-changing buds, blossoms, fruits, insects and, yes, nesting birds as well, buried in its midst in summer, with loitering sparrows and foraging blue tits visible within the barer parts of its framework in the cold months.

The car on the roadside is increasingly obscured by the hedgerow plants I installed. I got these 'whips' from Cambridgeshire County Council's nursery, a mix of thorns and field maple, with some hazel, dogwood, dog rose and wild privet. I was delighted to find an old hawthorn stump refusing to submit and sending up fresh stems, and traces of blackthorn too, when I removed some stray cypresses. The immaculately maintained elm hedge next door also sent a sucker under the path that separates our two gardens, to add to the diversity and help make the link between our two hedgerows.

I added some *cistus* plants, for a Mediterranean 'maquis' feel, for scent in the summer sun, and for year-round green and drought-tolerance. I also decorated the hedge bottom with primroses, and slipped a few snowdrop and bluebell bulbs between gaps in the plastic, disguised with some leftover gravel.

Elsewhere, the garden path has been lined with lavenders, broom and box. A cutting of gorse rooted well, added in the corner, where I should be able to see the sunlight radiating from its golden flowers. And nearby I squeezed in a plump foxglove, fattened and ready to produce a flowering spike the following spring. In due course foxgloves with gorse will remind me of Dumyat, the hill that glows as the summer sun sets over Stirling.

Sitting there, at the back, I would rue the years of prevarication that had left me still confronted by this mostly lifeless partition of unchanging green that was indifferent to the seasons; like wallpaper for the garden – albeit wind- and neighbour-proof. It would take so long for the replacement to grow, I had told myself. Could I face all those years of exposure?

And then I hit on a compromise solution. I would phase it out and phase in the new hedge. Brilliant!

So, I began my own back-door habitat restoration scheme, a bit like a scaled-down version of the RSPB's work to extract modern spruce from ancient bog land. Okay, it wasn't really much like that at all, but it brought it to mind. In the first tentative thinning of the cypress hedge, I removed every second tree, to be used as biofuel (some people still call this firewood). And I began to phase in the new hedge mix.

Predictably, it made slow progress in the first year. The remaining cypresses soon spread themselves into the gaps so, to hasten progress, I removed all their branches on the near side. It now looked like a cross-section of a cypress hedge – a bit Damien Hirst, really – but I figured that the surgery would lessen its competitive edge, maintaining the wind break while giving the new whips a fairer share of the sunlight.

And then, as the young mix inched higher, I bit the bullet and stripped the cypresses of their remaining branches, leaving the wood-ribbed, knobbly trunks in place as posts, as markers, dead woods, climbing frames for creepers, whatever.

The spring was a washout for many things, but for grass-growing it was nirvana, and grass types like bents and fescues soon bristled from the seedbed, at first a sheen of lime green, then a coat, and then a mop, ready for its first trim. I went for a seed mix to suit a thinner soil and endure the rainless phases of an eastern summer. I wasn't looking for Astroturf: I wanted character. This is on the southern side of the house, and I hoped the loose, fine soil would encourage delicate annual wild flowers and inhibit vigorous perennials.

Magically, creeping camomile appeared, and to help it establish and spread I carefully mowed around it, and the bird's foot trefoil that soon followed. Grasshoppers colonised, from who knows where. And the final seal of approval in late summer was a juvenile yellow wagtail, accompanied by a more streetwise juvenile pied wagtail, passing acquaintances blown in on a westerly wind, looking for insects on the sward.

So, that's it. My garden is finally laid largely bare again for all to see, inspect, comment on, gossip about. But they had better be quick, because the new-generation mixed hedgerow is coming. It is well on the way to realising my vision. It may not yet be ancient, but it is already species-rich. And I'm not too worried if it will never be 100 per cent year-round neighbour-proof. I like my neighbours. And besides, I figure they'll be too busy inspecting and enjoying their side of the new hedge, and what it produces, to bother looking over or through it at any strange fellas in deckchairs.

Notes made for successful hedge planting

As more and more of the stewards of our countryside realise the value of hedgerows in landscape, wildlife and amenity terms, so too can the gardener help to put back hedgerow species and the life they sustain. Most gardeners have boundaries to manage: perhaps a *Cypress leylandii* hedge that has been mismanaged or has reached unruly proportions. These walls of green can be great places for wildlife to shelter, roost and nest, but they are often a source of tension between neighbours and outstay their welcome. Long-term headaches can be avoided by replacing these with a more traditional, varied hedgerow.

Where privacy is important, a few *leylandii* have their place. Birds like song thrushes and dunnocks often like to nest in them. But there are also native species such as beech, holly and wild privet that keep their leaves all winter. The mixed hedgerow is a weatherproof alternative to panel fencing, but will also allow the pleasure of selecting the species to plant and of watching them grow and develop, season by season, year by year.

Here are some of my tips for hedge planting:

- Go for a rich diversity with a solid thorn theme running through it – hawthorn and blackthorn laced with holly, guelder rose, dog rose, spindle, wild privet, cherry plum, dogwood and beech, for example. I have also found yew to be a wildlife-friendly evergreen native alternative to cypress trees, and box can be good too, though slow-growing.
- Plant in winter.
- Put plants in at 45 degrees, to encourage a denser growth.
- Plant in two rows, ideally, spacing plants about 18 inches apart in each direction.
- Reduce unwanted competition from grass and other plants by using a recycled mulch, such as old plastic sacks.
- Don't water too much, except in the first year or two during droughts.
- Prune hard each winter, down to a strong shoot, to promote thick growth and prevent gaps low down.

- When established, trim the hedge on alternate sides each year, but not when it is flowering or fruiting.
- Taper the sides into an A-shape to let light reach the bottom.
- Consider laying the hedge when it has matured, about a decade on.

POUR YOURSELF A LARGE ONE

Garden ponds can be idyllic. They are refuges for increasingly uncommon things, sequestered from the cut and thrust of the outside world, with its pollutants, its vagaries of weather, its drainage operations, its large predators. Anything that holds water can bring life to a garden, whatever its size. You learn about birds, and much more besides.

You can learn a lot about the principles of providing water by putting out a bird bath – any small, shallow, bowl-shaped receptacle. You realise it needs regular topping up and cleaning. That algae swamps it – in warm weather – almost as quickly as the birds get into the habit of sipping from it and immersing in it. And that the smaller and shallower it is, the faster water evaporates from it.

A cool, shady damp corner can add a new dimension. I've provided piles of sticks, logs and leaves and piles of weedings or grass cuttings on an old polythene sheet. Amphibians and insects gravitate to this. Any old receptacle will do for amphibians to hang out in through the warmer months. A basin, bucket, sink, planter or bath tub sunk in the ground and given a bit of overhanging cover will surely sustain life.

Among debris in the back garden of my house I found the original cast-iron bath. Standing in the corner, it was unsightly. Sunk in the ground, bordering the lawn, it became a habitat. I added pond-weeds in pots, to help oxygenate it. Partly shaded, the bath retains its water effectively. I added slabs on one edge, to allow sparrows to sip from it and me to peer into it.

The first summer, a small frog took up residence on the lip of the shallow end, and could be seen until the chill air of autumn sent it into cold storage. I looked for it this spring, and sure enough in March it resumed its bathside vigil: soaking up the warmth, absently engulfing unwary insects, getting steadily bigger, plopping into the weedy drink if I got too close. Perhaps next year it'll journey the 20 feet to one of my 'real' ponds to breed.

In a previous garden, the first pond I made was too shallow. In my haste and excitement, I dug a big hole, lined it with old carpet, slid the butyl liner into place, added a thick layer of soil and turned the hosepipe into it. Result? A half-filled bomb crater effect.

Frogspawn appeared, some sort of thumbs-up, and the initial algal bloom was overtaken by pondweed proliferation. But, deep down, I wished it held more water and was properly shaped, and that the surface was flush with the surrounding landscape. Pond plants soon turned my starter pond from consommé to salad. Mental note: too much soil in pond.

Enter Boswell, next door's usually mild-mannered golden retriever. One afternoon, in the vicinity of my pond, he answered some primeval stirring and wrecked it. I consoled myself that this was the excuse I needed to start again. With a bigger butyl liner. You need more than you think.

Pond (mark II) was in a different league. With so much more water capacity, it maintained a more constant temperature. Channelling rainwater from the roof via a water butt and lengths of old guttering meant there was less of an algae problem to deal with in the early stages. There's also something really gratifying about saving and using your own water. And I was able to make a better shallow shelf around the edge – which is important for marginal plants and for allowing birds and other visitors access.

Among its graduates was one *enormous* beetle, which I took to be a great diving beetle, devourer of tadpoles and fish, but found, on netting it, to be what the *Observer's* book told me was the even bigger – but vegetarian – great silver beetle, described as local and scarce even in this, the 1963 edition of *Pond Life!*

A southern hawker dragonfly visited to lay its eggs. This large greeny-blue and black species does its *ovipositing* – as it's called – with great delicacy and precision, in this instance on some dead wood at the water's edge. Two summers on, a mass exodus took place as, one after another, gruesome little monsters dragged themselves up stems and squeezed out of their skins as adults, much as they must have done in Jurassic swamps, only smaller.

But perhaps the biggest thrill was a small grass snake, little bigger than a large earthworm, winding through the duckweed. I recall watching it ducking under, and a newt flipping out.

And then there were the wild flowers that the damp margins produced. The diversity in such a small area was extraordinary. Loosestrife, irises, rushes, mimulus. The breeze across the surface could almost have been whispering their names, carrying with it aquatic smells – the mint and the mud – that even our vestigial sense can detect.

Where I live now, I have applied the water gardening experience in a more rural setting. I've been greedy, and, as well as the bath tub, I have installed a large planter, one large pond, one smaller pond (I patched up the liner perforated by Boswell), and one pre-moulded fishpond, which was there when I arrived. I made the latter less formal by taking the paving slabs from around it and replacing them with turf from another part of the garden. This makes it slightly less rectangular and may even provide more natural food for the fish, which keep well hidden, but are definitely still in there. I can tell that by the appearance of the water, which is never clear, and never seems to have any life in it except the fish, which make the occasional swish as they sense me approaching. Murk – and otherwise lifelessness – is often the sacrifice you make if you want to keep fish. I think a wild-life pond holds more surprises.

I've come to realise just how important ponds are for farmland birds, especially seed-eaters. The pond nearest the open fields at the end of the garden is a regular watering hole for corn buntings, gold-finches, greenfinches and, in particular, linnets. Linnets eat nothing *but* seeds, from the day they hatch. Common sense tells me that an unrelieved diet of seeds would be a thirsty one, especially in late summer. Talk about spitting feathers. Small wonder ponds prove such oases. My pond has even brought in a reed bunting. Yellow-hammers are nearby all year but, if they come to drink, they must do so when I'm not around.

Most old farm ponds have, regrettably, been dried up by changes in farming. I'm told by my neighbours, who owned Coldharbour Farm along the road until they were bought out in the 1960s, that the playpark across the road was a pond at one time, where livestock and horses would drink, and no doubt the swallows and martins would collect mud for nest building. Now the birds must wait for puddles to form after rain on the unmade car park.

I've been reading a local history book, about the World War II airfield used by secret agents that lies between our houses and The Lodge. One misty morning in 1940, a stray bomb landed near Cold-harbour Farm. My neighbours were milking at the time, they tell me, and the blast blew the chickens off their nests. The crater can still be seen, and today it holds water. Perhaps it makes up for the lost farm pond. I wonder what life has been put back by this, an act of war.

THE MAN WHO FELL TO EARTH

Writing for the RSPB magazine (first titled *Birds*, then relaunched as *Nature's Home*), you meet some interesting people.

'I read your article on garden ponds in *Birds* magazine with interest,' writes Alec Milne of Newbattle, near Edinburgh. 'Twenty years ago, when the moment was right, we took heed of the blackbirds and chased the children away.'

In his letter, Alec goes on to describe retiring to an old cottage. 'It was in a very dilapidated state, and the half-acre walled garden completely overgrown. It took seven years to clear. My wife Diana, who moved into retirement better than I did, and who is younger and has far more essential energy, progressively assumed her present role of the complete organic woman, so that we are virtually self-sufficient in potatoes, apples and salad.'

Alec describes his water gardening endeavours, comparing notes with what I have written. But halfway through, his subject changes to something quite different: 'I read your article carefully,' he writes, 'and all was well until your last paragraph, which really hit me.' My last paragraph contains that reference to a water-filled World War II bomb crater in a local field. From this, Alec identified the spot: 'Tempsford! One night in May 1943, diverted there, I crash-landed my Stirling bomber off the runway. I ended up piggybacked in extraordinary fashion on top of a Halifax…'

I am by now very familiar with Tempsford's old airfield. It is a three-mile walk from my front door, along country lanes and bridleways on the route of an old Roman road, flanked by wide open spaces enjoyed by skylarks and the now-returning buzzards. The airfield is now used mainly by the resident hares, which I often see loping across it. It is best known locally for the night-time missions flown from here in World War II by agents in tiny aircraft called Lysanders. I hadn't associated it with bombers. I have often tried to imagine what it was like here then. Now I have someone telling me first-hand, who actually lived it. It suddenly doesn't seem like such a long time ago. Alec explained:

There is some sort of membrane in the brain of ex-servicemen that separates the reality of their present life from what was once. The Old Soldier's Syndrome. Forgive me, but I can't stop, 55 years on. I became fascinated by the Lysanders, for here were aircraft flying on missions that were completely beyond anything that my courage and skills could cope with. The pilot had to fly and navigate this failed Army Corporation aircraft into the heart of France, find a small field, pick up people and get back… trying not think about intercepts over the French coast, unpredicted weather patterns, low-lying fog, getting lost, running out of fuel, dropping oil pressure. Nor of the ever-present possibility of betrayal.

This once-secret airfield, at the foot of the greensand (hence Sandy) ridge, is about three miles, as the Lysander flies, from The Lodge. The runway remains, the centrepiece between the horizons under big, bulging skies. It probably looks more like an airstrip now than it did in wartime, because then it was made to look derelict. The thick clays have been drained, and the damp scrub replaced by fields of wheat and oilseed rape in all but one area. The calls of the nightingales deep in the thickets carry a long way on calm summer nights. In late summer and autumn the reed buntings and yellowhammers spill out from this tailor-made nursery to forage in small groups on the stubble and the seed-strewn edges of the runway. Short-eared and barn owls visit too, I am told, although I have not yet been lucky enough to see them here.

For the duration of the war, passing enemy aircraft never sussed that the airfield was active. The bomb that made the crater of which I wrote had actually been intended for the Barford power station a bit further north. The barn remains too. Agents were issued with their supplies from here. It lingers today as a simple memorial. Inside there are poppy wreaths, and yellowing press cuttings pinned to a board. It is a touchingly restrained, poignant memorial for quiet reflection on the intrepidity of those who flew by moonlight, like the tawny and little owls that are nowadays the barn's inhabitants, and which litter its shelves with their droppings and pellets.

On a bright, brisk Sunday morning Alec and his sister, who lives at Barford, come by my house and we make a pilgrimage to the airfield. Alec is, understandably, quiet on the visit. I try to imagine what he might be reliving. The Old Soldier's Syndrome, as he had described in his first letter to me...

There were no casualties. We retired to the mess to await a pick-up back to base, Waterbeach. Any fitful sleep was shattered when the Polish crews of three Halifax back from a supply drop to Belgium clattered into the mess: the first time I had heard a foreign language spoken in earnest.

At that period I had too much on my plate to think about anything but personal survival. Later, I was posted from Downham Market to Newmarket to what now would be called a rest and recuperation unit, and from there renewed my acquaintance with Tempsford. I had some reasons, now forgotten, to fly there. I know that one such was to take my flight commander. I was with him when news of his posting came through. He went deathly white, as though he had received a death sentence, as indeed he had. On what must have been his first trip, his Hudson was lost... this is the Syndrome at its worst, one goes on from one thing to another...

The memory endures of the larks singing, while the airfield went about its business of servicing and refuelling with all its quiet industry, preparing for night and loss.

Alec assures me afterwards that he found it quite uplifting to revisit the airfield. 'But it wasn't a social occasion, more a homage to lost youth, and so I enjoyed a contemplative time. Reading the obituaries, noting the aircraft lost and where.'

In Alec's eye is the glint of a man who knows that living should be thought a privilege, and he has a humility borne of his sense of luck, and his vivid memories of those less fortunate. After the war he became a pioneer in homeopathy – nature cure, he prefers to call it – and is still, at 80, a passionate advocate for organic husbandry. His cottage garden on the banks of the River Esk is idyllic. I am lucky enough to be able to visit him there one sunny Sunday afternoon in July, for a home-grown lunch and the benefit of his wisdoms: surviving war, nature cures, organic gardening, wildlife, affairs of the heart. He's a man who has learned how to live and let, or help, live.

Note

One afternoon as the sun sinks at the end of the runway, and I am showing two friends this place, a white bantam dove appears, some distance from the nearest dovecote, and lands in the middle of the runway. My friends, having never seen a white dove before, are completely fazed. At the time I find it a little less unusual than they do, though of course the symbolism is not lost on me. But I didn't know then how close it was to the spot where Alec fell to Earth.

Shrewdunnit

'Do you know anything about water voles?'

Phyllis from next door has surprised me at the garden fence.

'A bit,' I answer modestly. I actually know quite a lot about water voles, having lived at one time beside a stream that still had them.

'Why?'

'Well, something's been attacking my goldfish,' she explains, 'and I wondered…'

I am able to tell Phyllis straight away that she can eliminate the water vole from her enquiries. 'Water voles are vegetarian,' I say authoritatively. They do eat meat sometimes, but right now that feels like a technicality.

'Oh… well, we do have *something* coming to the pond.' She takes me to her back garden to have a look, explaining that some of her fish – large goldfish – have been found dead, with head injuries. Unfortunately, she hasn't kept any of the casualties to show me, but we arrange that if another one goes belly-up she will put it aside for me, for a post mortem. I might have theories of my own, but I think I'll have to bring it in to The Lodge; take it over to the 'boys in the lab'.

We don't actually have a lab, but I do know one or two people who are expert in such matters. They're not just expert on birds – although there is a lot of that, of course. No, there are plenty of staff here who reckon they know a thing or two about things like fish, as well as fowl.

Now, it might strike you as a bit odd, someone bringing a large goldfish with head injuries into work. But it's that sort of place, and I guess I'm that sort of person.

Phyllis describes the creature she has seen acting suspiciously around her pond. I am thinking water shrew, but water shrews are normally found by running water – where they are found at all.

'Whatever it is, it'll have to go,' Phyllis declares.

I plead that the evidence is circumstantial, and that, in any case, she'd have a job catching a water shrew. It wouldn't be likely to take a cheese or chocolate bait. They like their food alive and wriggly: small fish, for example. *Small* fish.

Notwithstanding the size of the victims, I did think it feasible that the culprit was a water shrew. People at work were much more sceptical; but we really needed a fish…

Then one February morning a water shrew turned up in my bath. In the garden, I should add. In the old cast-iron bath that I had sunk at the edge of the lawn. From the corner of my eye I caught sight of movement in the water and across the rim of the bath. Hmm, I thought, creeping closer for a stakeout.

I didn't have long to wait, or time to regret my lack of pre-packed sandwiches, staple diet of detectives. The suspect reap-peared and slipped swiftly underwater, a silvery podule among the pondweed, causing considerable turbulence as it foraged. It was a water shrew, all right. How exciting. A shroud of bubbles kept it dry, and made it so buoyant that it had to cling to the weed and paddle like mad to stay under. When it ran out of breath, it popped out of the water onto the rim of the bath like reversed footage of a shrew jumping in.

I radioed Dan, the lodger, for backup. OK, I just went inside and got him. I wanted him to corroborate my story. A water shrew is noteworthy, to say the least – to get such good views of a live one even more so. This is a big moment in a wildlife garden. Dan fol-lowed me outside, but all was quiet on the water front. I went back indoors but, intrigued, Dan hung around, and was rewarded with clear views of the shrew in the pond and herbaceous border.

I drew up an all-points bulletin: black glossy fur above, ivory white below, quite large – for a shrew – and typically hyperactive; a bit spivvy-looking, really. Water shrews come armed: they have a poisonous bite, or rather toxic saliva with which they debilitate their prey. They also have long, tactile whiskers for detecting prey under-water, and can eat half their body weight every day (which isn't a lot of weight, but is a lot of beasties).

Then a spooky thing happened. Dan was at a dinner party that same evening. Conversation turned to recent downpours and flood-ing, rats flushed out of sewers, that sort of thing.

'Next thing you know, we'll have water shrews in our baths,' someone said. Someone who wasn't Dan.

'You're not gonna believe this…,' says Dan, 'But I actually saw a water shrew in a bath today.'

He says they believed him.

I said I believed him.

The water shrew, or at least one that fitted the description, was occasionally sighted thereafter. I saw it clambering on a sedum plant, and it beat a shuffling retreat from the outhouse one afternoon when I interrupted its search for spiders.

Of course, there was no actual proof of the water shrew's guilt. And, in any case, Phyllis hasn't reported any more mutilated goldfish. I assume the water shrew and/or its kind are still at large, and I'm pleased that harmony prevails. Even if it means that I never got to bring a dead goldfish into work to have its head examined.

TALES FROM THE BACK DOOR

I sometimes think mine might be the only garden in this part of the world that doesn't have cats in it. I almost never see one here. Perhaps once in six months I get a visit from a dowdy grey farm cat from up the road, but I think it knows where it stands. As soon as my face appears at the window it makes a sharp exit. I don't dislike cats, but I can certainly live quite happily without their effects. Ditto grey squirrels. And rabbits. This a rural, residential road, about a mile of it. It's a bit of a peninsula, I suppose, with open fields on three sides.

Where mammals are concerned, I do have bank voles; loads of them – or maybe just a hyperactive handful. I also have wood mice and shrews, although they, by habit if not by number, are less often seen. And while none of these is quite on leg-nuzzling terms with me, they are quite confiding, in a myopic, 'well, he hasn't killed us yet' kind of a way.

Most mornings a vole will be sharing breadcrumbs with the sparrows, dunnocks and blackbirds in the shady corner at my back door. They and the birds are quite accustomed to each other, and uninhibited, often standing off at opposite ends of a crust. The vole will sometimes try to drag the bigger morsels under cover, snagging them on the daisies that sprout between the flagstones.

Occasionally a wood mouse will brave the daylight, especially after a cold night. And the shrews' long crinkled snouts will protrude comically from under a log, sniffing out the richer of the kitchen scraps. One morning while eating breakfast outside I looked down to find a shrew scrabbling in vain to get a grip on the edge of a yoghurty bowl I had placed on the ground.

The voles get everywhere. I have had them on the window frame, which they reach by climbing up the Virginia creeper, and I see them foraging in the bramble I have trained up the wall of my outbuilding, and which fruits prodigiously. If you stay still the voles are untroubled, such is their short-sightedness. Many people confuse them with mice, but they have a much shorter tail, a rounder face, smaller ears and shorter legs. They are blunter all round, and run as though on tiny wheels.

I occasionally have a house mouse indoors in the winter, which has to be evicted using a – so-called – humane mousetrap. Received wisdom is that you must take your mouse at least a mile away or it will find its way back to your house. In my experience, the poor mouse that you set free is invariably soaked in its own urine, trembling and frail. You don't have to be a zoologist to work out what the local mice will make of it. Nowadays I just put mine outside.

The only pet I ever kept, apart from house spiders (and they don't really count), was a white mouse I allowed myself to be emotionally blackmailed into taking from a colleague. By not taking it I was condemning it to death, she told me in a businesslike kind of way. I called it Vermintrude, which worked as a show name, I thought. Verm for short. I got her (although in truth I couldn't confidently sex it) a lovely big cage full of things to climb and explore, and a wheel to run in.

Before long Verm, or her sunflower seeds, was being visited by a local wood mouse. It couldn't get into the cage, but instead would gaze longingly into it from beyond the mesh. The visitor wasn't difficult to tempt under a bowl, propped up on a stick, attached to a length of string, attached to my finger. The difficult bit was sliding an LP record underneath the bowl, and the prisoner, and then getting it into a large bin for the short drive into the countryside. I figured the bin had to be deep. I've seen how high mice can jump. Trouble is, as I attempted to tip my captive – gently – into the bin, she leapt from the LP and proceeded to do circuits of the rim, with me close behind trying to tip her – gently – in.

I eventually donated Verm and her spacious living quarters and adventure playground to a worthy local cause – a small boy – who might have more of the time and patience required to keep the cage from reeking.

Phyllis next door reported a rat one day, in a state of some anxiety – she, not the rat – but I played it down. The odd rat isn't going to do any harm, I thought, and until it starts doing something antisocial, or shows up with 20 of its mates, I will live and let live. The man who lived here before me had told me that a rat took up residence in the outbuilding, which was a bit messier then than it is now. One day he was leaning out of the window when the rat ran up his leg and his back and jumped out of the window via his shoulder. He decided then that the rat had to go.

He called in Fred, the old country boy, from the other side next door. Old Fred could turn a neat trick with a small snare, and one day, reminiscing while puffing on his pipe, took great pleasure in telling me just how big the rat was (which of course he caught). I can't remember the exact statistics, but they were impressive, even if a rat is a lot of tail. I half-imagined Fred posing with it for a photograph at the village fête – winner in the snared rat category.

I have never heard of a humane trap for rats, or of anyone driving a rat in a bin out into the countryside to give it a fighting chance. With any luck, I will never be faced with this challenge.

Note

Alec Milne, the man who fell to Earth (see page 12), told me a great story about the homing abilities of mice. Some friends of his in Scotland were being visited by a mouse. They captured it, took it away and released it. In no time at all a mouse answering its description reappeared in the house, with very similar habits. Surely it couldn't be the same mouse?

To see if it was, they hit on the idea of putting a dab of nail varnish on the suspect's head after capturing it and before releasing it again, one mile away. It reappeared in the house. They captured it again and released it two miles away. Again it returned. They then took it to the other side of the Tay. And guess what? They never saw it again.

SURVIVORS

From my bed I have views across open farmland to a wood in the near distance, called Esme. I value this 'arm's-length' everyday link with a bit of wildness more than I could estimate, as well as the up-close connection allowed by the permissive path around the wood, provided by the estate. It's an important site locally for the community to connect with nature.

I've been noticing the dieback of old oaks in the fields around me in recent years, and wonder if perhaps they are reaching the end of their natural lives. But while exploring in Esme Wood I began to notice tall, slender, sky-craning, younger oaks dead where they stand, and some that have keeled over, dry as breadsticks through their bases, reduced to powder. I got some forestry experts out to have a look. They pointed at some bore-holes in the bark, small enough to have been left by drawing pins, and noted some fungi, and scratched their chins. Of course, it's difficult even for an expert to know what might have finished off a tree, from the multitude of possible suspects.

My own instinct is that uncertain weather might have been the tipping point. We know drought is stressful to many types of tree, as is undue saturation, and that plants in general aren't keen on unscheduled fluctuations. All of these things might just give the opposition the upper hand, cause the sylvan immune system to pack in. After that? Take your pick of executioners.

The good news is that we found a grown-up elm in Esme, skulking like a refugee from the onslaught of Dutch elm disease within the wood – a tall, thick, mature elm, with distinctive bark. 'Huge elm, with rifted trunk all notched and scarred,' as John Clare described ones like it, at a time when they dominated the landscape. I'd describe this tree as Plasticine-coloured, fluted, like a hastily whittled stick. So how did it survive, while a country-wide latticework of these trees disintegrated all around it?

All the variants of elm trees have been vulnerable to the disease, but some more than others. I discover there's a type that was hybridised not far from here, called the Huntingdon elm (some people call it the Chichester), which has a reputation for resilience. Several specimens survived in Bedford, although they too may be nearing the end of their natural lives. There's a theory that the four that survived while all elms around them succumbed may have been preserved by their proximity to petrol stations – it is possible that the atmosphere here wasn't to the liking of the bark beetles.

There is much about trees we don't know, or can't know. Like the rest of us, a tree is an organism under steady assault from, and waging constant war against, an army of browsers, nibblers, borers, rotters, suckers, pathogens and viruses. Its immune system is worked remorselessly, and its resources must be channelled through its lifeblood vessels of xylem and phloem – the capillaries that transport water and nutrients round the tree. Dutch elm disease kills – fast – by blocking these tubes.

I went back to get a leaf sample from the Esme elm, to see if I could identify this tree more precisely. I've made a few enquiries and discovered that I may even be able to get a DNA reading from a lab, to find out if it matches the Bedford trees, and other examples in cities like Norwich and Cambridge. Perhaps we can ensure that new offspring are cultivated and installed, to maintain this token presence of elms among us in the future. There are other ways to keep elms with us. I nurture relic elms in my garden, in the hedgerow, knowing that while I maintain them, bonsai-style, at hedge level, they won't attract the disease-bearing beetle.

Poet John Clare was a great celebrant of the elm. Two centuries ago he wrote of how he loved:

> on the buttressed roots to sit, and lean
> In careless attitude, and there reflect
> On times, and deeds, and doings that have been...

JURASSIC PARKY

Morning is the best part of the day. The earlier the better, really, for me. And Sunday morning is the best part of the week; even if, like today, it is bitter cold, and the late winter rain, having slid down all night, has not yet abated. The ponds are brim-full. I tip the water that has collected in a wheelbarrow into them anyway.

The rain has slowed to an icy drizzle, wafting on breezes onto my furrowed brow, etching lines into my face, no doubt, as I take a short walk along the road from my front door, for fresh air and to stretch my legs.

I am looking for early signs of spring. The song thrushes are piping confidently, reassuring me that they are still around, even if they never visit for crumbs with their cousins. Walking slowly, I study the ditches and hedge bottom for signs of movement. And I scan the flooded fields for any unusual visitors. This will be a short walk. If I hang around I'll get soaked. I walk as far as the level crossing – the main line from London to Edinburgh. I pause to look at the brook, which is swollen to the scale of a small river, the colour of weak, milky machine coffee.

There isn't much around. The countryside is at its most unprepossessing and dreich. A day for waiting through.

And then I see something on the glistening road. I could easily have stepped on it. At first I think it's a newt, but it's too cold even for a newt to be out. But something about the angle it is holding itself at tells me there is living tissue there. I bend to look more closely and am perplexed to discover that it is a lizard. A *lizard*, for goodness' sake! Nothing could have seemed less probable, in this leafless landscape of mud and puddles. I've never even seen one round here on a summer's day. And it's almost too cold today even for warm-blooded critters like me to be out.

A car is coming. I quickly but gently scoop up the refugee. To add injury to insult, it has lost its tail. All of it. You could say I'm starting to feel protective. As I carry it back, it clings to my thumb with tiny claws, little bigger than the hooks on a burr. Its tiny black eyes are glazed. And it gapes slightly, here and there. I imagine a silent echo of Jurassic times. This is how its gigantic ancestors might have looked when one day an asteroid knocked their planet for six, and suddenly the climate or the atmosphere wasn't to their liking. The primitiveness of this little fella – in such a stark, wintry, contemporary landscape – is striking. This scores high on incongruity in every possible way. It looks like a visitor from another time; another geological time. I'm really pleased it's here.

Until now I had thought that a lizard couldn't actually function when cold, even if it wanted to. My understanding was that reptiles, before they have been charged up by the sun's rays, are catatonic. Surely that's the cold-blooded deal? But somehow this lizard is moving – impossibly slowly. Heaven knows how long it has taken to get even this far on to the road. I think it must have hauled itself clear of the rising floodwater in the ditch. Then survival instinct kicked in. The sense of its will to live, of struggling against overwhelming odds, is powerful. Its sheer primitiveness adds to this sense.

Perhaps the railway is a good habitat. Actually, this makes a lot of sense. The combination of the stones and slabs are ideal for alternately hiding and sunbathing, and the untreated vegetation of the embankments provides insect food. Plus, it is relatively undisturbed, bar the trains that thunder through. I assume that lizards are never tempted to bask on the rails themselves. If they are, the vibrations of the oncoming locomotives must bounce them off.

In my kitchen, in a bowl, the lizard slowly comes round from its state of numbness. After a couple of hours it is peering over the rim of the bowl. Another hour, and it has reached the edge of the worktop. Not long afterwards, it is safely ensconced in a cool outhouse, in a wooden box lined with newspaper and bark, to rest up for the remaining cold weeks.

This is a common lizard. Well, it's more common than our other one, the sand lizard. Technically, a third lizard can be found in the UK. It's got no legs to speak of. It looks like a dumpy snake. And we call it a worm. The slow worm.

Common lizards are actually widespread in Britain; it's just that they are quite hard to see. They give birth to live young, and our climate makes their lives a bit stop-start. If it's too cold they don't get up: it's as simple as that. If they aren't active they don't need energy so they don't need to eat. (It's a strategy that worked for me when I was an unemployed student, out of term time.) Funny to think that the lizard I once found on the high tide-line of a rocky shore in Wester Ross in north Scotland during a brief interlude of spring sunshine is the same species as one of those you see running all over the buildings and walls of southern France. Perhaps they live longer in Scotland, with all the sleep they get.

And mine is the same species too. Well, I say 'mine' but I'm only keeping him – Ronaldo – until his tail has regrown. Then it's back to the railway, to take his chances with the twenty-first century.

It's hard to believe – but gratifying to know – that there must be a viable population of common lizards just along the road from me. Just as there must be more than one Loch Ness monster...

Let's just say I'm a little less sceptical than I used to be.

WHITE FANG

Some days are cold enough to excuse the wearing of outlandish headgear. This Saturday afternoon is one such. A wan sun peers out from a gap in a grey-papered sky, and a piercing breeze forces a faster pace on a short walk. I parked at Eversholt, on the edge of Woburn's great park, near a stretch of the greensand ridge pathway that runs from not far south of here up to and beyond the north of the county, where I lived for a time in an old farm cottage.

The path leads from the road through a high gate and across rough pasture. The only grazers today are greylag geese, which move away from my approach like a ripple of iron fillings repelled by a magnet, closing again behind me. Little skirmishes break out among them as they regain their composure and re-establish rank.

Up ahead is a belt of young pines, widely spaced. Pausing within them I pick up on a hint of animal movement, of damp hair, blending well with the dun-coloured grasses. I lift my binoculars, exposing brittle fingers to the sharp air. Looking back at me over its shoulder is an oddly blank face, like that of a teddy bear, with black button eyes and nose, and large, cocked, furry ears. A stocky, shaggy creature which looks almost dog-like, as it turns its head to consider a retreat and I catch a glimpse of one of its greatly enlarged canine teeth, which is fully 8 centimetres long. It juts almost comically down by its chin. It's now clear I'm looking at a Chinese water deer. A cuddly toy with fangs.

China is obviously the natural home of this species, but if it could be said to have a UK home, then that would be right here at Woburn, where it was first introduced. It has now gone native, but interestingly it has not spread very far. The one I'm looking at is a matter of yards from the park perimeter fence. Its scientific name, *Hydropotes inermis*, means the unarmed water drinker. It is the only deer in Europe that never grows antlers, but it could hardly, with those choppers, be said to be unarmed. The males score great grooves in each other during the rut, which takes place here around December. The adults bark and whistle, and litters of sometimes as many as six young are produced in spring. They are tiny and striped, and vulnerable even to stoats if left unattended.

Water deer do like water and watery places, and have spread into the fens. But they are not confined to such places, and here at Woburn the land is mostly dry and rolling. This makes their lack of spread elsewhere seem peculiar, but in any event the UK now has a substantial portion of the world population of water deer. China's water deer seem not to be faring so well, and are little studied.

Pushing through the high deer gate into the park itself, I see more of these little deer: one running swiftly down a parkland slope, kicking up its hind legs as it goes and looking from a distance like a huge hare. I'd love to find a skull to show to friends and colleagues and ask what they think it's from. No doubt about it, this is a distinctly odd and endearing little animal, especially today, when it adds intrigue and a touch of the surreal to a stark, wintry, scenic – but almost equally introduced – landscape.

THE BLIND JACKDAW, PART I

It's Burns Night tonight – 25 January. I'm walking to the bus stop, when I find an injured jackdaw on the road, close to Esme Wood. It's a local hotspot for these sociable birds, which nest a little later in the year in the mature horse chestnut trees that line the road and provide handy cavities. They also use the chimneys of the farmhouse opposite.

I have to hold up some traffic as I fish for a plastic bag and ease the bird into it without making too much fuss. It is injured about the head, and apparently blind. Foregoing the bus, I take it home and put it in the back porch, setting down newspaper, and adding a low stick perch, water and a tray of seeds. One eye is gone, and the other is badly damaged. Despite his apparent blindness – he makes no response to sudden movements, but shuffles away from approaching sound – he is able to locate his food, which he pecks at readily, if a little inaccurately. I've decided it's a male, although the sexes are similar, and I call him Robert Burns.

Jackdaws made an early impression on me. They inhabited the lime trees at the front of the house we moved to when I was just five, and they were the mysterious birds up the chimney, the ones that provided useful kindling, dropping it down for us to collect from the grate. One day, the kindling bird put in an unscheduled appearance itself! It took a bit of catching after we'd eyed each other for a few minutes, its beady, intelligent eyes darting about the front room for a way out. Going back up the chimney never seemed to be an option. I liked jackdaws after that. They seemed impish and bold, and persistent. Goodness knows how much stick-gathering and dropping they have to do before these chimney nests find a solid foundation.

Chapter Two

February

The blind jackdaw, Part II

Robert Burns (Rab, for short) has now been in the porch for a week. He has made some progress, getting stronger and more livelier. I have read that jackdaws, and blind birds generally, can make very affectionate pets. But I know that I won't be able to do him justice, as would be true of any high-maintenance, social animal.

I take him to a wildlife park. I brought a blackbird here once, after finding it stunned on the road. Today they tell me they no longer take in rescued wildlife. Oh. Apparently a study has shown that nursing and releasing wildlife isn't an effective use of resources. The survival rate isn't high. I don't tell them, but I knew this already. I thought most people did. But there are also hygiene considerations now that may not have been considered when I brought them the blackbird back in the day.

So, rightly or wrongly, I take Robert Burns to the top of the ridge and, on the edge of a wood, I let him out of his box. The wind gusts. Still blind, but much stronger than a week ago, he jumps onto me and clings to my jacket, climbs onto my shoulder, then my head, and balances there in the wind for a few minutes. Could Rab suddenly be realising that my presence is preferable to the void beyond? As I am entertaining this thought, with a lump in my throat, wondering what anyone stumbling on this scene might make of it, he catches a gust and flies, perhaps for one last time.

He lands some way off, among the furrows of the field, and sits preening the cack off his wings that inevitably he picked up from being confined. I turn away and leave him there to live out his last hours, hoping that his end will be quick; when the buzzard mewing in the near distance moves in, maybe.

I could have left him in the road, or killed him and put him in the bin, but I made a judgement that this way would be better, for him if not for me. It is probably the normal and preferable fate for a wild bird to be predated. Mostly we do this rescue stuff for ourselves, I realise.

'Goodbye Robert, and good luck,' read my wife Sara's message when I texted her. And I shed a quiet tear, sitting in the pub with a pint, for all our deaths and final flights, symbolised in this bird, and because goodbye and good luck are the last things we can say to those we love when they fly off.

'I'm sorry,' a neighbour said consolingly when we spoke about it later. 'No doubt his namesake had something to say about loss and death, but you've done a pretty good job, it seems to me.'

As long as the chestnut trees and the chimneys are there, and the pastures beyond, his fellows will come again.

ROLL OUT THE BUMBARREL

There's a bird at the window, tinier than any bird I've ever seen in this country. Perhaps only the hummingbirds I've seen in California might run it close. When I say it is at the window it really is *at* the pane of glass, flying at it with a fury that adds further to the tragicomedy of the scene. It looks like a tiny pompom, this bird: the bobble off a woolly hat. Or a huge bumblebee, perhaps. It takes me a moment or two to register what it is: a long-tailed tit minus its key defining feature – the long tail.

Why this inconvenienced long-tailed tit should be resorting to attempted bodily harm remains a mystery to me. Perhaps it's been traumatised in the incident that cost it its tail, although you sense that long-tailed tits, in their busy little extended family troupes foraging in tight hedgerows, flitting from tree to tree uttering their constant contact calls (not unlike the sound of someone sucking bits out of their teeth, I often think), are beyond the range of most cats and beneath the contempt of most birds of prey, other than as a snack on the run, a morsel on a cocktail stick.

But the incident brings home to me just how tiny these birds are, even with their lolly-stick tails poking out behind them. They weigh about the same as half a dozen paperclips.

I was pleased to work out that the nest of moss, cobweb, fibre and feather that I discovered in the evergreen (or ever-brown) berberis shrub at the bottom of the garden turned out to be the handiwork of long-tailed tits. It was an open cup when I first noticed it, like a chaffinch would build, but it later had its roof sewn on, to create the perfect domed structure that is the tiny tits' speciality. It strikes me as remarkable that this oddly flexible pocket can accommodate the parent bird as well as up to ten eggs and, later, nestlings. In our nearest ancient woodland I've noticed one of these nests 10 metres up on the branch of an oak tree, and one at similar height in an ancient forest in Poland.

Wherever the nest is placed, it must be pretty toasty in there as the time approaches for the young to pop out into the thorny world beyond the tiny opening in the side of the soft globe. It is thought that the folk name *bumbarrel* was inspired more by the nest than by the architects themselves. It's by this earthy local name that poet John Clare knew the bird, and found 'twenty in a drove' on a wintry heath, two centuries ago, an hour north of here.

It's cold weather that long-tailed tits must fear the most. Tiny birds like this are quick to chill, and not good at holding their heat. They are in constant need of food, which is tricky for invertebrate specialists like the bumbarrel. I found one dead on the pavement one chill morning. Again at first I didn't recognise it as a bird at all. It just looked like a tiny fragment of material, bedraggled on the wet ground. I lifted it and the sodden tail came free from the ground. I dabbed it dry and placed it in a spectacles case, and later after it had dried (to reveal again some of the pink tinges in its otherwise monochrome plumage) I preserved it in a bag in the freezer. Later I donated it to colleagues who were running a training course on how to handle and ring small, delicate birds. For this it would have made the ideal subject.

It is only recently that I've begun to notice them visiting the peanut dispenser at the back window. If they've been able to mimic the blue tits and master the one at the front (which is a thin plastic cylinder with a mesh base), they haven't yet shown any sign of it. This adaptation to coexistence with us seems to be a recent development, and may partly explain the current success of the species. While many birds have been declining in number, the long-tailed tit has been faring pretty well. A few years ago it even squeezed into the top ten of birds seen by the half million members of the public taking part in the RSPB's annual Big Garden Birdwatch, held over a weekend in late January.

One winter dusk a small group of them gathered near my back door as though poised to enter a night-time roost site. I watched closely in the hope of discovering where they might go, to huddle together and arm themselves against the sub-zero temperatures ahead. I thought they might even be thinking about coming into the house, as I'd left the back door open while doing some chores. They would have been very welcome. I'd have loved to see what perch they chose and how they would organise themselves. But after some kind of conference they flitted off into the dwindling light, to take their chances in the biting night.

I wonder if the tail-less tit lived long enough to grow another one. But the very fact he seemed to be on his own suggests he couldn't keep up with the group, and his chances therefore may have been limited. But it's a picture that will stay with me; that image of impotent rage, the little bird stripped of the very thing that defines it, identifies it, railing against its own reflection, fury perhaps doubled by the injustice of it all. Birds do attack their reflections, of course, but I've rarely seen this in species other than the chaffinch and once, memorably, vividly, a red cardinal versus itself in the glinting chrome hubcap of a Chevrolet in the Arizona desert sun.

Even with its long tail intact, the bumbarrel seems an unlikely survivor, in many ways, but a very welcome success story.

BIRD HOMES – THERE'S NEVER BEEN A BETTER TIME TO BUILD

According to tradition, the birds pair up for spring on St Valentine's Day. With this in mind, Valentine's Day marks the start of National Nest Box Week, organised by the British Trust for Ornithology

(BTO). The week is aimed at raising awareness of the fact that many of our birds need more safe places in which to nest. As naturalist-broadcaster Tony Soper put it, 'Britain needs more holes.'

The BTO has been sending out information packs since the start of the year. The packs contain useful tips on how to make nest boxes, where to put them and how to record their use by birds. All over the country, people keen to help breeding birds have been involved in putting up nest boxes. Nest box provision and monitoring has for some time been done on many RSPB reserves, in association with the BTO. You've probably enjoyed feeding the birds in your garden this winter. Helping them to breed is also very rewarding.

In the autumn I took advantage of the bumper acorn crop here at The Lodge and gathered a small box-full. I was lucky enough to attract to my garden not only jays, but also nuthatches. Unfortunately, I was unable to persuade the nuthatches to stay to nest (although this species sometimes uses boxes), and they and the jays retired to the woods as the weather moderated and the acorns ran out.

I took consolation from the pair of great tits which, for the second spring running, used the nest box I had installed eight feet up the trunk of a sycamore near my back door. I had the pleasure of watching the parents at every stage of the breeding cycle, and the magic moment early one Sunday in June when seven youngsters left the dark interior of their nursery to disappear into the canopy of the tree. While nuthatches may be difficult to entice, great tits and robins are much more willing nest box users. At the time I noted my top tips for putting up a nest box.

- The earlier the better – give the birds a chance to get used to your box. They may roost in it over the winter too.
- A nest box could be something else's lunchbox, so I always try to secure and disguise them from predators.
- It should not face south and the direct rays of the afternoon sun. It may be cold when it's put up, but spring can be hot – even in this country.
- Cleaning it out each autumn may increase its chances of being used again by nesting birds next spring.

Nowadays, bird boxes (or, more correctly, artificial nest sites) come in all shapes and sizes, much like the species that will use them. With a little imagination, there are more unusual tenants that can be attracted – perhaps not always birds – depending on where you are.

I've found that house sparrows will take to boxes with a slightly larger entrance hole than that required by the tits. Starlings will use something bigger still, and this may even deter them from nesting in your roof. Robins and wrens can be encouraged to use nooks and crannies in outhouses, as well as creeper-covered walls and thick shrubs. I've put out old flowerpots, teapots and tins in well-hidden spots, and created small alcoves, adding a few leaves, dried grasses or sawdust by way of encouragement.

I make sure there is always access for the birds. My old wash-house had a rat-hole at the bottom of the door, and the blackbirds that nested high on a dusty shelf used that when coming and going. Mind you, they did this even when the door was wide open.

I have tawny owls locally. For them I placed a conical linen basket with plenty of sawdust high up in a tree – but sheltered and secured with rope, and one night not long afterwards I heard a potential occupant calling from near this spot. While it may have inspected the site, there has been no evidence of breeding – yet. Tawny owls will use barrel-type boxes or something along the lines of the typical stable-door design favoured by robins–only much bigger, of course. I'm no carpenter, but I made one of these from off-cuts of tongue-and-groove floorboard I found in a skip, and I have given it to the reserve manager here at The Lodge, where tawny owls are resident.

I'm always alert for farm outbuildings near habitat that might be suitable for barn owls, in which a nesting tray could be installed. This idea can be sold to local farmers using the 'free pest control' angle. Little owls will also use artificial sites. Stock doves, kestrels, jack-daws and woodpeckers can all be attracted to larger boxes, if you are lucky enough to have these species locally. Artificial sites, in moul-ded 'woodcrete', can be put up for house martins and swallows. The latter may not use these, but the cup may encourage them to build nearby. They can be helped in this by hammering a nail or two into a wall under a roof in an outhouse or porch, as the swallows' mud nest will require some additional support of this kind. Swifts will also take to specially designed horizontal boxes placed under the eaves.

Squadrons of shrieking swifts add a touch of drama to summer evenings, and for this alone they are worth encouraging. You should not expect more than one pair of the same species to nest within the confines of an average garden, but species that are not in direct competition will happily coexist. I know of one garden in which a nest box placed among clematis on the side of the house among a creeper had tits in the box, and spotted flycatchers on top. Another year, the tits had pied wagtails upstairs! However, what this garden didn't have was cats.

In nesting, as in other areas of their lives, birds know what's good for them. But – and I am reminded of this every time I think of the song thrush that nested on the Belfast to Limavady train while this was still in service – with a bit of research you will know even better.

RALLY AROUND THE ASH

I can measure how long I've been nurturing this garden by the height of the ash trees in the front hedgerow. They turned up soon after I put the hedge whips in, and I let them get on with it. They're taller than the nearest lamp post now, as thick in the trunk, and a similar colour. That's ash for you: prolific, quick to spot an opening, fast-growing, and why we have 80 million of them in these islands. It is from its pallor that the tree takes its name.

I mentioned these ashes in the winter issue of *Birds*, when reflecting on the legacy of Dutch elm disease and the lessons it should have taught us. As fate would have it, we were just about to learn that another fungal disease is already in our midst. Ash dieback threatens – if the experience of Denmark is mirrored – to infect 90 per cent of our ash trees.

It is in maturity that the ash, like most trees, achieves its full value and stature. When I think of the examples I know in Hayley Wood, our local remnant of properly old woodland, I am dejected at the prospect of their loss. These trees are all classical elegance, clean lines and open structure, limbs spread to the skies in swaying, balletic poses. It is because of this fusion of grace and strength that the ash has been known as the Venus of the Woods. Other, smaller ashes I know from local spinneys are still – by some distance – the largest trees in there, and the ones most likely to provide natural nesting holes for birds and other small animals for which such cavities are a crucial part of the life cycle. Nature can ill afford to lose them.

Land managers like the RSPB and others have plans in place for mitigating the worst effects of the arrival of the fungus, but what does the arrival of ash dieback mean for me and my ash trees, and for domestic ash-tree guardians everywhere? I will keep a close eye on them (there are two more out the back) for any signs of the fungus.

In a garden context, there are some consolations. Ash trees aren't typical garden trees, for the basic reasons that they can grow to be a hundred feet tall, and they are not especially good neighbours for other plants. My own ash trees would have to be curtailed before too long in any case. I had it in mind to pollard them – that is, to cut them at ground level and allow them to send up several new shoots, which in due course can be harvested as poles for various domestic uses, such as stakes for hedge-laying, etc.

Ash wood has long been valued for its great strength and suppleness. Taken at the right age, the wood is as strong as any of comparable width, and even the youngest poles are favoured material for the handles of hammers, axes and other high-impact tools. I fear that a lot of ash trees will be pulled down and burned, like the elms before them, but I would hope that, where possible and practicable, productive use can be made of this valuable timber.

For all its utility, the ash isn't the most valuable tree for supporting biodiversity. Anticipating the none-too-distant day when my ash trees have outgrown the garden, I have other trees following more sedately in their wake. Succession planting, I could call it, although it's a bit of an over-claim. There are two box plants in the hedge, and these can be small trees if spared the clippers on top. There's an ornamental cherry that is slowly gaining height, and one hawthorn in the hedge that is substantially more vigorous than its fellows. Out the back, the bird cherry owns the place in spring when bearing its translucent white petals, and throngs with thrushes and doves when it puts out its blood-red fruits. I can also recommend a weeping birch. Inspired by the magnificent, contorted, ossified old specimen outside the library at RSPB HQ, I planted one on a late winter Saturday, and by Sunday there was a redpoll sitting in it.

Alongside the bird cherry is a small but perfectly formed rowan – also known as the mountain ash but no relation to its lowland namesake. For a garden, I'd recommend this as perhaps the best ash backup plan of all. It looks similar but grows more sedately, and rewards the patient – and the garden fauna – with nourishing flowers and berries that the ash cannot match. It's a tough little tree, unfussy, and is even thought to bring good luck. Because of biosecurity failings, allowing the movement of infected plants from affected countries, and the arrival of an unscheduled fungus with which they haven't co-evolved, our ash trees are going to need all the luck they can get.

A TREE AMONG TREES

I already mentioned that there's a wood half a mile from my house. I can see it from bed, an inviting clump of oaks, ash, hornbeam and conifers, with a few chestnuts and limes in the mix. Local people of long standing know it as Home Wood. The Stuart family who were the estate's former owners called it Esme, after a family member. The permissive footpath forms a loop around the wood that can be walked in about 20 minutes. At this time of year the woodland floor is open, lacking much in the way of undergrowth, in common with a lot of small woodlands where muntjac deer are present. But among the tall trunks of the oaks and others there is one smaller tree which forms the centrepiece of the wood at this time of year, because it is now that it flowers, and forms a spectacular, glowing mass of white blossom which glows and sparkles like snow crystals in any sunlight streaming through the boughs above. At such times it hums with early insects seeking an early season sugar hit. There is something particularly heartening about this little installation within the leafless late winter wood.

I looked it up in the book and confirmed that it's a type of plum – a species called the cherry plum. It is a naturalised tree here now, having been brought to Britain from continental Europe a long time ago. It's pretty much the first of our trees to come into flower, ahead even of the sloe-producing blackthorn which is a more familiar feature of our hedgerows. Its vigorous root is sometimes used as the base onto which cultivated shrubs can be grafted.

Cherry plum's scientific name is *Prunus cerasifera* – cherry-bearing plum. What's unusual about this local specimen is how it has been able, in this situation, to grow as it pleases, and I suspect it's really quite an old tree. Although dwarfed by some of its neighbours, it has sprawled upwards and outwards to reach an impressive height, though not quite the 50 feet that the books say is possible for this tree in the wild state. I wonder if it is a lingering trace of a former hedgerow or boundary. Many of the other trees nearby look like colonists of an abandoned field, and nearby there are some relic foundations of an abandoned settlement.

In late summer the cherry plum produces small red fruits that are modest but edible; a useful source of nutrition for newly-fledged thrushes. Wood mice and bank voles no doubt clamber around on the leggy limbs to reach these prizes too.

I realise now that some of the early white blossom that signals the end of winter in local hedgerows isn't blackthorn after all, or damson, but this plant. Unlike those two, it seems not to send suckers out all over the place, and can be a bit easier to keep in line in a hedgerow. I have bought a couple of rooted cuttings to add to my hedge at the back, keen to bring some of this late winter blossom even closer to home.

RETURN OF THE SNORER

One familiar bird species that's dwindled in my life in recent years is the humble greenfinch. I can partly blame myself for this, as they were always very keen on nesting in the *Cypress leylandii* hedges in my back garden, which I've been phasing out. But the main reason they have all but stopped visiting the bird feeders in the front and back gardens is that they seem to have been greatly diminished in number locally, even through the winter.

The greenfinch probably deserves a greater share of the limelight than it has been given. It quite likely suffers a little from comparison with the other, more ornately plumaged, finches. But the greenfinch can be a striking bird, especially the male when he reaches peak condition, with his flashy yellow rump and wing-bars.

They've always been a feature of bird tables, adapting well to exploit the rise of the peanut dispenser, but versatile enough to take most of the things the householder offers.

Greenfinches went into decline due to a parasite called trichomonosis, to which they seem particularly prone. It's a microscopic parasite that is passed on via food fragments and has the effect of blocking the host's gullet. Birds with the affliction may look lethargic, fluffed up, and as if they are having difficulty swallowing food. They may have traces of food or dampness around their bills.

Greenfinches are among the worst-affected birds, but the problem affects many others.

I've been finding the odd casualty in the garden, dead but mostly unscathed. It's a reminder that hygiene is important around bird tables and bird baths, where one infected bird can leave a deadly calling card for others. I prefer to avoid using a bird table, unless I have the time to regularly scrub it clean (which I often don't). I like to scatter food on the ground, where the birds have a reasonably clear view around them and local cats can't lie in ambush. I regularly tip stale water out of the bird bath, give it a rinse, let it dry out from time to time, and fill it again from the water butt. Woodpigeons are especially guilty of pooping in their bathwater – and the parasite is also prevalent in pigeons.

As daylight began to fade in the late afternoon of a bright, freezing winter afternoon I noticed an unusually large flock of finches swirling overhead and coming to land in and around a bed of miscanthus – a tall, reed-like plant growing in unseasonal swishing luxuriance in a damp hollow within this area of open, frosted parkland. I crept closer, till I could see they were almost all greenfinches. I've never been so pleased to see them. It was a bit like stumbling on a reunion of old friends. The greenfinch has always been there, a familiar fixture in the places I've lived, and I've always had a soft spot for it.

Since then, one or two have returned to the feeders in the garden. I've seen the males once again doing their comical song flight, like a child mimicking an aeroplane, arms held outwards and back, tilting one way then the other. *Wa-hey, wa-hooo*, you can almost imagine them shouting. This is clearly a song flight in the early stages of its evolution.

I can also hear again their characteristic wheezing song, the adenoidal drawl, which has returned to the tree tops in my neighbourhood. I told Sara I would describe this sound as a succession of weird noises that someone might make when snoring. 'I can confirm that,' she replied, without missing a beat.

BUILD IT AND THEY WILL COME

Recently, I've been removing plastic tree guards near the village, now that these have done their job of protecting what were (a decade ago) newly planted trees and shrubs. While keeping the browsers' teeth at bay, some of the trees have, sadly, been garrotted by their protectors. This is most often plastic coils, which can fail to break off and so 'choke' the trunk.

With plantings like this it's important to carry out this 'after care', which the authorities may not have time to do. Having identified the local need, I got in touch with the county ecologists to offer my services as a volunteer, and they gratefully accepted.

I discovered great tits nesting in one plastic cylinder, and of course I left them in peace. I then found robins nesting in another. Both nests were on the ground, squeezed between trunk and plastic wall: a slightly odd choice of nest site for both species, smacking a little of desperation. It underlines the lack of suitable cavities elsewhere, so I quickly installed conventional nest boxes for both. I even installed a large old flask, presumably lobbed out of a passing vehicle. I tipped the glass fragments into a bin, and wedged it carefully into a choice spot. Within a fortnight it was occupied by nesting blue tits.

One of my other successes has come from an unlikely source – a job lot of old bricks that I intercepted before they went to the tip. Some of these rescue bricks are lovely, paprika-coloured, flaky old things – probably imperfects, or rejects, from the former Bedford brickworks, deemed unsuitable for proper building. Others are 'Cambridge buffs' – more khaki-coloured. I hit on the idea of building a brick pillar for a vine to grow up. If you place four bricks in a square formation, a brick and a half each edge, it frames a typical nest box-sized gap in the middle.

I mixed the sand, cement and water and, after digging foundations two feet deep, began to lay the bricks and build the column upwards. It was a bit of a *Generation Game* effort to begin with, as I got to grips with the brick-laying, but I improved with each layer.

When it was four bricks high, I used one broken brick to leave a small gap in the side of the column, for a nest entrance hole. Before I laid the next course of four bricks I put in a wire mesh 'floor', which would also serve as a roof above the ground-floor apartment. I repeated this every four bricks up, to create four of these apartments, one on top of the other. The nest hole entrances are on different faces of the pillar, one for each face. I capped off the column with a slab. Ta-da! The Blue Tit Hilton.

That pillar has been in place for well over a decade now, and it has had blue and/or great tits nesting in it every year, usually in the third-floor apartment, but also in the fourth and the second. Every year the birds seem to be successful. The nestlings are secure from woodpeckers and squirrels, the contents well insulated, the pillar built to last. It is also well ventilated, like a termite mound, with its regular openings to the outside world. If only all new-builds could have bird cavities built into them.

I had cause to reflect on my modest, domestic-scale efforts recently, prompted by an unlikely source. It's a short film called *Midway*, which graphically and simply conveys the tragic effect that discarded plastic is having on an albatross colony in the Pacific. The spectacle of all that debris covering vast areas of the ocean, strewn across the island among the nests and causing slow death to the chicks and adults, is deeply unsettling. The image of the birds' decomposed corpses, revealing the cluster of plastic objects they have swallowed (in the mistaken belief that they were edible), is a powerful illustration of the unintended result of our carelessness.

If only all that rubbish could be scooped up, taken out of harm's way and put to use. What if it could be recycled into nest boxes and other homes for wildlife? Maybe the US Navy could ride to the rescue. Governments could help make the recycling part happen. The public could get involved by purchasing the recycled bird homes, as well as by helping with local beach clean-ups. Imagine a nest box that helped garden birds and albatrosses at the same time. You've got to love the idea of helping two (or many more) birds with one box.

RETURN OF THE TREE SPARROW

I've long held, in the face of scorn from chums who live more scenically or higher up than I do, that my wee bit of country road here in semi-rural north Bedfordshire is a pretty decent spot for wild birds. It's unspectacular. Nondescript, even. Spliced by the A1 and the East Coast Main Line railway, perhaps. Flat too, generally. But the rivers (Great Ouse and Ivel), the greensand ridge, the gravel pits and the presence of mixed farming activity all contribute to a range of habitats that can still support a lot of the farm-dependent species that are declining elsewhere.

Corn buntings, for example. There are more singing at the bottom of my garden in spring than are left in Northern Ireland and Wales put together. Two, that is. Linnets abound, especially in an oilseed-rape year, when they are joined by reed buntings. Yellow wagtails – 11 at one sitting this year – are regulars among the cattle. Cuckoos, turtle doves, lesser whitethroats, yellowhammers, swallows – all seem secure. There are even lapwings, the only ones I know of breeding for miles around, on my cycling route between here and

The Lodge. With foreground interest like this, even the most prosaic backcloth has plenty to distract, and stops me pining for the glens.

I could nearly add to this impressive roll-call of local farmland favourites the formerly widespread and now curiously uncommon tree sparrow. I say 'nearly' because they were present locally not long before I arrived to live in these parts. The Station Road tree sparrows were probably the last surviving breeding colony in the whole county, for ten years or so, according to my source Richard Bashford. Richard also works for the RSPB. This refugee population dwindled to nought in the early 1990s. I visited the site down the road and over the railway to see what a tree sparrow habitat looked and felt like. Eerily empty, I have to report.

So you can imagine my delight when, late in the winter, a small flock of these enigmatic little birds was discovered foraging on a stubble field near my home, by Graham White, an RSPB expert on the conservation management of farmland. Richard Bashford – him again – and I wondered if they could be encouraged to return to breed. For that they would need two things: more food, and somewhere to nest. Seeds, and holes. And insect food when there are offspring to nourish. Not much, really. You'd think there'd be more of it out there.

So, working quickly, and with Amanda Proud of the Ivel and Ouse Countryside Projects, we organised 21 RSPB nest boxes which, with the landowner's blessing, we put up in a spinney near where the sparrows had been discovered. We also set up feeders. The spinney is mainly thorn scrub, with some fairly well-developed ash trees. My impression is that there are very few natural nest holes in the whole area. Tree sparrows need nest holes, as a rule, preferably in groups. They also seem to like being near bodies of open water. We aren't too far from rivers and gravel pits here. So it was just a question of waiting to see if what we had provided would prove helpful.

The uptake of the nest boxes was staggering. Well, I was staggered, at any rate. Not, unfortunately, by the tree sparrows' response, but by that of blue and great tits. The foraging sparrows must have returned from whence they came, perhaps unsurprisingly. But how about this for a vote of confidence from the local tit population? In that first spring, 12 of the 21 boxes were occupied (and a further one by bees), producing more than 60 young birds. And this, remember, from a spinney with practically no natural carrying capacity for hole-nesting birds – though clearly no shortage of caterpillar food.

The demise of tree sparrows has been a little mysterious in its country-wide comprehensiveness. Longer-standing members of staff here at The Lodge recall a time when nest boxes were put up here specifically to attract nesting blue and great tits, and tree sparrows would commandeer the boxes instead. This tended not to be popular. No one thought, in the early 1970s, that the ubiquitous tree sparrow could become a stranger to these parts, and so much of the rest of the country.

Their decline is linked to changes in farming, but it is not straightforward. Tree sparrows have declined before in this country, recovered, and declined again. Their population dynamics are volatile, and a little difficult to fully explain. What we do know is that between 1970 and 1998, 95 per cent have vanished from our countryside. But the good news is that, since then, they have shown signs of picking up, helped along by local recovery initiatives.

Tree sparrows are easy to overlook, especially when there are few of them around, and if – like me – you haven't had a chance to get to know them. They are superficially like house sparrows, but are more clean-cut, and have a telltale black 'ear' patch. They chirp differently too. This is what led me one day to discover a few of them in an Avebury farmyard. I wasted no time in reporting them to the RSPB's then tree sparrow man, Richard Winspear. He – unsurprisingly – already knew about this 'cell' of the fugitive species. Well, he would really, with so few left.

Our nest boxes are still in operation, and the output of great and blue tits has doubled now to over 120 each year. It shows what a difference a few safe nest sites can make to the fortunes of hole-nesting birds. We are still hopeful that one day perhaps a tree sparrow or two will return to take up some of the nest boxes on offer, to reclaim their place on the local farmland bird roster. And we will remain contrite that we ever took their presence on it for granted.

A SIGHT FOR EYESORES

The early-morning commuter train rolls into King's Cross station, north London, swallowed by the immense, cavernous concrete and iron maw of the great city. It's grimy, oily, noisy, dingy. The carriage is packed with passengers wearing bleak, blank, withdrawn, tired and

– in some cases – sullen expressions. It mirrors the surroundings, although buddleia – the butterfly bush – is doing its best to lighten the mood, wild nature clinging to the walls of the concrete gulley, this escapee from suburban gardens, with its crevice toe-holds, thriving somehow despite the lack of light, moisture, soil and fresh air, offering nectar when it flowers to any passing butterfly or bee (though it seems unlikely that many would pass here, this time of year).

I pause to fish for my ticket, to let the hordes clear the ticket barrier further down the platform. Bizarrely, there is birdsong issuing from somewhere up among the concrete and iron walls. It's a familiar song, yet oddly out of place for Britain; a trill, with a curious scratchy, grating quality in one of its phrases, but appropriate to the setting. It's clearly audible in the respite between train station tumult, grinding trains and tannoy announcements.

I don't see it today but I know what it is. It's a black redstart. It's roughly the same size and shape as a robin, but it looks as though it has been held by its russet-coloured tail (or start, hence the name) and dipped in soot. This gives it a striking black and red appearance (which often signals danger in the animal kingdom; the presence of a toxin, a species not to be messed with). The black redstart is simply streetwise, urban, a survivor.

Strange to think, in this situation, that this is one of the rarest breeding birds we have. There are fewer than a hundred pairs thought to be present in these islands. Perhaps as many as one-third are resident in London. They can survive here, but not in many other places. That's kind of weird. Why here, and not in plusher surroundings? After all, just across the English Channel this is a widespread bird. I can barely think of a single stay anywhere in urban, continental Europe that hasn't involved befriending at least one local pair of these birds. Hardly a farm, village or ancient monument is without them, no block of masonry or roof tile has not known the touch of their feet. They seem to take over where our robin leaves off, although they keep their distance from us, seeming always wary and twitchy, content to keep an eye on us but beyond arm's reach.

I think the limits on where they can live and nest in the British Isles are set partly by climate and temperature. They need those vital few extra degrees of warmth you get in inner cities, along coasts and river valleys like the Thames, and perhaps they also steer clear of the demure but passive-aggressive (when it wants to be) robin.

It's well recorded and recalled by some that the heyday of the black redstart in this country followed the unlikely circumstance of the Blitz. Immigrant birds found the rubble and ruins of our major cities greatly to their taste. These must have been the closest thing they'd found here to the rocky crags and screes that had tradition-ally been their home. After the bombsites were cleared after the war and sent on trucks and trains to outlying areas (I often wonder which parts of pre-war London I am walking on near my home in north Beds when the hardcore base of local bridleways is exposed by passing feet), the black redstart had to look elsewhere.

The later decline of heavy industry and shipyards may have offered a different kind of sanctuary. They also took to power sta-tions, sewage farms, derelict warehouses and various other gaps and brownfield sites. It seems that no location is too ugly. You sense that location finders for episodes of *The Sweeney* might just have fol-lowed the black redstarts – if they like it, then it provides the kind of dystopian post-industrial backdrop needed for a chase scene or other denouement of gritty social realism on television.

I can relate to this bird when I reflect on my 1970s childhood in west central Scotland. The local adventure playgrounds of my youth, I can now see, were ideal black redstart habitat – abandoned foundries, railway sidings, scrapyards, coal-yards, spoil heaps (on a scale that felt like Ayers Rock/Uluru) and even the odd unofficial dump. It's all cleared up and sanitised now, and probably wouldn't hold much appeal for the black redstart today.

Luckily the black redstart can adapt to up-and-coming areas too. Employees at the Bank of England showed me some that were be-coming increasingly regular visitors within that stout edifice, and I found on a ledge there what could have been a nest – empty now, but in the sort of position the birds often choose. I'm not sure what the birds have made of the recent gentrification of King's Cross, but I'll be keeping an ear open for them in the hope that they've adapted once again, and are coping with all that shiny newness.

PHANTOM

Berlin. Late February. As chill and still and drab as all the Cold War, spy thriller clichés. I am here with 'Altenkamp!'. That's how Rainer (Altenkamp) answers his hands-free, as we drive to the fourth and last of our destinations this afternoon, here in the east of the sprawling city. This is Rainer's 'precinct'. This is where he does his stake-outs, stalks his quarry, makes his notes. We aren't looking for dissidents, however. Those days are gone. We are looking for goshawks.

Improbably, we are in a playpark. And not a very big one. It makes a change from the first three venues of my whistle-stop tour – all cemeteries. We found evidence of goshawks in all three – plucking sites, nests, tantalising goshawk calls.

The park is dotted with people. The quiet is punctured by the cries of children and small dogs. There is a tennis court, a round-about and swings. Mallards loaf on a tiny duck pond, ice still intact around its muddy, scummy rim. It doesn't look promising. I still have an image of the goshawk as a bird of remote and expansive conifer woodland, where they remain strangely invisible. The trees here, however, are towering in places. In one, Rainer points out a gos nest from last year. Further on, we spot what must be this year's: another huge, dark cone against the grey, in the highest fork of a beech. And I notice dark feathers on the ground. They catch my eye because some are still stirring in the faintest breeze, not wet and stuck to the grass like in the graveyards. Fresh. There is a trail of them. And I notice downy feathers too, and some of these are still airborne.

I absently follow these round in the air with my finger (I realise now this probably looked like the exaggerated, gormless gesture of someone in a pantomime). Without realising it, I am looking up open-mouthed and pointing at the source of this feather trail: a hooded crow, prone on the branch of an oak, 10 feet above our heads, in the firm grip of a juvenile female goshawk.

It is a hyper-real scenario. The phantom of the forest, the grey ghost, the bird you normally see well only in books or glass cases – glass-eyed – now close, animate, fiery-eyed, moving, pulling and tearing, twitching as she dips her head. Purposeful, focused, alert and aware, yet somehow not really looking at us. Looking beyond us, or through us; as though maybe we are now the ghosts, the phantoms. A little disconcerting. Haunting. And quite amazing.

'Don't point at her!' hisses Rainer. Of course, I immediately feel like the gauche, rookie cop, liable to give the game away in his enthusiasm after a prolonged investigation that has led finally to the clinching encounter. I pull my hand away abruptly.

'We need to not look at her – she might not like it,' he whispers.

'We should take turns to look over, while talking to each other – like this...' As he demonstrates the ruse, I sense that Rainer, even after 15 years of study, is nearly as excited as me, not old and cynical like the formula veteran cop. In a way, I'm also gratified to confirm that I can still feel like this myself. I'm like the kid that once was me, seeing my first buzzard, up close.

We attempt a rather awkward, stilted semi-conversation while I at least am struggling to disguise my excitement, stealing glances at this mythical bird, come to life. The goshawk – 'the bird you know is there, because you do not see it', as they say in rural Germany – plain as day, relaxed as a pet, more beautiful than books, pictures, films and of course taxidermy can ever hope to emulate – is right here before us: in a city centre playpark.

It becomes steadily clear that she has not batted a raptor eyelid. This is confirmed when a pram-pushing couple stop immediately below the branch and, as one, look up at her and, yes, point. Perhaps they too have noticed the crow's stomach on the path, discarded by the dining hawk with the bulging crop. Or maybe they just couldn't miss her.

She is 26 inches long, lean, muscular, saffron-tinted and streaked with chocolate-coloured arrowheads. She has that goshawk glare, which makes her look invincible. Perhaps she is. Perhaps the routinely persecuted goshawk has at last found real sanctuary, so close to us now that no one could find it in their heart to hate it, far less shoot it, or trap it, or poison it, or put it in a glass case. In Berlin, at least, the goshawk is now out of the woods, back in our lives, and no longer considered a threat to the state.

Chapter Three

March

The law of the flies

Returning migrant birds like the chiffchaff, the swallow and the cuckoo hog most of the limelight in springtime. It's understandable. We are always lifted when we see and hear them again, increasingly uncertain as we are that their homecoming (as we see it) can still be guaranteed.

We know the avian migrants have been in Africa, and we're getting better at working out exactly where they've been. But do we yet care enough about the flies that bind? There is the obvious stuff, like the blundering bumblebee, rampaging through the dead nettles like a man half-asleep and hung-over, in myopic pursuit of sugary drinks and energising solar warmth. These early spring risers are young queen bees. 'The buzzing bees are out!' I can still picture a neighbour's child running up the garden to let everyone know what he'd seen, and the excitement in his voice that the long winter might actually be over.

And that other airborne nugget of spring, the brimstone butterfly, that materialises as though from the fresh air itself. The brimstone seems always pristine, like a daffodil or primrose that has sprouted wings to get nearer to the sun, to explore the world. You imagine it must just have hatched, but in fact these early fliers have spent the winter slotted into a wall of ivy or an evergreen shrub somewhere, trying not to be noticed. This is the butter-coloured fly that gave its name to this entire group of insects, perhaps because it is often seen first, and makes such an impact, at least in southern Britain. Or perhaps there were just many more of them, once upon a time.

I find nowadays that I can get a quiet, inner buzz of gratification from other, even earlier, signs of spring from tinier, less feathery creatures, going more modestly about their work. Perhaps it's that I feel more directly responsible for their re-emergence, their life cycles being more permanently linked to my own, to the fixtures and fittings of the garden. But it's also sense that these small things – dormant and torpid and latent in the winter landscape – are the mostly invisible threads that link all life together.

Of the humble earthworm, Charles Darwin himself wondered 'whether there are any other animals which have played such an important part in the history of the world'.

I'm not sure if it's exactly what I intended or envisaged when I planted my front garden more than a decade ago, but the car park is now transformed into a kind of arena. It is edged on all sides by stout hedgerow, border plants, climbers and the south-facing wall of the house. Centre stage is a bird bath, but otherwise the stage is clear, and set, for whatever might emerge from the wings, the gods, or even below stage, to announce the advancing seasons.

And here's a current favourite. In the dwindling light of a still day in early March, there are animals that gather here to dance. They assemble in mid-air in a loose cluster, bouncing up and down like puppets on elastic. As a group they look like they are moving fast, but if you fix your gaze on just one, you realise that its pace is quite leisurely. It could just be the arena effect, but they recall a tribe, celebrating the end of winter, worshipping the earth from which they have emerged once again. All they lack to complete the illusion is a drumbeat. They are quite silent, and inoffensive, and don't bite. They ease away gently at my approach, bobbing and weaving. But what exactly are they? And what are they doing?

A quick leaf through an insect ID guide suggests they are, in fact, 'dance flies' (or bobbing gnats). There are 350 species in the UK; it's hard to identify precisely at species level. In any case, I haven't brought a specimen in for full inspection. I note that their emergence coincides with my elderly and poorly neighbour's first Spring venture outside. Meanwhile, the kids in the neighbourhood are boisterous again with the lengthening and vaguely warming days.

Reading on, I discover that the dance flies pogo-ing over the lawn are the males. The females are sitting nearby, unseen, as though on the edge of a dance floor, watching. When the mood takes them, they fly up to join in, to select a male, presumably on the basis of his moves…

It gets better. The male has other powers of seduction. He can produce silk, and wrap gifts with it – usually an even smaller fly – which he gives to the female before mating. In some species the male sometimes employs deception, and presents an empty silk-wrapped package. Or it may contain something inedible. I should also mention that the male runs the risk of being eaten by his partner. Fair's fair.

They may be a hazard to the open-mouthed cyclist, but I find the presence of flies like these comforting: even the early house flies, which gather on the sunny brickwork to get revved up, and turn up on the wrong side of the window, 'to stand on the sky, and try their buzz', as Ted Hughes put it. I take pleasure in shepherding them out, so that they might go and find something smelly, and run the gauntlet of the house martins.

Above all, the presence of early spring flies of whatever stripe, bounce or hairiness means that the main event – the headlining migratory birds – have a landscape worth coming back to. Not that insects are simply bird food. It's worth bearing in mind that some insects, like the common gnat, depend on the blood of birds for a living. It cuts both ways.

It's now more than 50 years since Rachel Carson wrote *Silent Spring*, which warned the world that some especially noxious insecticides, laid on thick, were threatening to silence birdsong once and for all. And while it was the birds that made the headline, Carson's point was also that we need to cherish the insects and the other small, voiceless and spineless things. Because if we do, we still stand a fair chance that the birds, and the singing to go with the dancing, may yet take care of themselves.

MAD FOR IT

I mentioned already that I live about seven miles from the RSPB headquarters at Sandy, in Bedfordshire. Apart from the greensand ridge on which Bird Central sits, this is a flat part of the country, with large, open, arable fields that allow access for combine harvesters the size of maisonettes. To some people this can seem like quite a featureless landscape. But there are aspects of it that I like – the sense of open space, the huge skies, the relatively low rainfall, the long days, with sun rising and sinking low on each horizon, east and west in turn. And there are definitely things about it that brown hares like. They may have declined nationally by 80 per cent in the last century, but this is one species that appears to be thriving around here.

If I am up early enough I can walk or cycle to work along quiet, single-track roads, bridleways and footpaths. One stretch follows the route of a Roman road called Hazell's Hedge, and this skirts the end of a now disused airfield; disused as far as we are concerned, but it is a brilliant place to watch hares. For them, the runways are just that.

By the standards of most of our wild mammals, hares can be quite easy to see, but difficult to see well. They are active by day, they live in open spaces with commanding views, and they don't live in burrows. However, they are good at spotting *you*, and are very good at putting a safe distance between you and them, by lifting themselves up on long back legs and moving up through the gears, from a canter to a gallop. Sometimes I do get quite close, briefly, as I round a bend on my bike and find one browsing by the path.

I was up early one weekend morning and watched a hare emerge from the gateway to the field opposite. Looking one way, then the other, it ventured out towards the road, then proceeded to lope up the street. I've no idea where it was going, but it appeared pretty sure of its route, and may just have been taking a shortcut to a new field for a spot of grazing. Once upon a time, a hare walking in a village street was taken as a warning of fire. In fact, it's one of the many life forms about which deep superstitions were held. It seems that hares, with their staring eyes, nocturnal habits and fooling about were inclined to spook the locals.

I have also been lucky enough to see hares 'boxing' in the fields that back on to my garden. Hares do this in the early spring when they are establishing breeding rights. In fact, it's usually the females biffing the males to subdue their premature advances. Their manic behaviour at this time earns them the title of 'mad March hares', which is the basis for the character in *Alice in Wonderland*. He was always in a hurry, and hares in spring are very restless.

You could say a hare is basically a rabbit built for speed, with powerful hind legs that give it added pace; that turn it from a sports car into a racing car, if you like. Hares can achieve speeds of up to 64 km per hour. Until 2005 the practice of hare coursing, which involves hunting hares using hounds, was still legal where the landowner permitted it. In many other places it was carried out illegally. I used to see shadowy figures with greyhounds operating out of lay-bys, although I was never clear how their activities would be any more cruel or damaging than those of legal hunts.

The outlawing of hunting by setting dogs on to other animals for recreation made hare coursing illegal. It's possible that since then hares may be slowly shedding their aversion to us, or that a gradual recovery of their numbers might bring them closer to where we live. I had this thought as I watched one trot calmly past the window as I had breakfast at a friend's house one morning. They've always seemed very active by day in these parts, and not just because I've roused them.

In the uplands of north and west Scotland, northern England and Ireland, the mountain or blue hare replaces the lowland brown hare. It's a separate but related species, and although the two can and do sometimes interbreed, these alliances don't produce fertile offspring. Both species of hare rear their young not in burrows, like rabbits, but in long grass or heather, in a simple 'bivouac' type of shelter, called a form.

In the Highlands of Scotland mountain hares are hunted by golden eagles. In these environs the hare turns white (or bluish-white, hence the name) in winter, to blend in with the snowy landscape and attempt to go unnoticed.

They are very tightly woven into the fabric of our landscape now, but brown hares aren't actually a native species in the UK. They are thought, like rabbits, to have been brought over by the Romans – although some people believe they may have already been here when the last ice age ended, and the melting ice and rising sea levels created the English Channel, which now separates us from continental Europe.

Brown hares have become very scarce in some lowland areas, particularly western, pastoral country, but here in the arable east they may still be present in decent numbers. Once you know where to look for them, entertaining views can be enjoyed in spring, especially if you sit still, downwind, and have some binoculars handy. You may even be lucky enough to see them going 'mad', and I can guarantee that at such times they will definitely be more interested in each other than in any onlookers.

STARING AT THE RUDE BOYS

Have you looked closely at a starling recently? The older I get, the fonder of them I become. They haven't, traditionally, been everyone's cup of tea, let's be honest, and I'll readily admit they weren't always mine. I have tended, like a lot of people, to regard them as the unwanted guest at the bird table – rolling in like rude boys in unruly mobs, gate-crashing the party, clambering on the peanut feeder, guzzling the grub in a vulgar, unrefined sort of way, scattering the civilised birds in all directions, then leaving without so much as a nod of thanks in your direction.

The term 'rude boys' was originally coined for the itinerant youth of Jamaica. When I was at school the concept had spread to kids here who dressed sharply, with cropped hair, tight trousers and boots. They were into ska music, a kind of souped-up reggae, which inspires a particular kind of jerky, angular dancing. The parallels with the starling are obvious – to me, at any rate, and to my brother Kevin, who first suggested the analogy. The juveniles often look like they're wearing wraparound sunglasses, for goodness' sake.

As if their lack of table manners wasn't sufficient grounds for disdaining starlings, they then became synonymous, for me, with exams. It always seemed to me particularly sadistic on the part of our academic institutions that exams were scheduled in May and June, when you least want to be cooped up indoors swotting, and sweating, over things like the Tolpuddle Martyrs and vectors. (I swear I haven't seen a vector since.)

In my experience every school exam was carried out in the tense, hushed atmosphere of a prefabricated classroom, while nesting starlings wheezed and rasped and squawked somewhere in the roof, singularly failing to observe decorum. It was much the same at Stirling University, where we also sat exams in May, and there they were again, gurgling under the gutters, ferrying grubs and worms from the daisy-covered lawns to the eaves, while yours truly chewed on a pencil and dreamed of liberation.

Despite these associations, I am learning to love starlings.

In late summer they are forming into groups, probing the roadside verges open-beaked, or gliding in loose flocks between feeding opportunities. Their opportunism and versatility appeal to me. In a north London street one quiet Sunday morning I watched them tidying up a tiny front garden where there had been a party the night before, a noisy gaggle of them acting like a sanitation squad, chortling and chattering and squealing, juveniles begging for scraps rather than looking for it themselves.

And then on a visit to Carnoustie, on the mouth of the Tay, I notice there is a starling on every television aerial, speaking in tongues, looking skyward, as though communing with extra-terrestrial intelligences.

Compared to our other garden birds, the range of their vocalisations is incredible, really. How often I have looked up, expecting to see a kestrel, a buzzard, a lapwing, curlew or swallow. Instead, there is Mr Starling, with his multiple personalities, jabbering his bill and bristling his beard, spangled in sequins, iridescent in a slightly oily way in the sunshine, watching the sky to see who is watching him, who is passing, who might come down for a closer listen, and perhaps a closer look at the nest cavity he is advertising. On my house they inspect every possible opening, including martins' nests (which they break, in a clumsy way) and sparrow boxes, which they have no hope of squeezing into.

The starling gets its name from 'stare ling', thanks to its beady eyes. It is amazing to think that until relatively recently this was only a winter visitor to our islands, much like redwings are now, for example, as evidenced by the Welsh name 'bird of the snow'.

I don't see the huge, kaleidoscopic flocks that you find wheeling over Brighton pier, but near me they do gather to roost in some tall cypress trees. When the starlings are in situ the trees themselves appear to hum and sing, as though charged with some kind of electricity, as the birds settle for the night, having a million conversations about who sits where, and what dangers the night air might hold.

The starling is perhaps the most reptilian-looking of our familiar birds. It embodies the link between birds and their ancestors, with their scaly appearance and beady eyes, stalking around on long legs and muscular thighs.

But even the starling – so businesslike, no-nonsense and pragmatic a feeder, so intelligent and varied a communicator, so sensible a nester, secure in its holes – is on the decline, diminishing in number by 66 per cent between 1970 and 2001. I suspect this is another reason why I find them so engaging, why I've grown to like them so much more. They're so in a world of their own, when you look at them, yet so much at the mercy of a world of our making.

WAKING UP TO BIRDS

I like telling people that I work for the RSPB. It usually brings some flicker of approval and some questions, opinions, anecdotes. I also like telling novices what I can about birds, fanning any ember of interest. Of course, it helps if there are birds around to illustrate the talk.

I'm in a reading retreat with the alluring name of Palazzo Montefano, near Bologna, on the fertile plains of north-east Italy. Its equivalent for us might be our Lincolnshire or Cambridgeshire fens – not a typical tourist destination, although the rolling hills of Tuscany are visible on the horizon.

'Oh, *you're* the bird guy!' Clark Lawrence, the American behind the reading retreat concept, exclaimed on the first evening, as we sat round a burning log fire. He had just made the connection between me and the emails I'd sent some time earlier.

Clark, we all agreed over dinner, is a cross between the actors Tim Robbins (*Shawshank Redemption*) and Anthony Perkins (*Psycho*); a little disconcerting when you first arrive, it's dusk and the big empty tiled hall is lit only by candles. Clark's Palazzo exists to promote culture of all kinds, with its shelves of books, its great acoustics and its wall spaces hung with or awaiting artworks, and Romeo the resident stray cat padding noiselessly across wide tiles.

Replete – or perhaps overwhelmed – with thoughts of art, I wake to the relatively simple pleasure of birdsong this morning. I am in a room which, with its high, domed and frescoed ceiling, is the shape of a panettone. Through a gap in shuttered windows I can just see the morning mist clearing from among the daffodils. I smell that sweet river smell that seems to typify rural southern Europe. Clark and Rachel are already on the wide doorstep, with hordes of sparrows around them, thrilled with the light and warmth of spring. Still-bare Lombardy poplars ring the garden, branches brushed upwards, like the heads of brooms. A solo goldfinch is in full twinkling voice at the top of a near one.

'You've got a goldfinch,' I announce blearily. Rachel cranes upwards to look, and Clark, appetite whetted, slips indoors to fetch a bird book from the library: *Ucelli d'Italia e d'Europa*. We haven't even had breakfast yet, but he is hungry only for knowledge. Starting on page 1, he wants to translate the names of the birds into English. All of them. This is a test of my attention span and my knowledge, especially since some of the photographs are a bit iffy (I maintain).

Marsh tit. Or is *Parus palustris* willow tit? Reed warbler. Or is it sedge warbler? Tree pipit. Or is it a rock or meadow pipit? Grey wagtail. I'm sure the photo is yellow wagtail. The *cutrettola – Motacilla flava* – looks like a yellow wagtail, and *ballerina gialla – Motacilla cinerea* – the grey. Willow warbler. Is it *lui grosso* and chiffchaff *lui piccolo*? *Sylvia trochilus* has pale legs – a willow warbler, I think. I will check when I get home. And so it goes on.

Clark and Rachel tell me about their owls, their woodpecker, their egrets (including the one that turned out to be a polythene bag). I am learning too. Little owl: *civetta* – the Italian word for a flirtatious girl. A garden warbler is a *beccafico*. And, I am pleased to discover, the Italian name for magpie is *gazza*.

Clark's excitement mounts. Kingfisher: 'We have those!' Nightjar: 'Is that something you pee in?' Coot: 'Those babies look like they've been through the washing machine, or scalded!'

The game ends on the hooded crow page: 'Take it away from me!' Clark thrusts the book in my direction and his face in the other. 'It's eating something dead in a river!' he shrieks. I scribble the last of the names over the pictures of the hoodie – *cornacchia grigia*.

Trauma over, the questions continue. 'How do you get birds to come to a bird house?' he asks me. 'Italian birds don't come to bird feeders. Isn't that *weird*?'

'Do English and Italian birds speak the same language?' he continues.

'Yes,' I reply, 'although accents can differ.' He looks at me sceptically. It's true, I assure him. I mimic a cuckoo as an example, with the changed emphasis in its call (more stress on second syllable) I have heard in some places.

Theory lesson over, we watch the garden. Some of the birds from the pictures materialise. A jay squawks and bounces down onto the grass. I hand Clark my telescope. 'It's beautiful…' he whispers. 'Look at the blue! What's he got in his beak? It's huge!'

The telescope also brings to life the presence of green woodpeckers, landing at the base of the trunks, crouching by the chicken coop licking up ants, and clinging to a telegraph pole just outside the garden, perhaps to have a look around. We make the link between that laughing call and these avian manikins with the parrot colours.

We hear the drum of a great spotted woodpecker, which Clark has noticed before but thought was a sound effect from the sawmill. Rachel tells me she thought that 'lesser spotted' meant not so often seen. Like me, she originally came here for a few days. She was able to stay for a year and now helps to run the place.

We look at starlings on the topmost spray of a few of the poplars, running through their repertoire of overheard gurglings and jabberings, and clacking their bills. We try to get them to mimic our whistles, without luck.

Great tits explore the stumps where past storms have pruned the poplars. Of all things, a male hen harrier appears from the side of the house, slides through the poplars as though on a wire – causing a momentary interlude in the sparrow din – drifts across the garden and out over the neighbouring field and farmhouse, wobbling in that controlled harrier way. A passing stranger, I think: the local birds show momentary uncertainty but little sign of recognition, by scattering or scolding. The *gazze* didn't escort it out of Montefano airspace. We were lucky to be looking in that direction at that moment.

A chiffchaff calls and as we eat lunch it comes to the poplar under which we are sitting. I am able to interrupt conversation to point it out. It's too close to focus the telescope on. The first house martins and swallows circle high overhead.

After lunch we slump in stripy deckchairs in the sun, to assimilate our pasta. I really like deckchairs. I hear Italian voices, the faraway bark of something small and yappy, the urgent strains of a distant sawmill. A tiny rasping draws my eye to a wasp, basking – like me – in these first rays of spring. It is chewing the arm of my chair. Oh well, there is wood enough for us both. The Italian for butterfly is *farfalla* – I like that word. A swallow-tailed one zigzags past.

If I squint I have views of barn-scale, square shuttered buildings with tiled gabled roofs. Tiny figures are hazy on the horizon, hoeing, timeless, almost placeless apart from the Italian murmurings that fluctuate in the still air. Cars beetle along powdery tracks. A neighbour stops by on her horse. And I am sure I hear a golden oriole calling briefly, flutily, hauntingly, from a poplar in the far corner.

Weela wee-o. Weedle-a wee-o.

I suppose I should be reading. But there's a lot to be said for falling asleep to birds too.

LIVING WITH THE HAWK

I am pottering in the back garden; playing in the dirt, really, totally absorbed, in the guise of doing minor chores. My daydreams are interrupted by a bird commotion, the kind that makes you think 'hawk' even before you've seen one. I turn as indeed a hawk arcs round the house and earthwards on fanned wings, passing only a couple of feet over my head, accompanied by a forlorn cheeping. The cheeps are issuing from the bundle in its clutches.

The sparrowhawk lands gently on my neighbour's lawn, about 15 feet from me. I have a clear view through the trellis on the fence, and from there I watch, heart beating fast, as the male hawk subdues its struggling captive, a house sparrow.

The resident birds are gathered; clacking, pinking and trilling their indignation. The hawk's only acknowledgement of the fuss is to nonchalantly duck the one dive-bomb launched by an incandescent male blackbird from the roof of the greenhouse. The blackbird has more reason than usual to be alarmed. His fledged brood has been loafing around the lawns in recent days, plump and indiscreet.

The sparrow's struggling ceases, and the hawk begins to unwrap its prize. It dips delicately, and calmly, while the row around it rages on. It flicks the down aside and pulls the wing primaries out one or two at a time.

This male hawk is little bigger than the blackbirds haranguing it; certainly leaner. Standing on long legs, it is handsome with its russet-barred chest, slate-blue back, long, barred tail, and intense, purposeful but slightly anxious expression. A bird, but quite unlike those that it has noised up: indifferent, aloof, unfeeling, yet severe.

Like David Beckham about to take a corner kick, to fire the ball into the goal with deadly accuracy, in front of jeering opposition fans, the hawk is inured to such abuse. *This is what I do. This is what I do well. I don't expect you to like me for it.*

My emotions are mixed. I find it impossible not to feel sorry for the wee bird that has been caught. For many people, I think, there is something hard to accept about one bird eating another; we find this less acceptable than what the cat brings in. And something seems unfair about a bird that looks so expertly predatory picking on something as innocent as a sparrow – because when you see a catch it looks easy, and slightly devious, the victims look so helpless and vulnerable, and you are usually as taken by surprise as it is.

But this I think overlooks the hawk's skill and work-rate. It belies how difficult it is, in fact, to catch a fit and healthy sparrow, or any of its garden compatriots, all of which are almost constantly alert for danger, and always telling tales – *the hawk is in the neighbourhood* – scuppering the ambushes, tipping off the targets. Without the element of surprise, the deadly game of chase cannot be won by the hawk. The hawk must be daring, take risks, withstand hunger, bruising branches, thorns, cats, crows. It earns its living; it deserves its place in nature.

You don't go and see hawks: they just appear, and disappear usually as quickly. I have seen them steeplechasing across back gardens, skimming fences, sheds and cypresses in turn. I have seen – and heard – them crashing into shrubberies; seen them vaulting hedges on the nearby fields and coming to land empty-taloned. And I have watched them sitting on the gable end of the outhouse, beady eyes glinting, scanning, hungry – ravenous, quite possibly – sizing up the terrain. And then they dive, as though into water, like a seal off a rocky headland, slipping downwards and porpoising off across the assault course of suburbia.

They appear to me quite often. I like this. I am old enough to remember when there were none, then when seeing them became a rare treat, and then when it became more commonplace, because the countryside had cleansed itself of the deadly, persistent toxin, DDT, and you knew this because the hawks were back.

But what about the sparrows? You see a sparrowhawk, and it looks – on the face of it – to be bad news for sparrows. It must mean there are less of them. Well, it could hardly mean that there are more. Or could it? There were no sparrowhawks in many areas in the 1950s and 1960s. Look at the breeding bird populations in an English woodland, and compare the years in which the sparrowhawk was common, then when it was absent, and the years when it was present again. You see no difference. How come? In a nutshell, because raptors eat the surplus offspring; those that once would have succumbed to starvation, illness, hard weather or a combination of these factors. The same numbers survive to breed the following spring as ever did. If the habitat is good, the bird populations are viable.

I have a feeling that the behaviour of garden birds is a little different now than it was in the days when sparrowhawks were only seen in the pages of field guides. The return of the hawk may have made the birds it chases more skittish, more wary. There's an added edge to life in the garden. A drama, a fearful dimension. It may not be pleasant to witness sometimes, but it's nature in the raw. They may look murderous, but in a strange and counter-intuitive sort of way, hawks are not representative of death. They actually stand for health, of a kind, and therefore life. This is not much consolation if you are a sparrow in a hawk's claws, but a truism nevertheless.

REFLECTIONS FROM A LIBRARY

It's spring 2011, and I've been spending my lunch breaks poring over books in the RSPB library. It's no more than a large room, with a bay window overlooking the formal garden, but it houses one of the biggest collections of ornithological books in the land. Today, the serenity and learnedness of the scene is interrupted by an irregular and persistent tapping sound. I turn to find a pair of chaffinches attacking their reflections in two of the window panes above me. I have noticed this in previous years, and it strikes me as odd that these particular windows are singled out for assault, from one year to the next.

When I raise it with him, I am astonished when librarian Ian Dawson (aka IKD) tells me that chaffinches have done this at these two windows every year for the 33 years he's worked here. That's a long time – and could be even longer, in pre-Ian days – and who knows how many generations of chaffinch.

This behaviour is not uncommon in chaffinches, and other species. It's the focus on these particular windows over such a long time that's intriguing. Is there something about the particular reflection cast by the glass that exercises the birds?

I have two or three colleagues who I like to bounce these tricky questions off. I enjoy the range of theories that can emerge, from the considered to the facetious.

'I didn't know that,' replies one, almost as long-serving as IKD. 'Amazing. Presumably reflections, but why chaffinches? And 33 years seems a long time for the presumed necessary conditions to prevail.'

'You could be missing the point,' replies another. 'Perhaps it knows something about IKD that we don't? Maybe Ian did something terrible to a chaffinch way back. Fringillids have long memories.'

'Your trouble is you don't care what birds *think*,' I tell him. 'But consider yourself quoted in a leading scientific journal.'

'But perhaps they'll stop, when Ian retires,' I propose. Cue *Twilight Zone* music...

I make enquiries more widely at The Lodge to find out if anyone else has seen chaffinches do this at other windows here, to establish the exclusivity of this spot/behaviour. I don't uncover any other examples, although quite a few people know about the library birds.

A year on, IKD has retired... and perhaps the long line of lairy chaffinches has retired with him. But no. The chaffinches are back. So much for the theory of IKD's personal chaffinch magnetism.

Having ruled out the librarian variable, I seek the views of Professor Tim Birkhead, author of the acclaimed *Bird Sense:What it's like to be a bird*, on what it is about our chaffinches and/or this window that might explain this long-standing, localised delinquency.

'How can the behaviour can have been so sustained over such a long period?' I ask him. 'And across such a large number of generations of chaffinches? I don't know of chaffinches attacking any other windows here, or of other examples from elsewhere of such repeated behaviour at specific windows over a long period of time.'

'Interesting,' says Tim. 'I'm sure it happens elsewhere as well. Although chaffinches are very long-lived for a small bird, it is (obviously) unlikely to be the same birds.'

'I did wonder if there might be some particular reflective quality in this glass,' I add, 'such as it being old or warped or magnifying in some way, but there is really nothing obviously remarkable about the panes.'

'It could just be that the local circumstances promote this behaviour – as you suggest,' he replies. 'The way the window reflects the light; the proximity of the window to where the bird might nest, etc. Who know? Because of the nature of the window, the bird might perceive its image in a very specific way. Why not have the window re-glazed and then sit there for another 33 years? Seriously, the only way you'd figure this out is to do some kind of experiment. Putting a laminated film over the glass might do it. However, if it was something about the window, then it is surprising that you haven't had other territorial birds doing the same thing.'

'Thanks Tim,' I reply. 'I'll get the step-ladder out, to get a closer look at the window. I'll let you know if I find my reflection grotesque and menacing...'

I update IKD, now relaxing in retirement, but ever willing to indulge such queries. 'Good to know the habit is alive and well,' he replies. 'A good sign that spring is on its way!'

He has dug out his notes on the matter. He's also already done an experiment like the one suggested by Prof. Birkhead. 'One year I attached a mirror with double-sided sticky things to the inside of the window to see if the clearer reflection would deter the window tapper,' he reports, 'but as far as I could tell it made no difference at all: the attacks continued at much the same rate as before, for several weeks.'

I've always been a bit more interested in what animals are doing, and therefore thinking, than has been good for me. I'm sometimes envious of those who shun such preoccupations, and carry on with the pursuit of black-and-white certainties, such as what and how many of them there are.

In the end, though, I like what is unknowable in nature, especially when it's right under the nose of all that accumulated knowledge, in book and brain, at RSPB HQ. That nagging, tapping sound over your shoulder, which will be well known to quite a few authors and researchers who have used this library in spring. It's almost as though those damn birds have got something to tell us.

THE AVERAGE BIRD

Watching blackbirds in action around the bird table, you could be excused some puzzlement at the success of this species. Because although the blackbird has been, without question, extremely good at what it does – that is, being a bird – it can come across as a bit lame of bird brain, frankly. Not the sharpest beak in the pecking order, shall we say. And this in spite of its apparent obsession with trying to peck its fellows.

Take today. A heavy fall of snow in the night has brought the birds out in force to refuel. I've provided a scattering of seeds and scraps in a small area of cleared snow, below the feeders in the ash tree out front. As many as six blackbirds are in attendance, and they must of course be hungry after a night in sub-zero temperatures. I know I am. But instead of getting on, like the starlings and sparrows, and me, with the serious business of eating food, they are so intent on fussing, posturing, squabbling and hassling each other that they hardly seem to recall what brought them here in the first place. Or to notice the steadily dwindling piles of seed, as the more community-spirited and focused of their relatives crack on with trying to stay alive.

It is as though the blackbird doesn't mind who gets it, so long as it's not another blackbird – male or female. And when just one blackbird is left, it stands there gormlessly, as though smugly surveying the lack of rivals, and ignoring the curious lack of food.

And yet the blackbird, in terms of numbers at least, is right up there with our most successful birds. It survives in every corner of these isles, from the Hebrides to the centre of London, from mountainsides to dense conifer plantations. It loves suburbia, and is ten times as numerous there as in farmland. There are an estimated six million-plus diligently defended blackbird territories here. And then there are the blackbirds that join us from northern Europe in winter. Some of my six may be German birds.

It's not bad going for a bird that at times can seem so bumptious, highly strung, neurotic, belligerent, proprietorial and, it must be said, self-defeating. Perhaps these traits are common to a lot of high achievers. These are birds that live life with reckless abandon, throwing themselves under garden forks, turning up in our kitchens, flying into patio doors. They also eat practically anything, from apples to tadpoles, and will nest practically anywhere too, and not, in many cases, discreetly. No, the blackbird plonks an eye-catching bowl of straw and any other debris pretty much wherever takes its fancy, often decorated with domestic refuse. Active forklift trucks, traffic lights and public lavatories are among the zanier choices recorded.

Some moss was seen; I thought it laid
By boys to make each other stare
But bye and bye a nest was made
And eggs like fairy gifts were there.

John Clare, from *The Blackbird*

I'd guess blackbird nests are most people's first close-up encounter with birds as things that nest. Even as a small child you will sooner or later run into a blackbird nest in a place that even a toddler can't miss. It is, as Mark Cocker puts it in *Birds Britannica*, 'often a long-remembered detail from the paradise of childhood and our first magical encounter with the reproductive strategy of the whole class *Aves*.'

And blackbirds get away with this recklessness because they tend to nest a lot – three or four times in a season. One story brought home to me how hell-bent the blackbird is on reproducing. This was a description of a female blackbird gathering straw for her latest nest. As she did so, one of her offspring from nest number one was following her, and begging, beak agape. Momentarily confused, the female bird paused for a second and then shoved the straw into the fledged bird's gullet. One way of cutting the avian apron strings, I suppose.

It wasn't always such a widespread bird. There is evidence that in past centuries the song thrush was the more widespread and familiar of the two. The blackbird took until quite recently to extend its coverage to the whole of north Scotland. And although blackbird numbers are now falling slowly, it has some way to go to match the rate of decline of its more retiring cousin.

I'm sure some people reading this will be starting to feel a little protective of good old *Turdus merula* by now. And of course I should point out that I do actually like the blackbird a lot. It has at least one redeeming feature. Its song. It is perhaps for this reason alone that we forgive the blackbird its foibles, and overlook its gaucheness. The liquid fluting of a blackbird is the backdrop to all our summers. Hear it in winter on the TV, and you are transported straight to the village green, the orchard in blossom, to a mood of drowsy well-being on a long spring evening.

The blackbird is arguably the identikit bird – average-sized, generalist diet, lives anywhere, gets on with people. Its niche could be said to be its very lack of one. By comparison, all other species seem a little particular. It's an average job, but something has to do it.

And it is just this – the sheer average-ness of the blackbird – that makes it so successful, so ready to adapt, to fit in, to improvise, in the jungles of suburbia and beyond. It's generally been good at being a bird, in an uncertain, humanoid world. And who, in the end, needs brains, with a talent like that?

THE NOT SO RATTY RAT

Old Frank was a countryman, by anyone's definition. He'd lived for most of his life in this row of cottages of which Johnny-come-lately – I – was now sharing a part, for a year's tenancy. He was nearing retirement age, although it was unlikely that he would in any conventional sense ever actually retire. He would just carry on being the odd-job man for the estate, smoking his pipe and vaulting the gate of a morning, until it was time for him to leave.

He stopped me one morning. 'Cat brought a big rat in, last night,' he announced, with a hint of pride, through what was left of his teeth, confident I'd be interested in such a development. I followed him to his back door, a matter of yards from my own. The 'rat' was laid out in a dish. It was quite large, right enough, but not unduly so, for a rat. It was a little ruffled, but with no obvious injuries. There were features of it that did not say 'rat' to me. The tail, for instance, was much too short. It was furred, not bristly. The nose was blunt, not pointy. This wasn't a rat, as such, although in fairness to Frank he may well have meant water rat – which is the old countryman's name for the water vole that we were looking at. Kenneth Grahame's vole was called Ratty, after all. Confused? It's been happening for a long time. *Wind in the Willows* is now more than a century old.

'It's a water vole,' I offered, adding, 'Brilliant!' Not brilliant that it was dead, of course, but you know what I mean. In any case Old Frank didn't seem too troubled by the distinction. Mere semantics, he might have been thinking, if not in so many words.

There was a brook at the bottom of the garden. I like to think that I would have discovered water voles here soon enough, but it took the dead one to alert me to the possibility of them. I paid an evening visit to set up a vole vigil. What surprised me was just how easy it was to watch them here, on the banks, as they scurried along their well-worn paths, by their burrows, and even in the water itself, as they torpedoed along, stirring the mud.

Unlike with real rats, it's not hard to sympathise with water voles. Plump, short-sighted, set in their ways, easy to find, active in broad daylight, cute, harmless, disease-free (probably), not in the attic, vegetarian (mostly – I was interested to read that they do eat fish from time to time). What may also surprise you about water voles is that they are not confined to aquatic places, and can thrive equally well on dry land.

Their decline is well recorded – thought to be as much as 90 per cent in just two decades. Among the main causes have been loss of habitat, persecution – I am sure in many cases in the mistaken belief that they are real rats – and their vulnerability to predation by the American mink. Water voles are evolved enough to make well-defended dens with underwater entrance holes, but these are no protection against the introduced mink. Entire vole colonies are wiped out by these formidable predators.

My local colony seemed pretty secure, but shortly before I moved on, disaster struck, in another guise. The drainage authorities dredged the brook – as dredge they must – and transformed this 100-metre stretch of waterway into a denuded trench. I discovered the desolation on my return from work. I was shocked to see forlorn and visibly traumatised voles clinging to the near-vertical sides of the newly-scooped ditch. They really did look as though a bomb had hit them. The following spring, it became an offence to damage water vole habitat under the Wildlife and Countryside Act – too late for my voles, but likely to help them in future if they could recover.

Ten years have passed. I returned to the scene one bright breezy day in early April, to see if the voles had recolonised. Ten years is a long time in weed-growth terms. This year's surge of nettles had just started, through a tangle of dry stems. So, there was plenty of vole cover at least. I carefully walked the bank, and could see on the opposite side what looked like vole tracks, droppings – and, yes, even burrow entrances, both in the mud of the brook itself and higher up.

There was a telltale splosh, and a swish of mud, and the distinctive shadow of a vole shooting downstream. This was my only glimpse, but I'm delighted to confirm that the banks on both sides are once again pockmarked with holes and laced with vole pathways. There is something about this little stretch of brook that works for water voles, and keeps them going when they have gone completely from all but one in ten of their former haunts. Water voles occur on at least 41 RSPB nature reserves, and thrive in carefully managed reed beds. We hope that from these safe havens they might be able to spread and recolonise well-managed wetland systems elsewhere.

Incidentally, I was also very pleased to note on my visit a little plume of smoke from up by the cottage, issuing from the unmistakable form of Old Frank. There was no sign of the cat, mind you.

THE SPIRIT OF FENTON

I'm not sure why I laughed so much when I saw Fenton, the black Labrador, in what is by now a legendary piece of amateur footage. It has even gone viral, viewed about 10 million times on the Internet.

In fact, I'm not sure it's even right to laugh at it, but laugh I – and so many others – obviously have. I'm not actually sure why it's even funny. I've been trying to analyse the reasons.

First, it's worth mentioning that not everyone has found it funny. Comedian Paul Merton, for example, national treasure and observational surrealist, was surprisingly – but completely – nonplussed by it. In fact it was on his show, *Have I Got News for You,* that I first saw the clip, and caught on to the phenomenon. It was by this time already such a big deal online that it was making broadcast news headlines, in that oddly democratic way that everyday incidents can climb the news agenda.

In case you haven't seen it, the clip opens with an idyllic rural scene. It's a view of Richmond Park. Fallow deer are relaxing in the meadow, among some scattered trees. The tranquillity is interrupted by the sound of a man shouting in the distance. 'Fenton!' comes the cry, in a sergeant-major, parade-ground bark, repeated every few seconds. There is increasing volume and urgency each time. The onlooker's camera-phone pans to the right, to reveal a lot more deer, beginning to stampede into view. Within seconds the gathered and now large herd is galloping away. Into shot comes the streaking black shape of what one can only assume is Fenton.

This is clearly a dog whose moment of glory has arrived. Suddenly the dappled deer are like gazelles, the manicured, sanitised park is the wild Serengeti. Fenton has reverted to wolf state. One can almost hear Attenborough's breathy commentary in his head. 'Seeing his opportunity, Fenton must hunt. The life-or-death struggle of Richmond Park plays out in the heat of the Middlesex afternoon...'

Behind him, and lagging behind somewhat, and at a much less impressive pace, comes the owner of the dog, and the voice.

'Oh, Jesus *Christ!*' he gasps, as the futility of his efforts to retrieve the situation become apparent. 'Fen-*tonnnnnn!*'

Just one man and his dog, in complete disharmony. You'd think a dog with such a distinguished name would at least turn round, let alone come to heel, when ordered to. There is another 'Jesus Christ!' or two for good measure. There is anguish in the blasphemy, the kind of oath normally uttered as death throes in a movie. Of course, it feels entirely out of proportion to the seriousness of the situation, viewed from the comfort of your living room.

The joke seems not, for some, to wear thin. An equally hilarious spoof has also now appeared in which these cries of 'Fenton!' are overdubbed on a sequence from Jurassic Park in which dinosaurs stampede across a primeval plain. There's also a TV ad in which a veritable Noah's Ark-worth of life forms are fleeing the unseen beast. The owner's cries are slowed and distorted the way dramatic moments and sounds sometimes are in melodrama, a parody of the over-reaction of the owner. It works well too.

So is it OK to laugh at the poor man's predicament, and inconvenience of the deer? Clearly, it would be better if a domestic pet wasn't chasing innocent ruminants in a public park; but the deer can presumably cope with a bit of a chase, and are unlikely to be outrun by a rotund family pet which has probably never caught more than a tennis ball or mauled more than a rubber bone in its life.

There is a road up ahead, so perhaps there is a danger there, but surely the menace of the motor car is ever present. The drivers can see these deer coming. In any event I think no deer was harmed in the making – no, snatching – of this little episode in the life of suburban England. No dog had to be put down. Fenton annoyed one person – his owner – or maybe two if you count Paul Merton, and delighted millions of others.

An out-of-control dog in a park – hardly sounds like comedy gold when described. You may agree, if you have got this far. I think the clue to the humour is revealed if you strip away the elements. Would it have been funny if the owner hadn't sounded so much like a sergeant-major? I think not. If the dog had been a pit bull? No. Clearly, had it been a Rottweiler or Alsatian it wouldn't have been so funny, or even funny at all. But then the owner probably wouldn't have sounded posh, and the dog wouldn't have had a name to match the Range Rover, Barbour coat and green wellies you imagine are back in the car park (for all we know, of course, Fenton's owner is a thoroughly lovely chap). And the dog probably wouldn't have been walked off the lead in a deer park. No, it has to be a black lab to work.

I think it's a joke at the expense of how we perceive the aspirational classes and their assumed status, their symbols. One suspects the cries of 'Fenton!' are in part for the benefit of any onlookers, although the owner can't have known that there would soon be 10 million of us, according to the views totaliser on YouTube; his illusion of canine control brutally exposed. I think we all snigger at the fantasy inhabited by most owners of large dogs that they are in control, that by shouting their dog's name often enough – while it ignores them and does what it wants – they are somehow in charge of the animal.

People who argue for and against the reintroduction of wolves, *Canis lupus,* to the UK may forget that we already live with 8.3 million of them, disguised nowadays as *C. lupus familiaris* in all its forms: some small, some large, some in handbags and some waiting to remove an inattentive post-person's fingers. But all, deep down, the wolf... with all its carnal cravings.

My parents-in-law reported one day seeing a Jack Russell terrier chasing two roe deer in a field and over the brow of a hill. Minutes later the terrier reappeared, the deer now hot on its tail. I'm tempted to assume that the deer came to realise mid-chase that, while their assailant smelled of wolf, this is where the similarity – and the fear – might end.

Finally, Fenton has reminded me of Rupert Pupkin's (*King of Comedy*) old adage – it's better to be king for a day than schmuck for a lifetime. We increasingly live our wild lives through the heroics or bravado of others, whether animals, action heroes or wayward sportsmen. For 45 seconds, unless you tutted disapprovingly, most of us were rooting for the black lab gone feral, and just maybe felt the rare stirring of our own inner Fenton.

A SONG FOR EUROPE

It's the last day of March at the tail end of a long, properly cold winter. It's late afternoon and the sun is sinking in a blue-white sky. Spring is present and detectable as light more than heat, and I'm walking home tucked into a coat, my breath visible on the cold air. As I pass under an isolated ornamental conifer in the front garden of one of our local farmhouses, I realise that among the assorted ambient sounds of the village there is birdsong – a proper, full-on song – that stands out. I simply don't recognise it. It feels odd that there's a full song of any kind – verse and chorus; the lot – although the thrushes have been warming up in recent days, and there's the odd blast of dunnock and the ever-present robins, despite the lingering chill. To hear something entirely unfamiliar is odd but welcome, like a foreign language at a family gathering.

Stopping to look round, I trace the sound to the top of the conifer – a scenic, drooping cypress of some kind; not the usual densely cylindrical shape of the ones that often form hedgerows. This is an elegant, open structure, with individual limbs extending out and down over the pavement. Pretty, but possibly the last tree in the vicinity you'd expect would support life.[1] At the top of this 40-foot specimen is the bird. I fish in my bag for the binoculars I sometimes carry, and focus in on the unfamiliar source of this novel, musical lilt.

I'm intrigued to discover that it's a redwing, and it looks very much at home. True home for a redwing can probably be regarded as the place it normally sings, and nests, and is therefore born, namely the far north of Europe, in the conifer forests of Scandinavia and beyond. This is the first one I've knowingly heard close up, in full, unrestrained voice like this. Redwings can be quite vocal in their winter flocks, and their utterances may include a sub-song, a partial version of what I'm hearing now. But this is the full performance. It feels like an announcement of the end of winter, because this bird will not be harbouring any serious aspirations to breed here, in a southern English village. But the urge to sing has obviously overcome it, and I can't help thinking that the choice of song-post might be significant – this tree has a Scandinavian feel about it. Viewed in silhouette against the western sky, its foliage appears draped on its limbs, like dollops of sagging snow, or ice cream.

I love that I have encountered something completely new amid the routine of life, without looking and when least expected, which in many ways is the best way to find these things.

I came across two dead redwings this winter; I assume they were casualties of the hard weather. One was brought to me in a box by a neighbour. The small consolation in the birds' death has been the chance to examine them close up, to admire the richness of their plumage. They resemble the song thrush, but their bold pale eyebrow and the smear of red on their flanks gives them a tribal, Norse appearance. I held the wings open to reveal the russet feathers of their under-wings, which seem to have been rinsed in ochre paint.

It is rare to get close enough to the birds to see these features, except when the hardest weather forces them into gardens and close to windows, for example. I remember the first redwing I saw this way,

---

1   A delve in the *Observer's Book of Trees and Shrubs* reveals that it's a Lawson's Cypress. In its native North America it is known as the Port Orford Cypress, found from Oregon to north California. Here, 'it has been planted solely with a view to its ornamental qualities'.

in the snow-covered garden at home, maybe in the hard winter of 1981. The bird on the ground looked disabled by cold, and the red smear on its flank like a wound. It is sometimes possible to approach them in a vehicle as they forage along roadsides or hedge bottoms.

These are tough little birds, and add a reassuring touch to the coldest of nights, as they pass unseen overhead, even crossing the most urban of settings, uttering their modest little *tseep* whistle as they go, keeping in touch with each other in their nocturnal squadrons. No matter how cold and inhospitable it may seem here, you can be sure it's a lot harsher where they have come from.

This thin whistling note earned it one appealing local name – the swine pipe. Pioneering Victorian ornithologist Alfred Newton noted this similarity to the note played by 'the swineherds of old when collecting the animals under their charge'. It is possible to stand at prominent points on the greensand ridge near here and watch the sky to see the great autumn movements of redwings and others. I was very pleased to discover that Professor Newton himself lived for a time right here, within a short distance of what would later become RSPB headquarters. He may have lodged in Hazell's Hall while being tutored as a boy nearby.

Friends of mine have rented a ground-floor flat in this old manor house, once owned by the Pimm family. It was requisitioned for a time during World War II and used as the base for operations at the secret airfield below, on the plain. The operations included some night-flights to Norway, of the kind that are routine for the unassuming but occasionally show-stopping redwing.

HAWK EYES

Like anyone else who attracts songbirds to their garden, I receive regular visits from sparrowhawks. They are usually just passing – or zooming – through, but occasionally they pause on a prominent perch, taking stock briefly before zooming on again. They tend not to be a bird you can admire at leisure. So it was with some surprise that one early spring morning I noticed from my back window what I took to be a hawk perched on the bird bath, close to the house. Very close. In fact, it was closer, more static and more exposed than any hawk I had seen before. I indulged myself in this unusually good view.

Several minutes elapsed. Apart from glancing occasionally to each side, the bird sat quite still, fluffed out, its neck hunched. It had none of the usual edginess that characterises a sparrowhawk. This was a bird not going anywhere fast. I had time to get my camera mobilised. I attached a zoom lens, and went to an upstairs window, where there was less chance of frightening what would normally be a very flighty subject. I was able to take a photograph, watch the bird for a while longer, and witness it finally flying off, which it did by vaulting the fence behind it.

Looking again at the photograph some months later, I began to doubt that this was actually a sparrowhawk at all. Clearly, my photo is not going to win any competitions. But a few things about the image did not square with my understanding of how sparrowhawks behave, and look. The jizz, which is to say the 'general impression of its size and shape', and demeanour, seemed wrong. I measured the rim of the bird bath – 12.5 inches – and, using this for scale, concluded that the bird was too small for a female sparrowhawk, yet did not possess the typical russets and slate-blue back of a male. It also lacked the manic stare of a hawk. This bird had started to look to me like a female merlin.

The case for merlin? Well, it seems the right size and overall brown colour. Its posture is falcon-like, and, though difficult to tell from the picture, it seems to have dark eyes – sparrowhawk eyes are yellow-irised and beady. And hawks tend to 'loaf' under cover, out of sight, in a spot from which they might also opportunistically launch an ambush on unsuspecting prey.

Merlins, meanwhile, are birds of open country. They hunt in the open, and they move around a lot outside the breeding season, as this was. They breed on open moors, as a rule. They are occasionally seen over the fields near my home. And while this wouldn't be a typical place for a merlin to perch either, again it could be explained by the bird selecting this resting place as the closest thing to a rock in the vicinity. The possibility that it was an escaped bird, a falconer's bird, also crossed my mind.

I have to declare an interest: I wanted it to be a merlin. That would be an exciting and unusual garden find. Clearly, my judgement was skewed by this partisanship. I 'hawked' (if you will) the photo around a few experts and interested amateurs. It was interesting to note the differing verdicts, from the noncommittal, to the certain one way or the other. There was roughly a split in the female merlin/male sparrowhawk camps. The length of the tail relative to the wing-tips should have been a clincher, but these are not easy to determine from the photo, even under a magnifying lens. Hawks have long tails and short wings, for manoeuvring in tight spaces. Falcons like merlins have longer wings, for speed in open flight. The jury remained out.

I found the photo again recently, and decided to reopen the file. For a final say, a definitive verdict, I decided to consult a man who, of anyone, really ought to know: he is a – if not *the* – world authority on sparrowhawks. He is the author of the monograph called *The Sparrowhawk*, published by T & A D Poyser in 1986, and studied these birds for 14 years in an area of south-west Scotland, Professor Ian Newton. Professor Newton has been chairman of RSPB trustees.[2]

I left the photo and the magnifying lens, and the details of time and place of the photo, with the dimensions of the bird bath for scale, with the RSPB Chief Executive's office, for Professor Newton to have a look when next he visited and had a spare moment.

I held my breath opening the verdict when it came through.

'It's a first-year sparrowhawk.'

And how could he be sure?

'You can tell by the white spots on the wings.'

And finally, the clinching fact, the one that explained the unusual site, demeanour and behaviour of the bird:

'From its stance, it is unwell – and therefore unlikely to make it into its second year.'

Riddle unravelled. Not only could Professor Newton identify the species, he could age the bird precisely and tell that it was unwell; and all from this grainy, ill-lit print. It explains all – the untypical plumage, location, posture and behaviour. I could forgive myself the uncertainty in making a positive ID.

Most birds don't make it through their first year. Only one fledgling, on average, from any nest survives to the following spring. Even the sparrowhawk must live and die by this principle. Of that, at least, we can be certain. Just ask someone who knows.

---

2   Note also that our contemporary ornithologist Prof. Ian Newton is no relation – that he knows of – to Prof. Alfred Newton (see page 68), but the coincidence is pleasing.

Northward Equinox

Chapter Four

April

Birds, bees and old balls

I have what is probably an unhealthy interest in football. I say 'unhealthy' because football is taken way too seriously (I know, I've done it myself), and is, in some ways, a distraction from the genuinely important things in life. And I realise that this may be precisely why my fondness for it persists. Distraction. Which probably isn't very healthy.

There may currently be more TV money in showing footballers doing their jobs than in televising conservationists in the workplace, but that doesn't alter the fact that football is not nearly as important as protecting the environment (or encouraging other people to do so), a purpose from which it regularly distracts me. To compensate for this, I have explored different ways of combining the two interests, to see which links, if any, can be established.

I had some early success last year with an old leather ball, which had reached retirement age; that is, it was punctured. When I was misspending my youth on the playing fields of Ayrshire we used to call these leather balls *clubbies*, for some reason. Other kids called them bladders, from an earlier time when the inner tube of a football was made from a real pig's bladder. In those days the ball also had a great, thick lace on one side, it weighed a ton (especially when saturated), centre-forwards had bull necks and Brylcreem partings, didn't flinch when heading the ball and flattening goalkeepers, and had names like Len, Nat and Wilf.

Anyway, after much deliberation I came up with a novel use for this tatty, deflated ball. I simply cut out one of the panels, removed the inner tube, and – *voila!* – it became a robin nest box, of course. I wedged it into a safe, sheltered spot in some trellis and bramble against the back garden wall, within view of the window. From this vantage point I could watch for developments, perhaps while pondering whether I really needed to get out more.

Spring came and, lo and behold, my speculative attempt was on target. There I was, spectating at the back window, getting psyched up for work, sipping tea, watching the sparrows come in for mixed seed, a dunnock poking around, a wren passing busily by, a blackbird fussing and a male chaffinch looking flash. A robin appeared in the gloomy bit at the base of the laurel hedge, chest out like a matador, perched imperiously on a lump of old drainpipe, beside a primrose. It had what looked like a handlebar moustache, which I worked out was a beak-full of moss. This could only mean one thing… It also had its eye on the ball, to which it made a blindside dash. Then out again, as fast.

Result!

I don't think I punched the air in triumph, or skidded on my knees on the hearth rug, cupping my ear as footballers do when they feel they have silenced their doubters, but I may have thought about it. '*Yooooou're* not singing any more…' But I've got to say there *is* something peculiarly gratifying about wild nature taking up your offers of help like this.

A couple of weeks on, the parent birds were coming and going with food for the nestlings, so I set up my camera for an action shot. I thought the resulting photograph wasn't bad, and I offered it to a couple of national newspapers – and got no response – and then to a Swindon Town Football Club fanzine, as this team is nicknamed the Robins. I never heard from them either, funnily enough.

We have our own football team here at the RSPB. We're called the Birdmen, which you may think lacks a bit of imagination, but

'Birdmen!' is easier to fit in to terrace chants (not that we have terraces... or chants, for that matter) and match-report headlines than any name that might reflect our wider biodiversity and sustainability agenda.

We're not bad, in a conservation context. We've had good results against English Nature, BirdLife's Secretariat, the BTO and others. We've won the Conservation Cup at Birdfair three times, and have donated the prize money to worthy conservation causes (wishing, as we did so, that other football clubs would do the same, given the huge amounts of cash sloshing around in the Premiership). We also have an annual fixture against the mighty Royal Society for the Prevention of Cruelty to Animals (RSPCA) FC, who draw from a larger player pool than we do, and have a proper kit. We hold our own against the Bunnymen, against whom we have played 10, won 4, drawn 2, lost 4.

Flush with my success – with the retired football – this year I installed another one in the honeysuckle near the front door. In no time at all it was occupied by robins, which again raised a brood by the end of April.

Meanwhile, out the back, a real buzz has developed around the first old ball. It has been adopted by, of all things, a bumblebee. If I go near the ball it vibrates loudly, having the acoustics of a stadium in miniature. So now, from the back window, I occasionally see this large bee to-ing and fro-ing through the missing panel. Which leads me to wonder what goes on in a bumblebee nest. Is the bee, like the robins, ferrying food back to a row of gaping mouths?

I checked the insect book and a whole new world opened up. Apparently a queen bumblebee lays about six eggs. The hatchlings are weaned on a supply of pollen and wax that she has gathered and continues to top up. The grubs soon pupate, and the queen weaves some additional magic by spinning a bright yellow silk ball around them from which, in a matter of days, the fully-formed worker bees emerge. They then take over food-collection duties while the queen concentrates on egg laying. Talk about a youth policy! If I could just get a photo, maybe Brentford or Barnet FC (both known as the Bees) might be interested.

OK, maybe not.

In any case, I am now on the look-out for another old ball, and I may be able to complete a hat-trick. Who knows, maybe then the agents will start calling, and we might be able to strike some sort of deal. Hatch of the Day, anyone? You heard it here first.

Watching the grass grow

'What do y'all do for ennertainment round here…?'

Small-town Bonnie (Faye Dunaway) is being teased by wide-boy Clyde (Warren Beatty) in the 1968 movie about the gangster couple.

'…sit around and watch the grass grow?'

Once upon a time I had the rare pleasure of being able to establish a wild grass and flower meadow. And sit around watching it grow is exactly what I did; that year and again the next. Clyde Barrow's southern drawl mocked me sometimes. But unlike Bonnie Parker, I rose above it. Watching grass grow may not be as Hollywood as being an outlaw in the mid-West during the Great Depression, but at least it's legal.

I was inspired to plant the meadow after reading about grasslands in Oliver Rackham's *History of the Countryside*. I found this engrossing tome in Cambridge, shortly after I moved there, in a bookshop little more than the bowl of a cricket ball from Rackham's college. (I was pleased to discover that my neighbour knew him well enough to refer to him as 'Ollie'.)

Rackham's scholarly book reflects both a deep appreciation of the activities of humanity that made this once-forested island so diverse and fascinating, and his dismay at the various pressures that have cost us so much of this cultural, historical and semi-natural diversity. The natural history of grasslands epitomises all that is best and worst about our partnership with nature.

Having been freed from the confines of a terrace in Georgian Edinburgh – for me an elegant prison – I was fortunate enough to find a sixteenth-century timber-framed, brick-floored cottage with a walk-in fireplace to rent just south of Cambridge. Its oak beams were warped and sloping; disconcertingly so. Where I come from in Scotland, you can watch exposed timbers rot. 'If a house has been standing that long, it's not going to fall down now,' they assured me.

In the large back garden were an old church pew for a bench and a near-fossilised apple tree, engulfed by bramble and nettles. Early in the year I set about clearing the way for a 'meadow'. I ordered grass seed from a company called Emorsgate. The small sack they sent me seemed good value, as it contained about a dozen types of seed, all painstakingly grown and harvested by enthusiasts.

In meadow growing, the approach is to prepare a light, thin soil and extract as much organic debris as possible, to remove excess nutrients. You can favour annual plants with just the right amount of grazing, or mowing, at the right times. You also need a bit of occasional soil disturbance. But not too much.

I sprinkled the grains on the tilth, stooping low to stop them from drifting away on the breeze. They seemed so lightweight. I wondered how many would ever make it to germination. I raked, trampled and watered them in. I added a pinch of wild flower mix, all the cornfield classics: poppy, camomile, ox-eye, cornflower, marigold, corncockle. Then I stood back and watched for signs of growth…

Doubts were fleeting. Annual wildflower seeds and a patch of exposed earth go very well together, with the application of a little water and spring sunlight. The smudges of green were all over it like a rash in a fortnight as I, leaning in carefully from the perimeter, removed dead leaves neurotically, and coaxed the sprouting along.

It was clear from an early stage that the feathery florets of corn camomile were enjoying themselves. They grew and grew through the spring: knee-height, then waist-height, and before long chest-height, like a crop doused in growth hormone and liquid fertiliser. And then, when they had strained every fibre and could get no closer to the sky, the whole collapsed in on itself in a resinous ruck, like revellers at a rock festival, drunk on sunshine and more besides, as though bingeing after years of enforced abstinence in the cornfields. Making up for lost time. Not so much a meadow as a mêlée.

Still, it had a kind of charm, and I enjoyed wading in to thin it out – till my limbs smelled of its heady sap – and ultimately to clear it when in late summer it had gone crisp and set seed. I had been aware that year one would be 'transitional', shall we say. Perhaps this bumper harvest would help to take some of the 'poke', or fertility, out of the soil. Wild flower diversity is diminished by fertiliser, and each crop takes some of this out.

Early in year two, a more even meadow was developing. The camomile was back, but in a much more orderly, less monopolistic way. Slowly but surely the distinctive spikes, racemes and panicles emerged, revealing their elegant inflorescences; engaging in various ways with the movement of air across them. Blue, papery ruffs of cornflowers glinted amid the graceful, bending stems. Field poppies provided stabs of scarlet. The rich pinks of corncockle added a subtler, pastel touch. By mid-July, at the height of a sunny afternoon, the whole thing was busy with insects, mostly hoverflies, but also little shiny beetles and honey bees, blue butterflies and skippers. Spiders waited to ambush them. Grasshoppers added percussive drama to the soundtrack.

Okay, I was playing at it. This wasn't real meadow management. We've lost almost all of our real meadows. Only fragments of historic grassland remain, with their characteristic diversity. We've lost the rest to ploughing, drainage, re-seeding, conversion to pasture, fertilising and agrochemicals, neglect and mismanagement. Meadows are sensitive to change; easy to destroy if handled indelicately, like an old master. You don't recreate them overnight.

'Evidently a meadow or pasture rich in plant life can be made in about 150 years,' says Rackham, 'less time than it takes to make a good wood, but impracticably long in terms of human whims and setbacks.'

Within three years, I had to move on. I expect the nettles and brambles have reclaimed the space since I left. It was good while it lasted. My dabbling introduced me to the distinctiveness of native grasses. They are relatively easy to tell apart. Some turn up in all kinds of places. Many have great names: sweet vernal, wavy hair, floating meadow, water whorl, blue moor, squirrel tail, small quaking, Yorkshire fog...

From these or their relatives, we have selected and bred the cereal monocultures that now dominate our landscapes. I can't decide whether it is we who have enslaved grass, or it that has enslaved us, as we spread super versions of it across the planet.

Can species-rich grasslands be economical for farmers, given the long-term care they need? I'd like to hope so. I was lucky to be able to keep an area of wild grass and do a little bit to keep the diversity going, and I had much fun and simple pleasure in the process.

We helped wild meadow grasses spread in the first place. Now we must meet the challenge of putting them – in all their wonderful, life-supporting varieties – back.

Just you watch, Clyde Barrow.

CRESTFALLEN
The lapwing is one of the most conspicuous avian symbols of the open fields of our farmland in spring. With its whoops and its

moans, its playing up and rolling around, its crest and its dapper plumage, it is something of a fop among farmland birds, a prima donna of the pasture. But for all its apparent exhibitionism, the lapwing's plaintive, haunting cries and its tumbles from the sky make it also an obvious metaphor for the vulnerability of our farmland birds.

Everything about the lapwing draws your attention: the *pee-wit* calls from which it takes one of its names, the noisy lapping of its cloak-like wings from which it takes the name you nowadays find in the guidebooks, the conspicuousness of its flocks, the proximity to human settlement of many of its breeding grounds. At least, that's how it's been until recent years. But if in the past the lapwing has appeared to seek our attention, it now demands it. Almost half of our breeding lapwings have been lost in a decade. The lapwing needs help.

I first got acquainted with lapwings while studying for O-Grades, as we called them in Scotland. I think we must have had time off for revision. Understanding the importance of regular study breaks, I spent a fair bit of time 'up the country' that May, clearing my head between bouts of algebra, osmosis and Aldous Huxley.

Damp and green, north Ayrshire is largely dairy country, the lush pastures punctuated by barley and silage fields. My lapwings were breeding on a disused quarry on a hillside: a perfect spot. It had damp areas, with tussocks of sedge and horsetail, and rubble-strewn areas colonised by wild flowers. Sitting birds had a good all-round view, and I had a clear view of them from the hedge bordering this marginal habitat.

The adults greeted me with sounds that can be best described as *girning,* a term my parents used to describe the peevish protestations of, usually, children. Usually me. As the lapwings girned, there was much scuttling and indignant flypasts, but within minutes of me settling down out of sight, they trotted back to their eggs and settled down. I think there were about eight nests; not a large colony, but big enough to provide reasonable security in the shape of early-warning systems and rapid response teams.

Smaller colonies are much more vulnerable. In early spring this year I visited the stone-curlew breeding site managed by the Norfolk Wildlife Trust at Weeting Heath. Besides stone-curlews, this heath also had a few lapwings, but the warden didn't hold out much hope of them succeeding. Unlike the stone-curlews, which sit tight on their nests, no matter the provocation from crows, lapwings have a scuttle-and-chase strategy, which means that while one crow is har-angued, another can steal in and plunder the nest. The girn of these few lapwings – as it always does – transported me in time to that wee bit hill in Ayrshire.

I remember the frisson that would ripple through the colony as a curious crow sloped clumsily past, on the off-chance. It would be met by an advance guard of rising lapwings and forced to duck and dive its way off the premises, neurotic calls crescendo-ing around it and subsiding in its wake. On one occasion suddenly a sparrowhawk was there, and in the dogfight above, it was hard to tell who was chasing whom. But the hawk was seen off.

I saw the youngsters at various stages of development, watched them scurrying about in search of invertebrates when the coast was clear, and freezing on the spot when the girning of the parents started up. As spring became summer, the youngsters would be lost to my view in the rising barley and hay, but the adults would maintain the watching brief.

I'm not harking back to a golden age of our countryside. I'm talking about the mid-1980s. But since that time, the apparent vulnerability of the lapwing has been confirmed in an alarming way. Research by the BTO and the RSPB has now shown the extent of the losses of breeding lapwings on farmland.

One note of optimism amid the catalogue of loss across the UK is the success of lapwings on RSPB nature reserves. In the increasingly lifeless and featureless expanses of farmland that stretch from coast to coast, RSPB nature reserves are proving oases of life, in which lapwings are able to flourish, as before. Ah, you may say, but it's easy for nature reserves to support wildlife. But the RSPB nature reserves in question are farmed, and could not succeed without farming. For example, Pulborough Brooks in Sussex, Vane Farm in Perthshire and Kinross, Ynys-hir in Wales and Portmore Lough in Northern Ireland prove the benefits of grazing at a level that sustains natural balances.

The lapwing is just one of a number of farmland species that are declining alarmingly; it just happens to be a highly visible example, one that is comparatively easy to census. The loss of wildlife from our farmed environment is not an inevitable price of progress.

Conservationists do not wish technology had never been invented. Technology can help us achieve the vision of a vibrant coun-tryside producing safe, wholesome food, and supporting vibrant rural communities and biodiversity. We all have a stake in ensuring this, and a role to play in influencing it, from the civil servant with an agriculture brief, to the farmer producing our food, to the shopper in the high street.

So come on, let's put the life back. Let's keep the lapwings girning.

MESSAGE IN A BOTTLE

I've been collecting corks for years. I suppose I've always had a *thing* about them – could never bring myself to throw one away, and not just at home. At parties and receptions I have always been the weirdo who is fishing them out of bins, or scrounging them off the bar staff, wandering around with them bulging out of his pockets. 'What are you collecting those for?' people ask. 'Don't know, really,' I tend to answer. 'I just, um, like them.'

Perhaps it's simply because keeping such things is better than throwing them away. Or my instinct tells me cork is a good thing. It grows on trees, and it regrows on trees after you've removed it: a substance produced by nature, thoroughly robust yet peculiarly light, buoyant and hard-wearing, yielding yet taut. I like the sound it makes as you ease it out of a bottle. Most people do, I'm sure, whether they realise it or not. Science cannot emulate it.

It didn't take me long to accumulate a whole bin bag full of corks, and they were getting in the way. I threw some into the garden, onto my wood stack, which is piled on a plastic sheet to retain rain for moisture-loving beasties. Here, corks swell up a little, and prove an ideal medium for moss to grow on. I also tipped them onto a pathway through the shrubbery, as though gravel, so that I could walk on them, barefoot.

I've seen cork growing in Andalusia, in the south-west corner of Spain, beside a jasmine-covered house called Finca Alma, high on a hillside on the edge of a whitewashed village. From here I could see Gibraltar and the narrow neck of the Mediterranean Sea, where the Atlantic Ocean keeps it topped up. If it didn't, the Med would evaporate in 100 years.

Cork oaks were part of the woodland mix around Finca Alma. The trees teemed with movement and birdsong, including a sweet warbling coming from the oaks beside the house. This turned out to be being produced by a woodchat shrike, a sartorial bird, but a butcher, with no right to sing so prettily, through its neat little hooked beak.

Every morning a square of sunlight on the bedroom wall let me know that there were blue skies outside, and from mid-morning onwards, when the thermals got to rising, returning migrant birds cruised and wheeled up the valley slopes, above the cork oaks, the almond and the orange trees. Mostly the birds were raptors – black kites, booted eagles and some vultures, which had laboured across the straits from Morocco.

On a visit to Tarifa's wind-buffeted sands I greeted the big birds funnelling in perilously low over the breakers to the safety of the sculpted dunes, where I reclined. Once here the birds were carried upwards again, spinning away as they saw me, carried to safety on the updrafts of dry land, before fanning out across the continent to rediscover Europe for the summer.

Among the procession past the house, I was delighted to see an imperial eagle, identifiable by its regal cloak across the shoulders, like a sable, or a mantle of ice from the sky. I was thrilled. There are only 130 or so pairs left in Spain. They are all gone from Portugal. Where they remain, they rule the cork oak woods.

Cork is the bark of the cork oak, and it is harvested from the trunk. In the woods I found terraces of oaks, some recently harvested, with trunks that looked like a cable minus its insulation. Bark removal like this usually kills trees, but not cork oaks. Even a narrow, bark-deep ring around the trunk of a sycamore will cripple it, eventually, but with cork oaks the skinning process can be repeated many times, as each time the bark regrows. The trees live to a ripe (and ripe again) old age. The farmers can sell the cork repeatedly, and the farming system around the trees is sustained, along with local people and the many creatures that subsist on the trees' limbs, leaves and acorns.

On the track down to Finca Alma I found the corky bark from smaller branches, like shed skin, hollow in the middle where the tissue had been eaten away and reduced to powder by nature's wood chewers and recyclers. The corky bark is much more durable and showed no signs of weakening. It is knobbly and waxy-waterproof, just like the skin of a toad. I was able to compare them, as in the night by torchlight I encountered the biggest common toad I have ever seen, as big as a galia melon, stalking – too big to jump – on the red earth, perhaps looking for the screaming – and I mean *screaming* – crickets, that were certainly too smart for me to sneak up on. I let the toad stalk away into the undergrowth, curiously like a gorilla in posture and attitude.

You may have noticed that nowadays wine corks are not always cork. At the start of 2001 I put the word out to staff and our network of 170 local groups that they might like to collect their wine corks. Between us, I thought, we might accumulate quite a few.

Through this I discovered that Peter Kirk has a thing about corks too. Peter is the leader of Macclesfield Members Group. He has been the driving force behind the collection of tens of thousands of corks. Hardly a popped cork in all of Cheshire can have slipped through his net and gone to waste. His enthusiasm is irrepressible. He makes my cork-saving efforts look like a mere passing fad. From many other friends and supporters we've been receiving regular contributions, plastic bags and envelopes full, and even on one occasion a chocolate box taped at the corners.

'What are you going to do with them?' they ask me. This time I have an answer.

We're going to do something creative with the corks: create some kind of sculpture with them, for publicity purposes, to promote the value of cork oakwoods. After that the corks can be recycled. We are aiming to enlist the support of an artist or sculptor, to turn them into something spectacular, to show the extent of support for cork and cork growing, and the things that cork supports and *represents*.

Science and economics aside (because someone will always dispute your claims), things like cork are just inherently, aesthetically, *instinctively*, better than plastic. Have a closer look, and listen, the next time you open a bottle. You may just hear it being harvested, and the warble of a shrike.

Note

I commissioned the artist Robert Bradford to create an enormous Spanish imperial eagle sculpture from the vast number of wine corks that our supporters collected. The sculpture is the size of a double-decker bus, and was on display at the Eden Project in Cornwall for a period, before being installed at the Pride of the Valley sculpture park in Surrey.

CROW MURDER MYSTERY CAUSES STIR AT THE *GUARDIAN*

A love of or interest in birds comes to different people in different ways, at different life stages. You don't have to fall for birds in childhood, although it probably helps, and of course prevents time lost in that bird-free wilderness. It also helps to have a mentor, but even this is probably less important than a profound, formative encounter with a bird or birds. Hard as I've ever tried to get my friends interested, no amount of pointing out and nudging in the ribs that I can do will ever be as powerful as a personal interaction or 'getting to know' experience.

I've known these epiphanies to take a number of forms, but they don't normally involve crows. I was therefore very interested in the stir that was caused over at the *Guardian* newspaper's HQ on Farringdon Road, north London, when a pair of carrion crows decided to build a nest in a plane tree right outside the office building. From the coverage given to this event on *Guardian Unlimited*, it was obvious that, having identified the birds with the aid of the RSPB website, the staff there had grown extremely attached to their crows and this nesting project. TV critic Sam Wollaston was reporting regularly on the progress of the 'G2 Crows', named after the supplement he works on.

'The effect on the office has been extraordinary,' wrote Sam. 'There haven't been such crowds around the windows since a couple were spotted having sex in the block opposite.'

A friend of mine called Matt works in the *Guardian*'s advertising department. He described to me with undisguised pride the grandstand view he enjoyed from his office of the sitting parent crows. Different departments on each floor had varying angles on the nest, and there was a certain amount of rivalry developing over 'ownership' of the pair. They were even given names. Sheryl and Russell Crow. Get it? The two young nestlings had names too.

I took an afternoon off and went down there to see Matt, call in on a journalist I had done some work with in the past, and say hi to Sam, who I had contacted through his blog. Needless to say, I also wanted to take a look at the nest. Alas, between arranging the visit, and actually getting there, disaster struck. In the course of that weekend, the nest became suddenly, mysteriously and, quite eerily, chickless.

The entire *Guardian* workforce was reported to be in shock.

Anyone emotionally involved was at a loss as to what could have happened. From all I could glean, conducting my enquiry over the phone with Matt and others, it was indeed perplexing that the young birds in the nest, only days old, in such an apparently secure situation, could have just *vanished*. Starved, died of cold, maybe. But *gone* altogether?

So, what might have taken them, in that urban situation, 30 feet up in a plane tree, miles from the nearest park? Surely not, at that height, a cat, or a squirrel in such a busy, largely treeless street? Surely not a tawny owl in the night, or a particularly daring magpie? Or even their own parents, if the babies had indeed died of natural causes? There had been no sign of them on the pavement below. Just an empty, wool- and litter-lined nest, and no parental activity, where just a day or so before had been a work in progress, a window on wild nature, an education and experience that many of these desk-bound newspaper folks had never had before.

I went ahead with my visit, which had now become more of an investigation. The *Guardian* has been an institution in my life for almost as long as the RSPB. My dad was a reader, back in the early 1970s. The paper was as much of an icon of the times as the scuffed old armchair, the dark-rimmed reading glasses, the pipe, and Harold Wilson or Eric Morecambe on the telly. To my young eye, the *Guardian* was a dense and dark adult thing that stained your fingers when you touched it and told solemnly of grown-up matters like trade unionism and foreign affairs. I was lucky enough to study under its former editor, Alistair Hetherington, at Stirling University. And I've been a reader myself for some years now and a regular user of the website.

It felt like something of a pilgrimage to be standing at the door of this national institution. I felt a twinge of guilt to be using it essentially as a bird hide. I began the tour at Matt's office on the third floor, for an aerial view of the empty bowl of sticks. Then to Sam's on the floor below for a side-on view. From there I was taken to the Comment and Analysis section, the one nearest the nest – and aptly enough where they compile the obituaries – although none was done for the birds at the time: 'just too upsetting,' said Sam. Here, I was asked a barrage of questions about birds in general and crows in particular. I had my leg pulled a bit too.

'So does the RSPB send someone out to investigate every failed nest then?' asked one of them, from his keyboard, winking.

'Well, we do what we can,' I told him. 'Although to be honest we are a bit under-resourced. Now, if I can just take a statement…'

And, as it happened, some evidence began to emerge of what was likely to have happened to Sheryl and Russell. Someone working over the weekend when the birds disappeared had noticed a spat in the plane tree between the resident pair and another couple of crows. Now, at least, we had proper suspects, an incident report and a motive: a rival pair, a border skirmish, territorial sabotage.

Well, you *can* grow to love them, but crows are crows, in the end: loving parents, no doubt, but opportunistic, aggressive, predatory birds. Not for nothing is the collective noun 'murder'. Rearing young in the marginal habitat of inner London is a dangerous business. It requires time away from the nest on foraging expeditions to distant bins and parks, allowing trouble in by the back door. The original four-egg clutch had become just two nestlings, and now none.

Crows aren't often top of most people's list of favourite birds. Their habits appear too antisocial for most tastes. They are widely controlled in the countryside. But for intelligence and resourcefulness, their abilities are not in doubt. And, for a few short weeks in spring, over at *Guardian* HQ, they were many people's favourite. It can come as a bit of a shock to discover that birds sometimes eat other birds. Even more so to think they might even be cannibalistic, on occasion, eating birds of their own species. I'm confident the *Guardian* team will get over the disappointment and use this as an introduction to the fascinating, if sometimes macabre, world of birds – as wild in our urban midst as anywhere else.

ONE FLEW UNDER THE CUCKOO'S BREATH

Keep it to yourself, but I was once sniffed at midnight by a kiwi. It remains one of the most unforgettable bird encounters I've had. The magic was a whole combination of things, but primarily the bizarreness of the creature, and the unexpectedness of the sound. I'm not sure I'd even heard a bird breathe before. They don't *sniff*, surely? Well, kiwis do. They have nostrils at the tips of their beaks, and they find worms by scent. My kiwi was sniffing at my torch, I concluded, thinking it was a glow-worm. I was in New Zealand at the time, it probably goes without saying. But I had a recent encounter much closer to home with a wild bird I got so close to I could hear it breathing.

One of the many pleasures of cycling is that it gets you closer to wildlife. As vehicles go, a bicycle doesn't fool forest creatures quite as well as a horse seems to, but for connectedness with the natural environment it sure beats being cocooned in a motor car. I was cycling to the RSPB HQ early one May morning and was pleased to hear a cuckoo calling up ahead, and far off, the way cuckoos usually are. It was between me and the greensand ridge, where I was headed, so I realised I might get a bit closer. Being on the bike, I closed in quite quickly. The *coo-coo*-ing continued. Closer, and louder. I could now tell it was issuing from an isolated chestnut tree. The path passes under it. I figured I would flush the bird any second. Still it called. Now I was directly beneath it. I couldn't see it in the thick of the candle-covered tree. Even better, it couldn't see me. And it was still in full voice.

It was like being locked in a sound room with the bird, a studio designed to amplify this extraordinary vocalisation, to throw it even further across the landscape. And the best bit of all – the kiwi moment – was that I could actually hear this cuckoo *breathing*. Don't ask me to describe exactly what this sounded like; all I can tell you is that it was clear that the first syllable of the word from which the cuckoo takes its name is a big breath in – or inhalation, like a snore – and the second a big breath out, or exhalation.

Is this widely known, or important, or even interesting? I'm not sure. I have told a few colleagues, of course, but it's not that easy to describe. It makes me wonder how much this basic need to breathe affects the structure of some other well-known bird songs. I've since sneaked up on my local nightingale – a bit easier to do, as it was dark. I was left wondering if the quiet, wheezing notes that immediately precede the most explosive phrase – *chup-chup-chup-chup-chup* – is the taking in of a very deep breath. Does it perhaps also explain how those birds with continuous 'songs', like the nightjar, are alternating sounds made on circular breaths in and out? The pitch does seem to switch, back and forth, suggesting that they do.

I had a rare and unexpected visitor to my road in June. It woke me in the night with a peculiar distant buzz, like static, or a faulty overhead cable in the distance. Opening the window, I worked out what it was: a grasshopper warbler. It had moved in to the tiny scrap of paddock opposite, where the horses had been absent for a while and the hawthorns allowed to grow. This was enough to lure the passing migrant warbler in, to try its luck in setting up a territory.

In the end, it stayed and 'reeled', as it's known, for a week, the first I've known to stick around here. It would sing by day, sometimes from a strand of barbed wire, beak agape, head turning this way and that, to throw the sound and see what might be watching. But its best performances were reserved for after dark, and all through the night. And I am sure this is another bird that sings as it breathes in and out. Like the nightjar, you can hear a slight switch of pitch; up, then down again. How else could it keep going for minutes on end? When I listened from the garden on a damp night, it sounded like there were two of them 'reeling'. I worked out that it was a combination of the sound bouncing off the house, and the atmospheric moisture. These birds are known to be somehow ventriloqual.

For us, singing while breathing in takes talent, practice and training. If you're going to try this at home, you could start with the cuckoo's song. And here's a tip – best wait till no one's listening.

LOOKING FOR THE ADDER

There are certain species we have come to think of as epitomising a particular type of place. Sea eagles and – well – the sea. Wild sea coasts, in particular. Hen harriers and moors is another example. Merlins and moors. Adders and moors/heaths. But I've had the steadily growing realisation that these associations are an artefact of our direct interventions with these species, and not our manip-ulation of the landscape so much as our pressure on the beasts themselves.

I had this epiphany – again – as I watched a small falcon menacing a flock of swallows and house martins close to the village and high in the sky. And it occurred to me that the reason this falcon so much re-sembles a merlin is that it *is* a merlin. The main consideration holding me back from this verdict was the sense that it was in the wrong place for a merlin – as though any part of the sky over our small isles is out of place for a bird so adept at putting the miles behind itself, and so nomadic when not tied to nesting responsibilities. And it also struck me that hirundines like the ones it was corralling ought to be an obvi-ous prey choice for a merlin, even though these little falcons are almost always linked to larks and pipits in a heathery context.

It's also worth noting that in other places – like the North American continent – these self-same merlins we think of as ground-nesters in remote uplands are familiar to many city dwellers, and routinely nest in trees – disused crows' nests, for example. I saw one of these American birds for myself, in Prospect Park, Brooklyn, of all places. I was led to it by an expatriate Scotsman called Keir Randall on a clear autumn morning. This is his birdwatching patch, and it was the first time he'd seen a merlin this year. Curiously, for a non-resident species here in the park, it was in the same tree frequented by merlins in past years. It was resting awhile on passage, and probably waiting for tired migrants to pass by, that it might waylay.

If my theory is right, modern generations of birds ought to be pretty quick to reoccupy the vacant spaces we've created historically through our pressure on their predecessors. Birds are, after all, extremely mobile as a rule. Perhaps before too long the occasional merlin over my village might turn into breeding merlins in a crows' nest up on the ridge. And the sea eagles might colonise the Ouse valley (this is a valley but not one with conspicuous flanks – you could easily miss it) through the wide open door of the Wash, beckoning to the Dutch population to overspill and reclaim their ancestral homelands, and settle once and for all the heated debate about whether or not they 'belong here'.

Adders, on the other hand, aren't nearly so expansive as birds with the wind under their wings. But I wonder if they are as catholic in their habitat tastes, when allowed to be. I've long been aware that adders were hunted out, on the heaths and warrens of the greensand ridge, by the nineteenth century. There was a bounty on their heads, and adder hunting must have been a financially rewarding pastime for young bounty hunters back then. Adders aren't particularly hard to find or catch, especially in the first warm days of spring, when they haul themselves out of their winter torpor and lie around getting charged up in the sun.

But it occurs to me that adders are simple creatures of hedge bottoms and woodland edges: all they need is a bit of bramble to hide among, some voles, frogs and lizards to eat, a few rocks or logs in which to give birth to live young and to share with other adders come the winter again. We've got all that right here (and what we lack in lizards and frogs, we make up for in bank vole profusion) in the village.

But will the adder ever come back, without assistance? It seems improbable, although my hopes were momentarily raised recently when I read in the biodiversity action plan for the species that one had been discovered in a neighbouring village. The not so good news is that this was more than 20 years ago. I wondered if it might have turned up there having floated down river, perhaps by accident, on flotsam (although I've found plenty of adders – or vipers – in and around French rivers), from the few places in the county they are known to survive. Well, I say 'survive', but they had to be reintroduced there, on a carefully managed fragment of heath set among conifer forest.

I went there to see if I could spot any at the reintroduction site. I chose the perfect day for adder searching, a warm sunny day in early April. Not only was the sky cloudless, but it was also noiseless, and vapour trail-less, although I was right under the flight path of London (Luton) Airport. Iceland's volcanic ash cloud had grounded all air traffic that day. It occurred to me that such a day as this could not have been experienced here since around the time the Wright brothers got their prototype aircraft off the ground. Perhaps the original adder population was still here then.

Female adders have been recorded travelling up to a kilometre to find a birthing site for the fully-formed live young they produce; there is no egg stage for the adder. But they tend to return to their place of hibernation. They don't, as a consequence, recolonise fast.

Another colleague reported finding an adder quite recently, also close to the river, and even further downstream. Maybe there *is* yet hope that the adder can find its own way back, perhaps using hedgerows as transport routes. But I'm thinking they need a bit of help to reach the relative sanctuary of restored patches of heathland such as that in progress at RSPB HQ.

I've always revered snakes, especially their movement, their presence, their stealth. I've spent many happy hours catching, watching and releasing them, once or twice in Scotland, where they are thin on the ground, but especially abroad. You'd have to be pretty unlucky or careless to be bitten by one, but care and respect are the watchwords, for snakes, like all wildlife, are deserving of our attention.

There's no doubt that the presence of venomous snakes adds a frisson of wildness and danger to a landscape, but I find this reassuring and indicative of a place worth visiting: a place civilised enough to maintain peaceful coexistence with some of the trickier, less universally popular, of our native fauna.

CELEBRITIES

The stoat, or rather the idea of it, has had me starstruck since child-hood. Until recently, my first-hand experience had been limited. I know all about the stoat's reputation, and had a childhood memory of one running in circles around a stupefied blackbird. An image of the beguiling dance lingers in my mind as the ceremonial rites of a feared and dashing outlaw.

Besides that, I had enjoyed only the occasional glimpse, the celebrity usually tumbling on to some man-made stage of tarmac, more by accident than design. These appearances have tended to be brief, with at best a pause to sniff short-sightedly in the direction of the audience, before exiting hastily, stage opposite. A reluctant star if ever there was one.

Of course, my fascination was heightened by the stoat's shunning of the limelight. For all we read and hear about those we admire, I imagine that few ever get an introduction. The dream is to venture backstage without intruding. Exactly how this is done is the eternal dilemma of curious naturalists and fans. As a mixture of both where the stoat is concerned, I have been privileged to make a recent acquaintance.

The grey mizzle of a Highland November on a well-managed gaming estate made for an unlikely backcloth. Shotgun reports and an incongruously large number of pheasants seemed to point to the likely fate of any rustler attracted to these woods and fields by pred-atory instinct. This was a living larder with a tightly fastened door. The gamekeeper would surely have seen to it, given the price on a stoat's head.

It was therefore with a mixture of surprise and delight that I greeted the first appearance of the stoat. I suppose I shouldn't have been so surprised. The signs had been there. When I arrived at my cottage I was greeted by the dried carcass of a rabbit jammed in a gap at the base of the front door. My ill-considered hypothesis had been that the wretched creature had got stuck trying to get out. I had not allowed the question of how it got in to vex me for too long.

By the same logic, a day or two later a bank vole lay down on the doormat and died there. Fortunately, my powers of deduction were not to be stretched a second time (otherwise the idea of a rodent's graveyard might have crossed my mind), because the outlaw had made an appearance by that stage, and I knew I was sharing its den. I wondered if I would be accepted by this member of the hole-in-the-door gang. Sundance. Well, what else? Fortunately, mine was not the bedroom that had been chosen for a latrine.

Gazing out absently at a classic November sky – threatening cloud rimmed by a hidden sun – I was suddenly aware of movement. Sundance was heading in my general direction, perhaps to inspect the lodger. I hoped there would be room for both of us.

His (I assumed it was a he, since it was quite large by stoat standards) approach can best be described as manic, with leaps and bounds taken where none seemed necessary on a circuitous route from A to B. To my delight, B was the front door. A wet furry parcel swung to and fro beneath his nose as he danced, no doubt obstructing each eye in turn, perhaps explaining his apparent lack of direction, and certainly his exuberance. I think he was just pleased with himself.

Within feet of the window he stopped abruptly. Standing upright and peering in my direction from behind his bounty, he reassessed the situation, and darted away to dine in private.

I was not to renew the acquaintance on that short holiday, although it was later that same evening that my cohabitant deposited the damp bundle on our doormat. I excused myself the conceit of imagining this to be a gift, because it had reminded me of the moment in *Falling for a Dolphin* when Heathcote Williams is presented with a fish by his brief marine acquaintance (although this is often in my thoughts). I returned the vole, placing it outside along with a titbit by way of humble apology for squatting in his winter hideout, and disrupting his meals.

As I was leaving I wondered at his chance of survival through a harsh Highland winter on the estate. Each distant report seemed to lengthen the odds in my mind. Sooner or later, surely, the posse would close in on him.

In April I returned. I was disappointed at the lack of evidence of further outlaw activity in the cottage. The upstairs latrine now appeared to be disused. I needn't have worried, though. On the last day of my visit I had company again. Sundance was back, with his Etta.

As I sat outside in the sun, I recognised the sense of frenetic activity that heralds the entrance of celebrities. They came into view ducking and weaving among the boulders and roots, jinking this way and that, as manic as ever – more so, if anything. I could see my own feelings of elation on that fresh, windy afternoon reflected in their mannerisms and unquestionable personality: that urge to run, leap and breathe fresh air, all the things that winter and city life seem to preclude.

In my enchantment I might have been a charmed rabbit, spellbound by the freebooting couple prancing before me in jaunty circles, happiness unabashed, black tail-tips fanned with the sheer excitement of it all as they rolled against the turf in serpentine coils, exchanging scents with the earth. They were, of course, oblivious to their reputation and the meanings I had attached to them within a setting shaped by the farmer and the laird. Perhaps they were just more trusting than me. I was moved by this feeling of trust, to have witnessed a private performance, to have met my divas off-stage. I realised they were simply carried away with the thrill of spring, but I could not shake the feelings of responsibilities of the guardian as well as the privileges of the spectator. I took with me a fresh awareness of what we see in celebrities: something we may feel we are lacking, and something of ourselves, if only mortality.

Passengers

I have taken sparrows for granted. Until recently, that is. A few recent events have shaken me out of my complacency.

In early spring I found a small cardboard box on my front doorstep. It contained a dead house sparrow. There was no note. I assumed it to be from a well-meaning neighbour. Sure enough, a few days later, a local farmer stopped on his bike and told me he was the provider. He said he had been finding dead sparrows under a roost site in the rafters of a pigsty.

The Institute of Terrestrial Ecology said they would have a look at it, although they normally analyse specimens higher up the food chain.

My local house sparrow population has seemed stable for the last three years, luckily. Up to 25 visit for dampened crusts at any one time. Mostly they are peaceable and sociable, sharing the crumbs and the birdseed in a civilised way. But from time to time there are squabbles, and the settling of disputes can be vicious. Mobs rampage into the hedgerow, and there some kind of conflict resolution takes place, amid a frenzy of chirping, all taking place hidden from view. Order is restored, with the group hierarchy no doubt reinforced or slightly rearranged each time.

House sparrows can't sing, as such, but their insistent chirping, the one-syllable urgent yelps, are as much a signal of spring as any fancy warbling: *THE - SUN - IS - UP: GET - OUT - OF - BED!* In fact, they chirp almost from the turn of the year, unruly and optimistic.

My sparrows nest in holes in the gable end between brick and tile.

'You wanna get those filled, mate,' the cavity-wall insulation man warned me one day. 'You'll get birds in there, and all sorts.'

His words are carried back to me on stormy nights as the prevailing winds hit the gable and things go bump in the roof space. It's not surprising that most home-owners are fastidious about wind-proofing (and therefore sparrow-proofing) their homes. But I wouldn't want to exclude my sparrows. I have wondered if I could provide them with alternative accommodation – perhaps coax them out of the roof and into something more, um, modern.

I got an old drawer from Treasure Trove, my local house clearance store, or, as I often think of it, the local museum of erstwhile furniture fashions – like the dusty props from *Abigail's Party*, Mike Leigh's 1974 play for television. Here, not only can you touch the exhibits, you can *buy* them, take them home and give them a new lease of life. I made a row of sparrow flats from the drawer, and the sparrows have already occupied an end terrace.

Besides my friend the farmer, many people have noted the recent decline in house sparrow numbers, and others have reported seeing them dying or finding them dead. The newspapers have been full of it. One has even offered a £5,000 reward to the scientist who can come up with the best explanation. There will not be one simple answer. *Passer domesticus*, so gregarious, is prone to infections. But it is also prone to the problems caused by farming and its escalating efficiencies.

Just as the house sparrow marched in step with urbanisation, so the tree sparrow was our comrade in agricultural revolution. *Passer montanus* likes trees, but it likes them well spaced out. The removal of dense forest for farmland suited it just fine – up to a point. In the UK it has become as elusive as the house sparrow has been familiar. It is by comparison a specialised, rural thoroughbred, refined and dapper. And, like many farmland birds, it has not found the UK countryside in the late twentieth century to its taste.

Growing up, I didn't have tree sparrows in my visual vocabulary. It's an easy species to overlook. I see now from the guidebooks that they do (or did) occur in Ayrshire, but I wasn't looking. The 1971 edition of the *Hamlyn Guide* (another junkshop retrieval) has a fully shaded distribution map, and describes the tree sparrow as common. But by the time I moved south the maps were being re-shaded.

In fact, I don't think I'd ever actually seen a tree sparrow in the UK until this occasion. Not properly, at any rate; not one I'd found myself. I struck lucky on a walk with friends across the Marlborough Downs. By the time we were descending to Avebury the mist had given way to bright sunshine, the slopes were sprinkled with angular rocks, scattered like eco-protesters in the path of any plough, and the skylarks were celebrating in anachronistic numbers.

On a muddy farm track we fell in step with the pagan drums of the spring equinox and the stone-worshippers gathering at the Red Lion up ahead. Then a sound from the farmyard brought me to a halt. A stray chirp had given the game away. A sparrow chirp all right, but with a subtle difference. I broke from the group to invest-igate. The farmyard I crept into was scruffy, but all the more alive for that – a treasure trove in its own right. And at the back, the prize among the clutter: the skulking bird. I was glad of my binocu-lars. These revealed the bird's chestnut cap and black 'ear' before it shrank away out of range. I had been rumbled. Further reconnais-sance revealed more of its band. I had found a safe house, a rural refuge, for a colony of tree sparrows.

On Monday at work I wasted no time in filing my report to Richard Winspear, coordinator of the RSPB's work on tree sparrows. 'Yes, we know about those ones,' he told me. 'That colony is part of our intervention project.' Intervention is the RSPB's term for emer-gency action to keep remnant populations alive. Conservation is usually about holistic treatments. Intervention is a life-support system – hopefully a temporary one.

I suppose part of me was disappointed. It would have been nice to have discovered a new population of tree sparrows; unknown, at least officially. But on the other hand it was reassuring to know that these birds hadn't been overlooked, and that they were already being, if not quite looked after, then at least looked *at*. On reflection, I realise it was foolish of me to even imagine these to not be documented. Between us, we can't really miss something so valuable: so few places to hide, so many browsers in the ancient curiosity shop.

For every 20 tree sparrows in the UK when that Hamlyn Guide was published, there are three left. There has been an 85 per cent decline since Abigail threw her party. The same book describes house sparrows as 'abundant'. They are now 64 per cent less so. That's why I've stopped taking them for granted.

When our partners in the settlement of town and country begin to depart the scene, it's time to pause. To look harder for tree sparrows. To look with fresh eyes at house sparrows. And perhaps to look at ourselves and ask where our journey is taking us. Then we can decide if we think it safe to travel alone.

CANARY IN OUR COALMINE

Perhaps more than any other bird, the familiar house sparrow has been our companion in the colonisation of the world. From old world to new, it has followed closely behind us, better suited to urbanisation than almost any other species, a comrade in agricultural revolution. It's pretty well qualified to play 'canary in the coalmine'.

And now it's in trouble. You've seen the headlines. The *Independent* is offering money for answers. Questions have been asked in the Houses of Parliament. So what has gone wrong for the house sparrow? I wish, as an RSPB man, I could explain, in simple terms, and point the finger at the culprits. If only. The conundrum is that the species appears to have gone into freefall in towns as well as in the country. That's a new thing.

I'm not a scientist by profession, although I do work very closely with scientists. I once flirted with ecology, for a semester, at Stirling University. Six months later my eye was roving. I felt imprisoned by books on cells, and I wasn't getting out enough, either to the woods to study ecosystems, or to the bar to study my contemporaries. I was, in the end, more interested in the movement of neo-realists than in the movement of water across semi-permeable membranes. So I switched to studying film, media, education and English.

I like to think that as a result of my background I inhabit a niche somewhere between scientists and the general public. I can let somebody else count the bugs, weigh the nestlings and analyse the droppings, and I can await the results. I admire the discipline, patience and rigour of my colleagues, even if it means it takes a while to get the full story behind things like the 50 per cent decline of house sparrows in suburban gardens in just 22 years.

I also live with house sparrows. Mine seem to be doing OK, although I've never formally counted them. For five years here, on the interface between town and country in north Bedfordshire, my sparrow population has seemed stable. So why is it different here?

I think about it from the point of view of my sparrows and their basic needs. Sparrows *like* us, in the end. They wouldn't have followed us round the world otherwise. They need a roof space to be born in. A bird box that simulates this will, of course, do. I am content to let them nest in three places in my eaves. I also have them in two bird boxes that I made from reclaimed wood. How many houses built in the last 20 years offer this basic concession to our sparrows?

Nestling sparrows need protein, in the form of insect food. Aphids are particularly important. I don't spray my garden, but of course many people do, instead of letting the sparrows, and others, do it for them. Some people think that unleaded petrol fumes are contributing to the loss of invertebrate food. If so, *mea culpa* – I haven't been able to give up the car – yet.

Adult sparrows aren't fussy eaters, but at the very least they need weed seeds and, better still, spilled grains from the harvest. Well, near me I can see where the feeding opportunities are, and there have even been winter stubbles, either because of the Countryside Stewardship Scheme, which compensates the farmer for not ploughing this up and planting again in the autumn, or because the ground was too wet to plough at that time. Either way it's good for sparrows, as these stubbles, once a common feature of the farmed countryside, offer rich pickings.

Sparrows also need company. They are the most social of our resident garden birds, which is a huge part of their charm. They find viability in numbers. It could be that when these numbers reach a critical low, the colony becomes unsustainable. The plug is effectively pulled. Colonies can also become isolated because sparrows just don't travel far – as little as a mile or two in a lifetime. I can't legislate for this – it's possible that the sparrows in my road could get 'cut off'.

Infectious disease is an issue for gregarious birds. I know that this has been an issue locally, as one of the farmers in my road brought me a dead sparrow (as I mentioned earlier), one of several corpses he'd found in his pigsty. It emphasises the importance of hygiene when feeding garden birds – which, if done properly, along with providing clean water, helps birds survive cold weather.

I walked through Kensington Gardens this week. A census of sparrows has been conducted there since 1925, when there were 2,603. This spring there were, apparently, four. Which is four more than I saw.

Needless to say, I'd be gutted if my sparrows weren't around, and I'd feel the quality of my local environment was greatly diminished. I, like many people, care about birds for their own sake; but also, ultimately, for the sake of me and mine. I did see feral pigeons in Kensington Gardens. What if they started to disappear too? People might not miss them quite so much as sparrows, but they might start to wonder what would be next.

CHAPTER FIVE

May

HOUSE MARTINS ARE GOOD FOR YOU

I moved into the house I live in now because it has house martins nesting on it. Well, partly. It was a factor. I thought, well, if they like it here, then there's a fair chance I will too. There were three house martin nests under the eaves at that time. This was in spite of the cat, which was about to move out, and which had been known to ambush the birds from an upstairs windowsill.

This house is the last in a row of five blocks, ten semis in all, built soon after World War II. When we moved in, ours was the only one in the row with martins. Why ours – particularly given the cat? Maybe the birds just like the flight path?

Soon after I arrived, the martins departed for the winter. In spring the three were reoccupied, after the winter-roosting sparrows had been displaced – and the birds seemed to be casing other bits of the wall, chattering excitedly. They were even shaping up to next door's eaves. And, sure enough, at midsummer construction began on two nests next door – the first martins on number 155 in 50 years.

One sticky evening, my neighbour drew my attention to a grounded fledgling. It was sitting on the garden path, more or less indifferent to us, with a slightly bashed wing. It seemed more interested in the ants that were running around, which it was catching.

I thought back to the grounded swift I once found in late summer. According to the blueprint, swifts aren't supposed to touch the ground from the moment they leave their natal home. This one had obviously nosedived on its maiden flight, and would have sat there on the pavement to die of passivity. Of not knowing what to do. Of being a swift out of air. (At least a fish out of water struggles a bit.)

I picked it up and took it to a wildlife sanctuary, to the veterinary experts. They knew what to do. They threw it into the air, and it – suddenly realising what and where it was – beat off to Africa, never to land again.

I know that martins can land on the ground and take off again but, feeling streetwise, I tried this launching technique with the young martin we had found. But in vain. Its almost weightless body fluttered silently to earth again: it was clearly too weak to fly. Giving in to sentiment, I took it into the back garden and gave it more ants, water and bedding. It ate a good deal, but only live ants. It wasn't interested in anything inanimate. I had to go out for the evening, and when I got back my patient was gone.

The following morning, there it was again, chasing ants on the patio. Slightly encouraged, I gave it yet more ants. But by the time I returned from work it was exactly where I had left it, dead.

I suspect this one was the exception. In late July, I watched as 20 or so of his generation seemed to be playing a game, trying to land on the top of a eucalyptus tree that swished violently in a strong wind. A telephone wire is right alongside this tree, but the martins were showing no interest in landing on that. Those that succeeded in grabbing a sprig merged with the foliage and became indistinguishable from it, as foliage and feather shimmered dark and silver, like a vision of Cezanne, leaves and birds harnessing the energy of the wind.

So what's having martins on the house got to do with the quality of my life? I suppose it's a bit like pet-owners who say that pets are therapeutic. Only with house martins there's less admin. No admin, in fact, bar the occasional sweeping up of droppings. The martins feed themselves and find their own balance, and the offspring move on (in the case of females) or inherit the site (in the case of males).

It's the gentle gurgling of the birds as they stir at dawn. The mutterings. The domestics. The way they swoop into their nests in perfect parabolas. The craft of their nest building, from the first dod of gobby mud pushed onto a vertical brick-face, to the strands of straw dragged in for comfort. It's their confidingness. OK, occasionally they seem to object to the window being opened four inches below, like they have the sudden realisation: 'Hey, there are *people* in there!', but on the whole house martins and hirundines in general aren't like our other 'garden' birds. They *belong* in that other medium – the air. Most everyday birds just have the option of it, sharing our land with us. It's not so much that martins are aloof; it's that they need have no regard for us. Their black eyes hidden in dark masks adds to their inscrutability.

It's the pure, simple pleasure of having them around, especially in late summer, when most other garden birds, in moult and having bred, are keeping a lower profile. As summer progresses, the martins are at their most boisterous, sometimes swarming overhead, surfing the breeze like a school of tiny, airborne porpoises, constantly chattering, negotiating. House martin social dynamics are complicated. They are a bit unusual in that the offspring of one brood will help raise those from a later brood. Of our other birds, moorhens and long-tailed tits also routinely do this.

From time to time a hobby fizzes through, scattering the martins, and no doubt thinning them out a bit too. Pleased as I am that my neighbourhood can support house martins, I am even more pleased that it can support hobbies; these exotic (to an Ayrshire man) little bandits of the sky, moustachioed, gallus (meaning confident and daring – as they'd say in Ayrshire, if they had them), firing off their six-guns and shooting up the peace-loving homestead.

And that migration thing. It fazes me to think of it. Really think of it, as I lie back on the grass at the front and try to make sense of the society above me. Today Bedfordshire. Tomorrow Bordeaux? Thursday Andalusia? Friday Mauretania? Saturday Gabon? ... Next spring, our eaves again? Life would certainly be poorer if they didn't come back.

THE LINTIE AND THE FURZE

I had well known yet oddly unfamiliar visitors to the front garden recently. I might not have looked twice at this pair of finch-shaped birds high in the ash tree, but something in their diffidence drew my gaze. They seemed to be nest prospecting – tentatively – and the small clump of gorse now established near the bird feeder might have been the lure.

There was no bird food left at this point in the day – none of the usual birds were around. When the light was right I could tell that the newcomers were linnets: the male with his rosy chest (like a lipstick-kissed tissue) and forehead eye-catching in the sunlight, the female attractively streaky. They checked out the gorse, then something spooked them, as usual, and they took to the skies again, scattering themselves to the wind.

Surely of all our so-called common and widespread birds, the linnet must be the one with which we're least well acquainted. I've had this thought several times, about this bird that never seems too far away, but always just far enough away to shun any advances. They come and go in the surrounding fields yet never visit the garden for food. It's as though, unlike its gold relative, the linnet hasn't quite forgiven us for the days when it was commonly trapped and sold in cages.

So I've been wondering what makes a linnet tick. What is it *for*? It's just a finch, in the end. It seems to occupy the open spaces between its relatives, the super-abundant, tame and sometimes cocky chaffinch, the renascent goldfinch, the skulking bullfinch and the disease-prone and fluctuating greenfinch. I guess it's more than most the farmland finch, the one that survives at the margins of civilisation – a bit of a gypsy, a wanderer, unattached to place, mysterious in its habits. I notice them more when the rotation of crops brings oilseed rape to the field next door. From time to time I re-acquaint myself with the male's exuberant medleys from the phone wires, as though he's channelling some of the current in the making of those twanging noises between trills.

I've wondered where they nest, where the focal point of their nomadic existence might be. They don't give many clues. What I hadn't properly grasped is that linnets sometimes nest in loose colonies and that, yes, for this they are deeply attracted to gorse. In fact, the linnet was known in the past as the gorse bird. Perhaps my modest little clump is now on their radar – it's the only bit of gorse for miles around, I'm sure, here on the fertile plains of Bedfordshire.

Meanwhile, up on the greensand ridge, from which I took my gorse cutting a few years back, there's a significant gorse reintroduction scheme happening – at RSPB HQ. I knew that the sandy heath was once upon a time the scene of gorse (or furze) harvesting, with this spiny shrub of our thinner, marginal soils having multiple historic uses in Britain and Ireland. It was used for everything from kindling to animal feed, medicinal uses to flavouring whisky, preventing stumbles (if worn correctly) to warding off mischievous spirits, curing horses and killing fleas. It was even a key ingredient of soap. Before The Lodge nature reserve was extended and the heathland restoration began, just one solitary gorse bush survived. Now, new clumps are pushing up from protective tubes. Once it really gets going, we'll wonder why it ever needed any help.

Mature gorse can provide a fortress for all kinds of otherwise vulnerable species. Dartford warblers are well known for their year-round reliance on it, and it can make the difference between breeding success and failure in shrikes, chats, wrens and long-tailed tits. The spiny litter beneath it provides sanctuary for reptiles and natterjack toads. Its profuse golden flowers will fuel sugar-deficient insects for most of the year. 'Set as lights upon the hill / Tokens for the wintry earth that beauty liveth still' wrote Elizabeth Barrett Browning in her poem, 'Lessons from the Gorse'.

The linnet isn't top of most people's list of species that might benefit from heathland restoration, but I'm hoping it's one that The Lodge might welcome back. Perhaps they'll set up a nesting colony, along with the less gregarious 'A-listers' like woodlark and nightjar.

Perhaps, too, more land managers should think about having a gorse clump somewhere in a quiet corner. Linnets need all the help they can get, with three out of five of them gone in Europe since 1980. It's often been described as a bird of 'waste' places, but anywhere that helps to keep the linnets with us is far from wasted.

No less than Oscar Wilde once told a story that Linnaeus, the 'father of natural history', when on a visit to this country, 'fell on his knees and wept for joy when he saw for the first time the long heath of some English upland made yellow with the tawny aromatic blossoms of the English furze...' I was also pleased to discover that he loved gorse so much he'd tried to grow some in his Swedish greenhouse.

Wilde, meanwhile, was obviously fond of the linnet. Of all the possible candidates it is the bird he chose to alert the Selfish Giant, through song, to the one tree in his garden to which spring had come.

BOX OF TRICKS

This is going to sound odd to anyone who knows how much I like making nest boxes, but part of me is opposed to the idea of birds using them. I wish they didn't need to. I'd much rather the blue tits that frequent my front garden were nesting in a knot-hole in an old oak, or the cavity of a twisted apple tree. However, like much of the landscape that surrounds me, I am lacking in such trees, far less the chance nesting cavities described.

At the start of the year I put up a home-made nest box for these blue tits. In a vain attempt to make mine seem a bit less like free-range pets (you've got to admire their cuteness and style – they've got us right where they want us, providing purpose-built homes, and fast-food outlets), I 'naturalised' its frontage with some cladding. This was a thin piece of pine with a perfectly sized knot-hole. I contented myself that this box was now the next best thing to a natural setting. I placed it among the stems of a climbing rose attached to a fan trellis, against the front wall of the house. I made sure the nest hole was facing the side, and towards the bay window, so I could watch any comings and goings from the comfort of my sofa. The foliage of the rose would shade the box from any direct sunlight – important for air-conditioning the box later in the season.

As per the blueprint, by March the box was being regularly visited by blue tits. Through April the perky pair ferried beakfuls of moss and hair into the box, and by early May I'd see tiny parcels of food being brought – I would guess, from one partner to the other – as eggs were being incubated inside.

Then, on the evening of Friday 5 May, disaster struck. I was returning from a bike ride, and I noticed, as daylight ebbed, one of the blue tits on the telephone wire leading to my eaves, in an agitated state. I looked to where the box should be. To my dismay I saw that it had come loose from the trellis and, although it hadn't slipped far, it was essentially upside-down in the stems of the climbing rose.

I hurried to retrieve what I could of the situation, and carefully removed the box from the net of stems that had broken and prevented its fall. I was prepared for the worst – that all or most of the eggs inside would be smashed. As constructor and installer of the box, I had to take full responsibility for the accident.

Fearing what might confront me, I gently prised open the front of the box. There was a tangle of nest material. And, lying in a row, like beads from a broken necklace, were the eggs – all of them, miraculously, in one piece. What I hadn't expected to also find in there was a parent blue tit, hidden from view in the tangle. It brushed my hand on its hasty exit as I reached in to gently lift the nest. I have no idea how the bird had sat tight during this upheaval, and in what position, but its coolness under pressure must have preserved the eggs, of which there were an impressive nine, little white misshaped pearls, flecked with pale freckles.

I gently gathered the eggs from the floor of the box and placed them back in the soft cup of the nest, smoothing down some ruffles, and pressed it gently back in position. I re-sealed the box front, and attached a new and more secure batten to the side, for re-attaching to the trellis. I had to work fast, conscious that with every minute the possibility of desertion was growing. I also thought that the birds would have to return to the box before nightfall – rapidly descending – or else the eggs would chill and the bond between birds and nest would be severed.

In all honesty I had no real idea how the birds would respond to the whole sorry episode. Birds are easily spooked while nesting, particularly early in the season, and especially if they have the option of cutting their losses and trying again elsewhere. With blue tits, in these parts, they usually only have one chance, one nesting effort per spring, hence so many eggs (in one basket, as it were). I was interested to read that in the north and west of the country, blue tits will make two breeding attempts per season. But not down here. They are synchronised to hatch their eggs when the caterpillar season is at its height, ensuring plentiful food for all those gaping beaks.

But the return of the birds seemed highly improbable, when I thought of the trauma experienced by the sitting bird and the period of time (I'd say half an hour) in which their home had disappeared altogether. But then nine *is* a lot of eggs, a big investment, and perhaps if one bird could cope, and would return, then the other would follow? Who knows how bird pairs arrive at such decisions: which has the casting vote, and how do they communicate this to each other? I watched the nest box from the living room until dusk gathered and fell, and all activity had ceased. I saw no further sign of the birds. The only movement of wings around the front garden was now that of bats. I called off the watch.

Next morning, I took up my seat on the sofa, a little forlorn, and fearing the worst. And then, right there, in the usual place, as though nothing had happened and all was forgotten, was a blue tit, hopping through the rose and up to the box, and in, and out, and away again. I watched until I saw two of them. Normal service was resumed. However the decision was reached, they had opted to carry on with their project, despite the rude interruption. It would remain to be seen if the eggs were healthy, and not chilled beyond recovery. But, so far so good.

Titbits were brought regularly through the day, and the indignation shown towards me if I went too near the window (after what had happened, you'd think they'd be cool about such minor matters by now) was reassuringly normal. I almost breathed a sigh of relief – but not quite. There would be other hazards ahead, and I still couldn't be sure the eggs were still viable.

By Monday it was clear that both birds were bringing food to the box simultaneously. There were obviously offspring inside.

The happy ending to this tale is that I was able to enjoy a good two to three weeks of further blue-tit hyperactivity, as the birds flew to and fro between my hedgerows and the box, and the fields opposite and the box, with caterpillars and aphid paste. I set up my camera to try to get pictures, and the birds never fully relaxed in my presence, or in the presence of the lens poking through the curtains, despite all we'd been through. I was even able to witness for myself how the parent birds would occasionally visit the peanut feeder to refuel themselves, and even on one or two occasions bring this fast food to the nest. But their obvious preference was to provide wild-caught protein for the brood.

I saw one of the youngsters make its maiden flight from the nest hole, and I took a photo of it. I couldn't be sure how many of the eggs had hatched, at least until the activity had ceased, and the family dispersed to the wider countryside. I was then able to take the box down, and replace it with something a little more failsafe. Inside the box was one slightly flattened nest, and no trace of any eggs. I am assuming they all hatched and made it to fledgling-hood. Quite how such a large family can be reared in such cosy confines is still beyond me, but somehow they do it.

Blue tits bridge the gap between domesticity and raw nature. They have probably done more than most species to recruit people to the cause of bird protection. There's a little bit of wildness and a little bit of tameness in these birds and, in the case of mine, this spring, probably just exactly the right amount of each. I've still got mixed feelings about nest boxes, mind.

VOICE IN THE DARKNESS

There's a bird that lives near me, but I've never seen it. It comes every year, in spring, and it sings within earshot of my garden, from early May through to early June. Drawn by its song, like a sailor to a siren, I can walk to it – get within yards of it, even. But still a view eludes me. It is a very plain bird, according to the books but, like most birds – even the plain ones – there are extraordinary things about it. Its voice, for one. And its habit of singing in the dead of night.

I'm talking about the nightingale, which is perhaps obvious. I should point out, though, that it's not the only bird that ever sings in the night (robins, and others, will sometimes sing by street light), and it doesn't only sing in the night. It is, though, the only songbird we have that prefers to sing in the dead of the darkest of nights.

The voice, of course, is extraordinary. There isn't much more I can say about this that hasn't been said before, by poets and romantics generally, but I will try. There is a precision to the notes, like a street vendor repeating oddly worded phrases. It's not the sweetest of bird songs, I would argue, but it has a clarity that pen-etrates to your core, slightly unnerving, like the incongruity of sleep talk. You expect people to whisper in the dead of night, or at least to lower their voice. The sleep-talker ignores these conventions, is free from self-consciousness. In darkness, you expect birds other than owls to keep quiet and animals to tiptoe. But the nightingale's voice is undimmed in the night-time – making you think that there's not that much to be afraid of, really. As long as you keep a thicket over your head.

Home for my neighbourhood nightingale is a small spinney with a stream and ditch, and thorny understorey, ideal for the birds to skulk and nest in. This road crosses rail tracks and forks to two dead ends. There is no station now, just the odd spike of evening primrose and a prostrate Virginia creeper to indicate that there were once a garden and walls here, before the railway reforms of the 1950s and 1960s. There is a spinney and a brook through a tunnel. The first nightingale I ever heard after I moved here 12 years ago was on a bright Sunday morning in early April. I was investigating the brook and a pool for frogspawn, when I heard the notes echoing under the bridge, a wonderful acoustic.

I can hear it from my bed on a still night. On one particularly misty night, after a very wet day, the sound from here was unusually loud, but I couldn't be sure which direction it was coming from. It made me realise how water vapour or atmospheric moisture catches and carries sound. A marine conservationist I know explained how it is like this at sea, where on still nights you can hear conversations on far distant boats. As a campaigner for a safer environment for albatrosses, he is a man who would know. Whales are able to communicate across oceans because water is such an effective conductor of sound.

Sometimes, if a competitor is audible, the nightingale's efforts are redoubled. I've noticed that these rivals often lack the range, volume and vocabulary of the holder of this spinney, but do enough to spur on their presumably more experienced rival.

I take people sometimes to hear it up close. There is always a strong sense of anticipation, like at a concert when you are kept waiting by the headline act, as the support acts – the young hopefuls – go through their repertoires. In the case of nightingales, robins, song thrushes and blackbirds provide a warm-up. Gradually they fade with the last of the light. They then begin their nervous chatter as the darkness sets in, and finally they fall silent, the proprietorial instinct to sing, to assert possession of a space, giving way to a fear of the dark and the dangers it contains.

There is usually a further delay, a long silence, before the nightingale takes the stage. This adds greatly to the anticipation. I wonder what the other birds make of it, if anything. Where do they go when they sleep? Where exactly, and in what frame of mind are they? Are they in some kind of torpor? How well, or badly, do they see? It is remarkably difficult to know where most of our songbirds go to roost, and it is fair to assume that they are in some kind of suspended animation brought on by darkness – a trance-like state over which they have little resistance. The night-time woodland is a place fraught with danger and uncertainty. And I think it is all of this that makes the habits, behaviour and attention-seeking of the nightingale so daring, arresting, uplifting, and more than just a little bit strange.

NEST BUILDING

I probably shouldn't have revealed this in a magazine (*Birds*) with an audited readership of 1.7 million people, but I used to build birds' nests. Eccentric behaviour? Perhaps. But then I was only about ten at the time. I had occasion to reflect on this recently, as I found myself once again nest building this spring. Okay, porch building, but the parallels with the birds around me seemed obvious, as I gathered reclaimed wood and improvised the structure.

I say I built birds' nests as a kid, but of course only a bird can build a proper bird's nest. Mine were pretty rudimentary efforts, as you might imagine, which only swelled my admiration for the magic birds can weave using only their beaks and tiny brains. And I took some satisfaction from the fact that with one small twig-based installation I fooled a friend into climbing a cherry tree to inspect what he thought was the real deal. Serves him right for risking disturbance of the birds, I reasoned.

Flush with this success, and growing in ambition, I then duped an actual bird – a carrion crow – into coming for a closer peek at another 'nest', the effect of which I had embellished with a cunningly placed and slightly egg-shaped pebble. And then – my proudest moment of all (and the one that finally ended my older brother Kevin's scorn about this nest-building foible) – a pair of song thrushes actually adopted a C.J. 'nest' in a bush by the front door of our house, and built a proper one on my foundations. You see, Kev? You see?

Nest building and the laying of eggs are among the many fascinating and endearing traits of wild birds. Unlike their other inspiring qualities – like being able to fly (mostly), sing, and be colourful and conspicuous (mostly) – we in conservation don't often talk about nests and eggs. These are things best kept private, for obvious reasons. Birds are sensitive to disturbance when breeding, as a rule. Even well-intentioned interest in their nesting activity can result in nest desertion.

Sometimes, however, the birds bring their nests right under your nose, into your space, and you have to find ways of accommodating them. This year, robins accepted my offer of an open-fronted nest box in my front porch. They have nested there before, in a plant hanger. In a sense, they were drawn to the site partly by the safety provided by me, and the fact that they were unlikely to be disturbed here by other predators. At the same time, they were clearly agitated, at least in the early stages, by my actual presence.

I think these were inexperienced birds, and to begin with they would flit from the nest whenever I appeared. As time passed, however, they grew bolder and would sit tight. In ten days or so the eggs hatched, and then downy fluff was visible above the rim of the nest (which is at roughly my head height), and then a pair of dark eyes, a comically wide and expectant mouth, even when shut, and ludicrous 'eyebrows'. The little face would shrink back when I appeared, but the eyebrows would remain risibly visible. You can only get away with such nestling buffoonery in the sanctuary of a porch nest.

It seemed to me that these comical eyebrows had barely had time to settle down into proper head feathers before the young were out of the relative security of the nest, and hiding behind the wheelie bin, and other inadvisable places. I checked the nest and two eggs remained, unhatched, probably chilled during the unusually cold spell of April. Or maybe it was during one of the extended absences of the inexperienced parents, who perhaps were having to forage harder and longer due to the cold. Or the eggs may simply have been infertile.

At the back of the house, a second brood of blackbirds was attempted in my lean-to shed, on top of the wood that I had piled there, and was in the middle of using. This obviously delayed what I was doing at the time, but I took ample consolation from being able to watch the female blackbird sculpting the mud cup of her nest using damp soil from a bucket I'd left out. I'd never before seen a blackbird doing this, and I could see how she used her body to shape the structure, as she 'shimmied' her wings and body.

My latest porch build is a job that's been pending for some months. I was struck by the sudden momentum that took hold of me as spring approached and advanced. Perhaps there is no great mystery in this – it's easier and nicer to work outdoors when it's warmer – but I suspect there is more to it – a more basic underlying reason why DIY stores are rammed on Easter bank holiday. I would guess you can find the answer in the rookeries around us.

Us humans don't breed on an annual cycle, of course, but spring, and longer (if not always warmer) days do give some of us 'the birds' urge to whistle', as Robert Louis Stevenson put it, and the birds' urge to build. How far you want to take it is pretty much up to the individual. Looking back, I can see that building birds' nests was quite an unusual thing for a young chap to be doing, but it will always be preferable to disturbing the real thing.

However you achieve it, you should encourage birds to share a little piece of your home, and let them build or furnish their own little extension. You can't put a (house) price on the rewards.

HAWKS AND THE CITY

I wrote a feature for the magazine *Lost in London* about the author J.A. Baker. From nine to five he was an office manager of modest means who became fixated with the peregrine falcon, and searched for them over a decade of winters back in the late 1950s/early 1960s in his native Essex. The birds had gone into a serious decline by that time, and he feared we would lose them altogether. He didn't live long enough to witness the birds' dramatic and welcome recovery, and indeed their return not only to the wide estuary of the Thames, but to the very heart of London too.

Perhaps we didn't know how resilient the birds would prove to be, nor how adaptable, though now it seems obvious that their fondness for mountain and sea cliffs, and the ducks, pigeons and gulls of the rural and coastal environment, might easily translate to our urban and inner-city settings, with their towering buildings and abundant prey.

For the last few years, I've had a bit of a fixation with another raptor species at least as dramatic – if not quite so conspicuous – as the glamorous peregrine, poster bird for nature restored. The bird I've locked on to is known by some as the phantom of the forest, in recognition of its spectral, cryptic ways. 'You know it is there, because you don't see it,' they say in Germany. I'm talking about the goshawk – *Accipiter gentilis*. The noble hawk. We have come to think of it as a bird only of remote forests, living as far away from humanity as it can get. But guess what? It can be even more adaptable to inner-city existence than its falcon counterpart.

A few years ago I found a goshawk. Not in the forest (though, trust me, I had tried there), but in a town. In a shop, in fact. A junk shop. The bird was stuffed and mounted. And in an odd, disconcerting, haunting way, it was still beautiful and alluring. My search proper began there. I had to know more about the species, and where it could be found.

I found out from German conservationists that the goshawk had somehow sneaked into cities like Berlin, and Hamburg, and had made these places its home. I went there to try to see this for myself. My resultant article on the goshawk I found there won me the 'Nature Writer of the Year' award from *BBC Wildlife* and since then I've been writing features to let more people know about this once cherished but much forgotten bird of prey.

I find that now I cannot walk in London without thinking of goshawks here too. I see goshawk habitat in these parks, large gardens, cemeteries and of course Hampstead Heath. They would love it here, just as they do Cologne, Moscow, Prague. I found a goshawk at RSPB Rainham Marshes – Stewart Goshawk, that is, of the City Bridge Trust, which supports wildlife conservation nowadays, as well as London's bridges. Well, you take your goshawks where you can get them – for now.

In lieu of proper goshawks, I've looked for and found other things, connected things. I looked for the author T.H. White, best known for his Arthurian novels wrapped together as *The Once and Future King*, which became a Broadway musical and a Disney classic. It also inspired the creation of Harry Potter. White wrote a less well known (but revered, by devotees of nature writing) book in the 1930s (though not published till 1951) called *The Goshawk*, about his battle to tame a wild gos, using medieval methods. King George VI is said to have died with a copy of this intense tale by his bed, in 1952.

By the late 1880s the goshawk was extinct in Britain, wiped out by trophy hunters in the age of the gun, although captive birds have always made bids for freedom and sometimes tried to nest. In an earlier age the goshawk was king, or at least travelled on the fists of kings, such as Henry VIII, who loved them. Royal hawks were kept at Charing Cross and on the site of what is now the National Gallery on Trafalgar Square. It was a huge complex with many staff, reflecting the importance and prestige of hawking at that time, and the skill and time needed to train and maintain the birds properly.

Goshawks were worth a fortune. They filled larders with food, such is their prowess at catching anything from hares to wildfowl. Peregrines will put on more flamboyant aerial performances, but if it's food you want, the *cuisinier* (as the French called it) is the bird of choice. Direct, no-nonsense, lethal in the chase; the goshawk is perhaps the most raptorial of raptors, the most versatile, rapacious. They can also be just a teeny bit crazy beneath that imperious exterior. And when their eyes flash orange, or even blood-red, they have something of the big cat's all-powerful menace.

One warm, almost continental, May afternoon I wandered into Hyde Park, one eye open for goshawks (well, you never know your luck) and the other on a map. I was looking for W.H. Hudson's memorial, hidden somewhere in a thicket in the Park. Mr Hudson is another conservation and literary giant, from the Victorian era, when the last British goshawks were shot and stuffed. I found treasure on the way – the Champions League trophy, glinting on a plinth, on public display before the final at Wembley. I could have queued to touch it, which would have been some kind of grail for me, but I preferred instead to maintain my search focus on William Henry Hudson. He loved goshawks too, although I am sure he never saw a live one, only stuffed ones in elegant drawing rooms. He hated that.

I found the shrine to him in that suitably sequestered green corner, as parakeets shrieked in the canopy above me – fitting, I think, for the theme of the sculpture. This shows his fictional creation Rima, the forest-dwelling bird girl, from his 1904 novel *Green Mansions*. It is the work of artist Jacob Epstein, and was installed in 1925, a few years after Hudson's death. The curtain on this piece was drawn back by Prime Minister Stanley Baldwin. It caused a bit of a furore, with the *Morning Post* describing the work as an 'atrocity' and the 'Hyde Park nightmare'. They even wrote that Epstein had 'sold his soul to the devil'. Epstein, it should be noted, was completely bamboozled by this reaction.

The goshawk also provokes some extreme reactions. In Shakespeare's day they were 'hell kites' to those who might lose a chicken or two to a marauding gos. W.H. Hudson records a woodland community in Wiltshire going into a frenzy when a large hawk, he thought almost certainly a goshawk, took up residence there. 'A fearsome, *tarrable*-looking bird,' as someone described it to him. After blazing away at the wretched thing for several days someone finally brought it down, Hudson recorded, remorsefully.

The goshawk is back in Britain now, secreted about our larger forests, intent no doubt on spreading to reclaim the landscape over which in pre-human times it was the alpha bird. So will the goshawk be coming back to London's forest of buildings any time soon? Well, it might not be soon, as it has to get across the farmed lowlands and suburbia first. But I feel sure it will rejoin us as and when we let it. And our lives will be all the more dramatic, balanced and enriched when it comes.

Note
A friend found my book *Silent Spring Revisited* in a bookshop in Cambridge, and sent me a photo of it sandwiched between W.H. Hudson and Richard Jefferies – for alphabetical reasons only, of course, but it was possibly the proudest – or the most humbling – moment of my life.

VISIONS OF CHINA
I drove to work today, which may seem daft when I have the option of cycling across country for half an hour instead. I did cycle yesterday, and on May mornings as beautiful as these you cannot go wrong; the air is alive with lark and warbler song. But today, as I took my place in the queue of cars at the level crossing near my village, I had what felt like a vision.

A tiny head and a black eye appeared in the shallow ditch to my left. The eye was ringed with white, a tapering eye-stripe curved into a fetching lash behind it. A bird's head, vaguely familiar. Wader? No: duck. Tiny duck. It looked furtive, uncertain of these cars paused alongside it. It crept up the bank. The female. Close behind, its mate, the male, or drake. Unmistakable now. Coloured like a bird of paradise, with crest, whiskers, plumes, affectations.

Mandarin ducks. Absurdly glamorous (the males, anyway) for birds that like to live in a ditch. Native of China, as the name suggests, crests raised, redolent almost of dragons, if that can be possible, in a duck. Imported decorations for our ornamental ponds and gardens, now gone native, feral in our woods and slow streams, a subtle tension of skulk and the spectacular. If there is anything more eye-catching than a bird like this, in peak breeding plumage, in pristine May morning sunlight, at close range, I'd like my eye to be caught by it.

Others in the village have glimpsed a pair in the wood, where there are small, weed-roofed ponds. I considered installing an old coal scuttle for the ducks on an overhanging limb, but then it's not my wood to embellish. They like to nest in a tree cavity.

I have been lucky enough to spend some time with author Christopher Lever, who had recently marked his eightieth year. We were visiting Ramsey Island to see first-hand the early effects that the removal of an invasive species – the brown rat – has had on the recovery of Manx shearwaters and other native species. A very positive effect, I'm happy to report. Brown rat removal tends not to be problematic, politically. Killing them is often an unpleasant necessity, and there aren't many voices raised in their defence when it comes to undoing the ecological damage caused by their unfortunate island introductions of the distant or recent past.

On our journey back to England we had time for a brief pause in the Forest of Dean, at a stretch of the River Wye that has become a stronghold for the mandarin duck. Christopher has recently authored the definitive study of this alluring species. We didn't find any that day, which wasn't unexpected, as our visit was brief. With the river soil-reddened and swollen, the ducks and ducklings were probably anchored safely in the lee of a bank somewhere. The locals assured us the birds were around.

Brown rats and mandarin ducks: both introduced non-natives, and of course the contrast in their impact and how they are perceived could not be more stark.

We spoke about Christopher's latest book and his particular interest in these ducks of far Eastern origin. I recall the enthusiasm with which he described the first time he set eyes on a pair of mandarins, as a young birdwatcher in the 1950s. It was in Windsor Great Park, on Virginia Water, where Berkshire meets Surrey. The birds made such an impression on the young man that he can trace his fascination for not only them but introduced species in general to that morning. He describes this formative moment in the preface to *The Mandarin Duck*.

Christopher Lever has now studied the history and ecology of introduced vertebrates for over four decades. Aged 79, he was awarded a PhD by Cambridge University for this work, as well as authoring and contributing to an impressive list of natural history titles. He hasn't been afraid to challenge the orthodoxy that if a species is introduced or non-native, it must be a bad thing. He considers such an attitude 'as irrational as it is misguided'.

I always sense from Lever's books that he is driven by compassion for any introduced species that finds itself, through human agency rather than its own pioneering spirit, at large in an alien environment. Compassion hasn't always been one of the stronger themes of conservation, and I admire him for it. He is intrigued by any newcomer's interactions with a novel set of circumstances, and mindful all the while that some introduced species do become severely problematic.

With a UK population of around 7,000 birds in summer, the mandarin looks like it is here to stay. It is a protected species here, though it may be vulnerable to lack of familiarity and misidentification (Google 'mandarin duck shooting' to find out more). Lever carefully itemises the history of the species here, region by region, and in Europe and the USA, and casts new light on how it has succeeded where, for example, the closely related American wood duck failed. Key to this may have been the shedding of its inclination to migrate.

On another occasion I came face to face with a resplendent drake, which was sitting quietly on a floating door as I canoed around a bend of a very narrow, overgrown tributary of the Cam. It was an Alice-in-Wonderland moment (I've had a few) still imprinted firmly on my mind. If I could, I would paint it.

The beauty and extravagance of the birds – especially the male – is beyond dispute (although some might consider it excessive), and of course they may sometimes look out of place here. But perhaps they look out of place, and improbable, wherever they occur, even at home in frozen Oriental wetlands. At face value, the mandarin duck is an unlikely colonist of these isles, but Christopher's monograph may make you change your mind if you think that this enigmatic species is mere ornamentation, or a misplaced trophy of the vain, any more than other birds. It was apparently present in south-eastern England 600,000 years ago.

I often imagine what it was like to be a bird lover in days of antiquity, to have been an enthusiast with the wherewithal to indulge a love of birds by importing exotic species for collections. Imagine unveiling a peacock, for example, to a crowd of onlookers who have never clapped eyes on such a life form. The impact of a pair of mandarins can't have been much less startling to nineteenth-century European eyes. They wouldn't look out of place in a beauty parade of Papuan birds of paradise. Lever's book brings out vividly the importance of these birds in far Eastern culture, across their native range in China, Japan and Korea. They have long been symbols of fidelity and love. It is a reputation well earned, in fact, as the male mandarin attends the nest site during incubation, and the family group for a week or two post-hatching.

In writing *The Mandarin Duck*, it is fitting that Lever has returned to the bird that first inspired his fascination with the fate and impacts of introduced species globally. It's not a controversial species – I don't think there are many charges laid at the mandarin's door, although some people he's met are against it, in line with their default position on non-natives. That said, I almost wonder if the sight of a male mandarin in his fullest glory might even be intimidating to other species. Mandarins certainly hold their own with other, bigger wildfowl, and I've watched them bossing more than their share of Berlin parks, for example. In the wild, as a skulking, woodland duck it doesn't have too many counterparts or competitors here, but of course it may occupy those rare and precious nest holes that other species might have used. But, generally speaking, the mandarin is a benign and pleasing addition to our avifauna, and it seems churlish to find objection to it, without good evidence.

Christopher Lever is a (if not the) world authority on introduced species, and his contribution to the literature on this important, emotive and often controversial area of natural history has been immense. With this work he has done a first-class job of enhancing our understanding of an extraordinarily ornate and tenacious species.

THINGS THAT GO BLEEP IN THE NIGHT

It's a damp spring night and I'm walking home from the pub. I'm not sure how many bleeps I might have been exposed to before they finally register and, recalling that I'm not abroad and that this is a bit odd, I stop to listen properly. I'm not imagining it or hearing things. The sound is quite high-pitched, you might even say electronic, with pauses of a few seconds between each. It's hard to pinpoint the exact source, but it seems to be coming from the garden of an old vicarage, which is between me and the river. I'm on the route of the old north road, and a milestone alongside it tells me I'm 55 miles from London. Traffic on the new north road (aka the A1) swooshes past 20 metres to my right, beyond our Millennium Garden.

I know from experience on the Continent that a toad must be producing this sound – a bit like the time pips on Radio 4, spaced out. I had heard there were colonies that had established in Bedford, but this is the first I've known they have spread the ten miles or so east from Bedford to my village.

A quick check when I get home confirms the identification. Midwife toad. A remarkable creature, which grows little bigger than a coat button, and so-named from the male toad's role in carrying the eggs from the moment the female spawns them till they are ready to hatch. He then deposits the emerging tadpoles in a suitable shallow pool. Mating takes place out of water, and the male uses one of his toes to help the female release the eggs.

There are five European species of midwife toad, and ours seem to have reached Bedford just over a hundred years ago, stowed away in plants imported from France, according to the Bedford Natural History Society. I wonder if they used the river as their route to reach my village, or if the local plant nursery might have transported some in a consignment of produce.

My friend Lizzie Infield farms cattle in the meadows alongside the River Ouse, and she has sent me photographs of a male midwife toad she discovered in its daytime hideaway under a rock in her garden. He has a cluster of eggs wrapped around his legs. Come nightfall in spring and summer he will emerge from the lair and forage for insects and invertebrates which he catches on his tongue, which is thick and rounded and gives the species its family scientific name, *discoglossidae*. The species here is *Alytes obstetricans*.

Midwife toads seem to be doing well, while locally the native common toad is not. The diminutive foreigner may be especially unpalatable to predators with its toxic skin. Its tadpoles lack this deterrent and are subject to the usual hazards in a pond.

On another evening I have reason to think the midwife toad might have reached my own garden, about a mile from the river and the local population centre. A loud electronic bleep is issuing from somewhere around the outhouses at the back. I trace it to my neighbour Dorothy's side of the fence, and I knock on her door to ask if I can pop round to have a closer look. 'I think you've got a midwife toad out the back,' I venture. This takes a little bit more explaining.

Dorothy gets the picture and approves the expedition. The sound is definitely coming from within the workshop that old Fred used to use, and as we home in on it with my torch beam it now dawns on Dorothy what the sound is. 'I know!' she reveals. 'It's that [bleeping] alarm thing!'

So not, alas, a midwife toad, but the government-issue smoke alarm (one that fits to a light bulb) she had removed from the bedroom as it was emitting these loud bleeps at inconvenient times of day (and night – they do this when the charge is low) and she didn't know how to make it desist. How we laugh. I remove the offending device, hoping to give it a new lease of life.

I've known other local people to call out British Telecom to investigate the odd and unexpected nocturnal bleepings of real toads, and I guess by now the engineers know when it's a false alarm and to save themselves a journey.

Introduced species can often be a nuisance if not a serious ecological problem, detrimental to native flora and fauna. But until and unless proved otherwise, the midwife toad seems a benign and endearing addition to the sound and colour of the village, a challenger to gender roles, and strangely in keeping (and bleeping) with the electronic age we have created.

OUT FOR THE COUNT

We have a pretty good idea exactly how many skylarks there are in the UK, and how many there used to be, and therefore by how much they have declined: which is by three-quarters in 25 years. We know how many lesser spotted woodpeckers there are too. But *how* do we know? Answer: I counted them. Well, some of them...

The radio alarm says 5 am. A thin wedge of daylight splitting the curtains tells me it's dawn. Dreams fizzle from my mind in the cold light of day. It's Sunday. It's May. It's time to go and count birds. I persuade myself that in an hour's time it'll be worth it.

6 am. I am right. It *is* worth it. I'm doing the woodland stretch of my one-kilometre Breeding Bird Survey (BBS) square, and the canopy is a free-for-all of warbling. I pause to make notes, to extricate one song from another, robin from robin from blackcap from blackbird from dunnock from wren from wren. I'm lucky that my square, randomly selected by the scientists at the BTO/ Joint Nature Conservation Committee and RSPB, is right on my doorstep. The BBS is how we know how many birds of each species we have, and how they are faring. The raw data is provided

by me and, nowadays, thousands of other volunteers like me. And counting.

My May visit is the second of three, between April and June. Each visit lasts two or three hours, and requires me to walk two straight-ish lines across the square. Line one begins with the woodland edge. I then emerge onto my street, with its teams of house sparrows, collared doves and house martins. The square straddles the A1. About a fifth of the square is on the other side, leading down to the River Ouse. In April I counted up the nests in the rookery. This is an extra task in the survey. Rook nests are relatively easy to count – before they disappear behind the unfurling leaves.

The river habitat boosts my species total. I can see kingfisher, common tern, grey wagtail, cuckoo, rabbits x 10 (the organisers want mammal info too). It's tempting to think, 'the more the merrier', but square discipline is important. If it's outside the square, it doesn't get in...

Line one complete, I nip down the edge of the square to the start of line two. Line two brings me back from the river past a church, under its bulging chestnut trees. I note with pleasure that the spotted flycatchers have come back, between pasture and graveyard. I cross the A1 again. I am walking a road between an unmanaged, sycamore-dominated strip of woodland on one side, and foot-high winter wheat on the other. My scribbling abates. By 9 am I am back home, clutching a cup of coffee and feeling righteous, if slightly glaikit. The write-up can wait.

The number of volunteers carrying out this type of survey work has been growing year by year. As it grows, so the coverage becomes more and more comprehensive, and the data ever more reliable. It enables the number-crunchers back at base to draw important conclusions. It is as a result of surveys like these that we know that woodland birds, on the whole, were faring reasonably well but are now in trouble, and that numbers of farmland birds are still in freefall.

The research provides us with a lobbying tool – accurate figures to push under the noses of the powers that be, or the sceptical. Bird population stats are recognised as a quality of life indicator. Life can certainly feel high quality on a sunny May morning – 'bliss is it,' to paraphrase William Wordsworth, 'in this dawn, to be alive.' You just have to hold on to that thought when the alarm goes off at 5 am.

CHAPTER SIX

June

HAPPY WHEN IT RAINS

I feel a certain amount of peer pressure from my neighbours to keep my front garden relatively 'tidy'. Relative to my back garden, that is, which has a kind of order, to me, but is basically organised wildness.

It is for this reason, I plead, that I came to be (lightly) trimming the hedge at the front in late June. Just to keep some of the longer shoots in check, you understand, as they were protruding over the pavement. The front hedge is a mix of hawthorn, blackthorn, dog-wood, dog rose and field maple (planted by me) and elm, which has suckered from subterranean sources. I assumed it was not yet stout enough for birds to be nesting in it. I had pruned it back to about three feet high early in the year, and by now its leaf shoots had brought it up to around six feet. In any event I had seen no evidence of nest building, and I do a lot of coming and going, not to mention gazing out of the window in its direction. Watching this ex-car port front garden transmogrify into a little slice of enclosed field has been a rare pleasure.

I was pavement-side with my rusty shears. Trim complete, it wasn't until I yanked a strand of bindweed out of the hedge that there was a flutter of wings behind the curtain of foliage, and a frantic, machine-gun piping started up from just the other side.

Song thrush! Unmistakable. Doh, I thought, embarrassed at my error of judgement, tinged with excitement that my hedge was already deemed suitable to be nested in, tinged with anxiety that the bird might desert the nest, tinged with a growing feeling, as the seconds passed, that she wouldn't. Her behaviour indicated that she was sticking around, that she would return, if I beat a conspicuous retreat. All the while her mate, presumably, was singing cheerfully away in the background.

I peered around the end of the hedge to see her sitting on my neighbour's fence post. I ducked back. She was between me and the house, so I sloped off up the road about 30 yards. She flew across the road to the fence opposite the garden, where she could see me, and for a few minutes I waited, and she waited, and watched, and flicked, and it became clear she wouldn't go back to the nest until I was out of sight. A car passed. I smiled sheepishly, shears in hand. No option: I did the walk of shame back down the road, past her. She didn't budge. By now she was silent, although there was still a little wing-flicking going on.

The next day after work I watched from an upstairs window as a song thrush searched the dry, patchy ground of the playpark opposite, walking and pausing, walking and pausing. After what seemed like a long period of apparently fruitless foraging it flew to the fence, and then, to my great relief, across the road and out of sight, into the hedge. She had stuck with it. At nestling stage, birds are much less likely to desert a nest. I was lucky.

I took it this was the same pair of thrushes which had earlier nested just outside the front window, in a shrub trained to the wall. Then, as now, they had escaped my notice until they began feeding their young, and then their presence was obvious as they followed a regular flight path into the nest from a dead branch I had planted as a perch, more usually used by sparrows.

They're amazingly discreet, really, apart from when the male is in full voice from the top of the willow across the road. I am lucky to have at times two of them duetting, from midwinter to midsummer. I liken their song to that of the nightingale, only it's more deliberate. The song thrush is a shy bird, modest and deferential, acquiescing to the boisterous blackbirds when their paths cross, a skulking forager for slugs and snails. They seem happy when it rains, if the singing is anything to go by. Dry spells send their food supplies out of beak range – at such times worms and snails get their heads down. The success of brood number two may hinge on summer rains. I will take some consolation from this when the rains come, assuming they do, and the covers are being dragged across the courts at Wimbledon.

I am very conscious of my luck in having song thrushes here, in the drier part of the country, a fact I attribute in part to the permanent pastures nearby, which also treats me to the swallows and yellow wagtails, among others.

Despite their shyness I sense these thrushes take some comfort and security from being able to nest in close proximity to the house. I am not often visited by cats and magpies here, but I have recently detected evidence of weasels. In fact, only two days before I found the thrushes' nest I had found a dead song thrush in a very strange place – seven feet above ground in the clematis- and hop-covered pergola in the back garden. Odder still was the absence of its head. I pondered this for a while, and wondered if the occasional 'sneezing' sounds I had heard in the denser undergrowth of the garden had been made by a weasel. I have seen one here before, a few years back now, in the winter, and on another occasion old Fred next door had reported one in his garden working the outhouse for rodents. Richard Bradbury at work told me he'd often known, from his field-work, weasels to eat only the heads of their prey. And they are well known to be able climbers. So that was it, then: the song thrush had probably been caught while roosting.

Song thrushes declined by a staggering two-thirds between 1972 and 1996. Little wonder, some people say, with all those predators around. But predators have always been around, just as song thrushes have always predated snails. I know that as long as there are good places to nest, like well-maintained (ahem) hedgerows, and dampish places full of molluscs and other nourishment, thrushes will go on producing more chicks than they lose. And that, in the end, is what the game's all about. It's pretty gratifying to be in a position to play the game alongside them.

BIRD EATS CAT

An anxious caller is put through to the RSPB's Wildlife Enquiries Unit one afternoon. She wants to know if we can tell her anything about owls. 'There's one on the garden fence,' she says. 'In the middle of the day.' This isn't necessarily strange, however, as there are day-active (or diurnal, as the experts would call it) owls in the UK.

'Tell us a little bit about the owl,' my colleague suggests. So the caller describes its plumage – brown and streaky – and our advisor tells her it sounds like a tawny. Sometimes they turn up in the daytime, having been woken from their roost maybe by small, indignant birds.

'Hmm,' she says. 'And how *big* are tawny owls?'

'About a foot tall, or so,' he replies.

'Oh no,' she says. 'This one is very much bigger than that.' And then comes the detail that clinches the identification. 'Oh my goodness!' – or words to that effect – she shrieks. 'It's just flown off with the cat!'

Brrrrrrrrrrrrrrrr.

The phone line has gone dead. We're not sure about the cat. Our correspondent never called back to complete the tale, so we can only speculate. But what we can be reasonably sure of is that the owl she described was an eagle owl. *Bubo bubo*, to science. It is not recognised as a native UK species, although bone deposits do place it here in prehistoric times. It is a bird that is often kept by falconers, and which sometimes escapes from them or is set free (illegally) when its appeal wears thin. It goes native quite readily.

If you've ever seen an eagle owl, it will probably have been in captivity rather than in your back garden worrying your pets. You will know that they are pretty awesome beasts, with their great, orange, penetrating eyes, ear tufts and sheer physical presence.

The eagle owl is actually native to continental Europe, mostly living quite secretly and well away from built-up areas. Its fearsome appearance and habits have not always endeared it to locals, especially the superstitious ones. It seems they are capable of crossing the English Channel, and much of what they would find to eat here is no different to the fauna of, say, Belgium, so there would be no reason why they could not thrive here. There have been well-known pairs established in the North York Moors, and the Peak District, in recent times. One escaped pair took up residence on a golf club house in Hertfordshire, where they enjoyed polishing off the local muntjac deer (which are actually native to China, as I mentioned earlier).

There appears very little limit to what eagle owls can catch and consume where other birds and mammals are concerned. They are especially partial to rabbits, themselves definitely non-native. But if they ever do become more widely established, it will give us all something to think about, and make us a little more apt to keep smaller pets under closer supervision. Some people might consider that no bad thing.

TOUCHING THE WEIRD

'It's like Arsene Wenger coming to train the RSPB football team,' was my reaction to hearing that Mark Cocker had offered to coach a group of conservation colleagues in writing skills. I mean no disrespect to them or their literary abilities (or to our footy players either, for that matter), but Mark Cocker is an author of considerable renown, as anyone familiar with *Crow Country*, for example, will attest.

I take my place in a group of eager students, wedged into a small office at our Strumpshaw Fen nature reserve, somewhere between Norwich and the Broads. Mark is holding forth on what it is to write, to discover, to 'puncture the meniscus' (the surface tension, as in water) that separates us in our everyday lives from the fascinating world that lurks beyond. To understand, perhaps, when a stick is not a stick.

I can explain. In our midst is a small table, and occupying most of its surface is a large glass-topped box. Visible within this is a pile of egg boxes, and prominent on the topmost of these is what looks like a fragment of birch stick, glued on. I'm itching to have a closer look, to delve into this box of tricks – or sticks. I have a strong suspicion that the piece of birch is actually a moth.

Closer inspection confirms that it is a moth. A buff-tip moth. It is one of those creations that would have you (if your attention were ever drawn to it) marvelling – boggling, even – at the bizarreness of evolution. That a mere moth can look so much like a piece of tree suggests a world of infinite possibilities. It has a frayed-looking, broken end (its head), while at the other end it looks like it has been cut with a knife, as though to be sharpened like a pencil, revealing a wood-grain effect within the flecked, grey-white bark. Its legs and antennae barely protrude. Sticks, after all, don't have such appendages.

The buff-tip has achieved this make-up, you suppose, for the purposes of being able to sit very still for long periods, and not be recognised as a potential meal (and scoffed by a robin, for example). Because of this, you could be forgiven for going a lifetime without ever seeing one – seeing only sticks instead.

There are other impostors among Mark's egg cartons. There are moths that look like leaves, like dead leaves, like droppings. There's even one (an elephant hawkmoth) that looks like a pink and green jet fighter aircraft. I'm not sure where evolution was going with that one, or who it was with influence in naming new species that got the elephant bit past the committee, but never mind.

'You've just got to go and find some weirdness.'

If only more of my teachers could have issued such instructions. This is Mark's final one to the dispersing group, as we are loosed on the nature reserve, our minds opened up to strangeness, perhaps as a child might find it.

A train ploughs through the reserve. Strange! Don't worry, it has a track to run on, but nevertheless...

There are three bee orchids by the car park fence, cordoned off with a length of coloured string, drawing the eye to them. I point them out to Sarah, one of the group. These are plants evolved to look just like bees, for reasons too strange to elaborate on here. That's not all that's strange about bee orchids. There is a Laurie Lee essay called 'A drink with a witch', and the drink she gives him is bee-orchid wine. Much oddness and witchery ensues, and I don't think it is just the drink talking. Apart from anything, imagine an age when there were enough bee orchids in any one place to make wine.

'You do this sort of stuff all the time,' says Sarah. Writing odd stuff, I think she means.

'Yes, but...' I don't really want to form a proper answer. I'm trying to think differently, today.

I wander across the railway line, enjoying the unusual legality of it. I amble down a leafy lane, past drowsy horses, looking up at corn-field poppies against a blue sky, crowning a steep bank. Further on, a flowerbed slopes uphill to a table mat-cute cottage. A handmade sign reads: 'Come and see the swallowtail butterflies, if you like,' or words to that effect. There are none present, but I like the kindness of the offer just as much.

Opposite, a gate tempts me back across the tracks, to what I take to be a path onto the reserve on the other side. I don't know it yet, but I am crossing too early. I'm not the first person to have done so, as there is a path of sorts through neck-high fen verdure. A swallow-tail bustles past my face, across the reed surface. I press on, hoping to intersect soon with an official path. This doesn't happen.

The fools' path peters out. Rather than plunge on, or retreat, I elect to stop for a bittern's-eye view of the fen. At an isolated willow, I duck through its fronds to the murky 'room' within. I perch on a low bough, above a small pool. There is a welcoming committee of bouncing mosquitoes, apparently jumping for joy at my arrival.

We share lunch – well, I have sandwiches and crisps, and they settle down in various places to try to have me. I get the hand lens out, to get better acquainted with these much under-examined beasts. What, after all, do moths have that mossies don't, apart from relatively vast expanses of pigmentation, and occasionally bizarre disguises? Determinedly open-minded, I home the lens in on the trouser-piercing mouthparts and – as it turns out – comically bulging eyes – of these small (and some not so small) man-eaters. Alas, I can't not think of the Gary Larsson cartoon, where one mossie, sitting on a stretch of flesh, is saying to another, which is filling like a balloon: 'Pull out! You've hit an artery!'

I toy with the idea of letting one of them sup from me, in close up, but hey, it might hit an artery. And how weird are we supposed to be getting here, anyway? I terminate the study.

Retracing my steps carefully, and climbing back out of the fen, I notice a derelict hut by the railway: a mossie-free quiet space in which to write up my notes for our feedback session.

Returning to the group, I meet Sarah again. I show her a broken branch I've picked up along the way. 'How about this for a moth?' I ask her, holding out the branch. Sarah doesn't think this is funny. Undeterred, I try it on Mark. He doesn't get it.

I guess sometimes a stick is just a stick. But despite my pale imitation of a joke, the lesson remains sound: it is always worth looking – and listening – a little more closely, to spot a little bit of oddness.

Note
The hawkmoth took me back to a childhood scenario: me retrieving a football from a ruck of rosebay willowherb, at least as tall as I was. And as I delved within these very everyday plants I found some monstrous-looking life forms: fat as my fingers, with enormous cartoon eyes. Caterpillars, it turned out, with these eye-designs intended to scare birds – and quite possibly small children. After a suitable period of getting acquainted, I took some home for adult input, and my mum got the book out so we could see these larger-than-life larvae, and the adult forms they would become. They were elephant hawk moths-in-waiting, as it turned out.

SEEING GHOSTS

I used to think that the barn owl was one of those birds you only see well on television, if you see it at all. And that this star of the small screen is, in all probability, a falconer's bird. Well, it's never flown like that in front of me, in broad daylight, in somewhere as scenic as the Somerset Levels. It always seemed like one of those birds that is probably out there, somewhere, most of the time, but it isn't about to let you see it. You sense, or you read, or you hear, that it is there, but it remains invisible to you.

For the barn owl, for me, although regrettable, this has always seemed entirely apt, because historically it was known as the ghost owl. To be honest I couldn't be sure I even *believed* in this ghost, that it was any more than a passing phantom, present occasionally but never actually resident in my neighbourhood. But recently I have seen the ghost; it has danced before me in all – or even more than – its reputed spectral glory, as amazing as I had been led or encouraged to believe, and it made me wonder how I can have failed to encounter it before.

There have always been barn owl pellets and occasional feathers on the floor of the airfield barn near my home, but the disgorgers of these large black lumps of fur and bone have always been mysteriously absent. It's the only shelter for miles around. A hangar for birds, really. Once I rumbled a little owl as I tiptoed in through the massive entrance. Those mad yellow eyes were glaring at me from a warped rafter, the startled face pivoted through 180 degrees. On another occasion there was a juvenile tawny owl scrambling for the exit, and another time I found a dead kestrel there. I sent it for analysis to the Centre for Ecology and Hydrology (cause of death: starvation). But the barn owl was never there, just the debris one had left behind – although I could picture one quite vividly.

And then, on the edge of an industrial estate on a November night, the bogey bird finally crossed my path. Once, up ahead. Twice, this time closer. I could see immediately that this was a special bird, and no pigeon, not just because of its size and pallor, but because of its overall jizz; its movement, wings beating stiffly and calmly low over the road, from one side to the other, and again over the road a little further up. Nothing else flies like this. It beat along as though on stiff polystyrene wings, each beat lifting it slightly, as though, no matter how gentle its down-stroke, the movement bobbed it upward.

I turned at the roundabout and made my way slowly back along the road. I was in luck. The owl had parked itself on a fence post, under a street light. I drew slowly alongside and stopped.

Moments like these, communing with raw nature, are like moments in showbiz to me. On this occasion more than most, because here is a barn owl, doing what barn owls do, at night, usually unseen, but suddenly here is one on a stage, in the spotlight. I am sitting ten feet away, in the front row, while the owl dances in the air, and while it sits. I can see its anxiety, feel its hunger, its uncertainty, its senses working, as its black eyes stare intently at the rank grass one moment, behind itself the next, at my car (not at me) after that. It leans forward, then shrinks back, then arcs into the air and scuds into the grass like a boomerang come to earth. Then up again, legs dangling, claws empty, to another post.

It is exquisite looking. Its narrow snout makes it look as peculiar among birds as Staffordshire bull terriers are among dog breeds. The extraordinary half-apple shaped facial mask is designed like the inside of an amplifier, because that's what it does: it amplifies sound to the owl's hidden ears, orders of magnitude more acutely tuned than ours.

This is a large bird, with a three-foot wingspan, and in this light it is as white as a gull, and even larger than life. I read, to my amazement, that they only weigh around ten ounces. This phantom of the night is actually one of the most widespread land birds in the world, found throughout the tropics. It is right at the limit of its durability here in the UK, unable to survive much further north than southern Scotland. It is not designed for cold, wet weather. I guess the lack of body mass makes it prone to chills and its buoyant plumage has little resistance to drenching. Barn owls tend to suffer in harder winters.

Barn owls are known to breed at any time of year, if rodent prey is plentiful enough, and they will hunt by day to provide food for their offspring. They may have benefited from recent milder winters, but they have suffered from a general loss of the hollow trees and vacant outbuildings in which they like to roost and nest.

I have resolved to strap some kind of barrel or box to the trunk of the eucalyptus at the end of the garden, to see if these barn or little owls might like the cubby hole. There aren't enough naturally occurring trees that are old and habitable. If you live near suitable barn owl habitat, you can help them by providing these places to roost, and maybe nest, especially near open grassland where mice and voles might proliferate. Believe me, a plague of these would be much scarier than a ghost owl in, on or around your house. But seeing is believing.

CLOSE ENCOUNTERS

Most people will be well aware by now of the steep decline of many of our bird species, unless they've been living in outer space. Something less widely reported is the apparent recent decline in some other flying objects: unidentified ones, or UFOs.

I'm not sure how troubled conservationists need to be about this one. Technically, it *should* be a cause for concern to compassionate types who care about life: even the not-as-we-know-it kind. The decline of UFOs, their extra-terrestrial occupants, and of the clubs and publications that report and discuss them, is, I suppose, like bird declines, another diminution of life's rich pageant (even if they are not, as bird numbers are, an official indicator of quality of life by which the government's sustainability performance is measured).

It's got me wondering. What would cause a UFO decline? Pollution of space, perhaps? I've heard there's a bit of a litter problem up there. But would space debris translate as fewer UFOs? Or maybe it's a kind of climate change. The emissions levels of UFOs might be high. Could they perhaps contribute to their own downfall? (Or should that be lack of downfall, since we're not seeing them down here any more?)

I saw a so-called crop circle this summer. In fact, it was more of a series of linked circles, near Norwich. These too, apparently, have diminished in number in recent years. If, as some claim, these are also the handiwork of cosmic intelligences, it may add further evidence of a decline. But could it be that the occupants of the flying objects have simply lost interest in us? Maybe they've seen enough of us and have given up on us as a lost cause, thinking they have nothing left to learn. And, with the loss of biodiversity, there's simply less to look at down here. Earth has become less interesting.

For all we know, aliens might have always been more interested in some of the other life forms with which we share our planet. Birds, for example. Perhaps those crop circles were designed to enable skylarks to nest better in cereal fields, as the RSPB's own crop trials at Hope Farm have demonstrated (although you'd have to say our skylark patches are comparatively minimalist).

Recent developments suggest that some birds are getting pretty advanced. They may even be emulating some of our technological and emotional knowhow. If some of the recent examples I've heard about are anything to go by, the interest of UFOs in planet Earth could soon be revived.

RSPB member Chris Dunn has reported being woken late at night by a bright light shining through the bedroom window. From the front door he encountered flying objects that turned out to be wrens. They were flying past the infrared switch to activate a light, which in turn attracted flying insects, which the wrens were snatching. When the light went out, the tiny birds would quickly reactivate it.

Another member, Richard Watson, has reported seeing robins at his local garden centre deliberately flying past an infrared switch to activate the door-opening mechanism and allow them inside. I myself have heard starlings imitating the sound of a car's electronic key in a London street. Clever, and everything, and I'm no technical expert, but is there a security issue here?

It's not just in Britain, either. My friend Edith Shaw emailed me from New Zealand. Her doctor, she says, went kayaking to Quail Island with his family. They were settling down to a picnic when a black-backed gull pinched his mobile phone and made off with it. He gave chase along the beach. A load of other gulls joined in the chase.

The gull with the gall, and the phone, finally let go and the doctor retrieved his property, which was none the worse for its unscheduled aerial excursion. His wife wonders if the whole scheme might have been an orchestrated distraction by the birds to try and get at their ham sandwiches.

Also at the criminal end of bird braininess, there is the blackbird that has taken to shoplifting grapes from a leading supermarket. And the grey heron that apparently pays regular visits to a chip shop in central Cork – stalking in, collecting its fish, and stalking out again. Bold as brass. This one, in fairness, has the owner's blessing.

Brains like this are one thing, but emotional sophistication is another. How about this, then: I recently heard author Graeme Gibson relate one of the stories from his *Bedside Book of Birds*. He told of the African grey parrot that he had once kept as a pet. It had been in the family home for a few years, a much-loved member of the household. Circumstances changed, and one day he decided that the parrot might be better off at the zoo, among its own kind. So he took it there, and saw it introduced to its new home, alongside other grey parrots. This looked, to all intents and purposes, like a much better place for a grey parrot to be. But, as Graeme turned to leave, the parrot leaned towards him, and uttered a word that he had never heard it utter before.

'Daddy,' it said.

As you might imagine, Graeme was pretty dumbfounded by the incident. Composing himself, he says that in response he mumbled a few reassuring words to the bird about how it would soon make new friends, settle in, forget him… But, agonisingly, he could hear it continuing to call 'Daddy' until he was clear of the premises.

There's quite a lot we still don't know about birds in general – like exactly how they navigate the globe so well – and, in particular, where some of them go to breed. It would be a great shame to lose any more of them. They might, after all, have something else to tell us, and, crop circles or no crop circles, whoever else might be paying attention.

RACHEL CARSON DAY AND THE NEW *SILENT SPRING*
If it were up to me, then 14 April would be designated Rachel Carson Day, to mark the anniversary of her death on a sunny spring morning in 1964, and the legacy of her life. I would also mark the occasion not with a minute's silence, or even a minute's applause, but with a minute's birdsong. The feature that follows was first published in the *New Statesman*.

I lost a songbird this spring. I had lived with it for more than ten years, near my home in rural Bedfordshire, 50 miles north of London. I had come to count on its unusual song from early each year, a sound rather like the reverberation of pebbles, issuing from its position high up on telephone wires over a remnant of pasture on the edge of the village. The bird was a humble corn bunting, a species quite easy to overlook, but a delight to hear, when the ear is attuned.

I felt privileged still to have it close by. This, after all, is a species that has steadily dwindled and retreated from the agricultural landscape of lowland Britain since the 1960s, finally disappearing altogether from Wales and Northern Ireland in recent years.

The corn bunting population stays with us year-round in

Britain. The birds gather in post-breeding flocks in autumn and winter to forage on any spilled grain and wild flower seeds. But it is becoming increasingly difficult for them to find this type of basic food in our agricultural landscape in winter because of changes in farming practice, linked partly – but by no means entirely – to agrochemical use.

I can hear another, more celebrated, songbird near my home. As a migrant insectivore, this bird tells a different but closely related story of loss. It is the nightingale and its continued presence and apparent success close to where I live does not reflect the calamity that has befallen it elsewhere. The nightingale, with its fabled, heart-warming and explosively defiant nocturnal warbling, is in retreat. It is following a pattern long established by our farm-dependent wild birds, and now seemingly mirrored by our African migrants adapted to life breeding in woods and parkland.

It is half a century since the American author Rachel Carson warned the world that we risked silencing the spring, bringing birdsong to an end through the excessive use of a new generation of synthetic insecticides. Serialised by The New Yorker *in June 1962 and published in full in the autumn of that year, Carson's* Silent Spring *is credited with inspiring the modern-day environmental movement. It arrived in Britain a year after its first publication, but its reverberations had already been felt.*

What characterised the particular threat that Carson identified and explained in such detail was the alarming number of dead birds and other animals being found in the countryside and even in suburbia. She concentrated on what was happening in North America, but similar processes were under way in the British Isles and beyond. The new insecticides, developed in wartime as potential chemical weapons and now let loose in the environment in what was, in effect, a widespread open-air experiment, differed from pesticides before and since. These products were proving directly lethal to birds, which died 'with their feet in the air'. Carson called these chemicals 'biocides': they were inimical to all life. It wasn't difficult to raise the alarm.

It was straightforward to make the case against the use of these synthetic insecticides, even though industry bigwigs mobilised a campaign to undermine and discredit Carson. Despite their wealth and power, they failed; her courage and stoicism throughout this shameful episode is all the more remarkable when one reflects that she was terminally ill, and had been for a long phase of the four years of research and preparation, un-aligned with any major institution, that she devoted to her book.

It took a decade for the US finally to ban DDT, just one of the products that were causing catastrophic declines in icon-ic species such as the bald eagle in North America and the peregrine falcon worldwide. In the tissues of these predators, the persistent organochlorines were accumulating. Problems of infertility resulted and birds began to disappear. Laboratory studies showed DDT links to cancer in mammals, but it wasn't until 1984 that the UK government followed the US and banned the substance.

Are we silencing the birds again today? If we take the group of species associated with the farmed environment, the answer is yes. As well as the corn bunting, species such as the skylark, lap-wing and grey, or English, partridge have declined since the early 1970s, which conservationists take as the baseline (the point when full and formal monitoring of the trend began). These are species of the open field and hedgerow, dependent on our sym-pathetic farming activity but increasingly silent.

Their difficulties have long been clear to conservation scient-ists. The declines began in the late 1950s and the 1960s, when Carson carried out her research, but the headlong crash in many bird populations took place from the following decade. Dismant-ling of old farm infrastructures, subsidy-sponsored drainage of ponds and meadows and ploughing and re-seeding of pastures all played a part. There has been a pattern of loss of mixed farm-ing (birds and other biodiversity thrive on variety, as a rule), with often prairie-scale arable fields dominating in the south-east of England and livestock retreating to the north and west. People have disappeared from the rural landscape, too, replaced by machinery that gets ever more enormous. With them has gone the wildlife.

It isn't just birds. Fears are mounting for the fate of honey-bees and bumblebees, and over the impact that their loss is having on the wild flowers and crops that rely on them and other insects such as butterflies for pollination, fruiting and seed pro-duction. A new breed of insecticides known as the neonicotin-

oids has been grabbing headlines recently; research indicates links to the collapse of honeybee colonies.

The products work by being absorbed into the system of plants. Bees ingest the chemicals through nectar and pollen. Several European countries are moving towards bans, but parts of industry are in denial once more, in an obvious parallel with and echo of Silent Spring.

If Carson were alive today, it is likely that the 'neonics' would be exercising her scientific and literary mind. The alternatives to these insecticides are likely to come with their own side-effects, however, creating wider, often hidden, ecological impacts. Crop protection remains a complex matter – yet how do we ensure that a balance is struck, to maintain ecological networks? These macro-scale issues represent the new phase of the conservation challenge in the UK and beyond.

Carson was not opposed to insecticide use per se. *Her message was of the need for moderation and care. She called for 'humility in place of arrogance' in the ways we apply science to the natural world, and to the farmed environment in particular.*

Scientists are increasingly worried about the fate of our woodland birds, some of which may be found in or near suburban settlements. The dwindling numbers of migrant species – such as turtle dove, swift, cuckoo and spotted flycatcher – have prompted researchers to place their African wintering grounds, too, under close scrutiny. The gentle, drowsy purring of the turtle dove will be the next midsummer sound to go, I fear, in line with the trend for this shy migrant species.

Advances in tracking nanotechnology have made it possible for turtle doves and even smaller birds to be fitted with transmitters and their progress monitored as they migrate. Scientists can work out where the birds go and where the 'hotspots' are. These are places such as coastal wetlands that may be vital staging posts on the migrants' journeys, and in need of special protection or restoration.

The threats to birds and their song are not confined to the UK, to Europe or even to agricultural land. One in ten of the world's bird species is threatened with extinction. At June 2012's Rio+20 Earth Summit in Brazil, delegates have been asking each other and our governments why we have collectively failed to halt the loss of global biodiversity by the original target date of 2010. Vows have been renewed to get it right by the new target date of 2020. We are approaching the stage where a second failure is no longer an option, if we are to prevent the ecological unravelling of the web of life around us.

Many people have noticed that there are fewer butterflies and bumblebees and that the windscreens and grilles of our cars are no longer as bug-spattered as they once were. Something strange is happening. In the 50 years since Silent Spring was published, we have replaced a specific threat and the grisly spectacle of dead and dying birds with a range of much less visible threats and a creeping – rather than a sudden – silence. If you listen carefully, you may hear the quietness mounting.

SOUTHILL REVISITED

Deep in the RSPB archive, I was unearthing grisly accounts of dead birds littering the arable landscape of south-east England around the time Rachel Carson was publishing *Silent Spring*. Leafing through a copy of *The Bedfordshire Naturalist* journal from 1963, I come across an account by Bruce Campbell of a nesting bird survey he carried out at a local estate, in company with then *British Birds* journal editor James Ferguson-Lees. They were repeating a survey first conducted at the start of the twentieth century. Campbell takes up the tale: 'On 4th June 1903, Jannion Steele-Elliott, the great Bedfordshire naturalist and his friend Ronald Bruce Campbell, my father, spent the day at Southill Park and found nests with eggs of 27 different species of bird, a feat which can have few parallels in British field ornithology.'

Sixty years on: 'On 5th June 1963, Jannion's nephew, Dennis Elliott, James Ferguson-Lees, like my father a Scoto-Bedfordian [...] and I celebrated the diamond jubilee of the 1903 visit.'

The three searched from mid-morning till around 9 pm, and only just failed to emulate their predecessors:

> *Allowing ourselves the blackcaps* [fledged young rather than the nest itself], *our tally was 60 occupied nests of 26 species. Considering the effect of the previous winter and that none of us knew the area well, whereas Steele-Elliott was certainly familiar with it, we felt we had not done too badly.*

With the 50th and 110th anniversary of this unusual and occasional survey fast approaching, I felt that it ought to be repeated. Working with Richard Bashford and Barry Nightingale, who has a permit to undertake monthly Wetland Bird Survey (WeBS) counts, we approached the estate. The necessary permission was generously granted by the Whitbread family.

We did a dry run in June 2012, to get the lie of the land and establish some parameters. It was clear that the emphasis of our survey would not – indeed should not – be on locating the actual nests of many of the species likely to be present and breeding, for an informal survey such as this, to avoid risk of causing disturbance. Times and of course ornithological conventions have changed.

And so, on 9 June 2013, the three of us met at 6am on the edge of the Park. In common with 1903 and 1963, our spring has followed a hard winter, although not on the scale of 1963's fabled three-month freeze. 'From a general comparison of the two days,' wrote Campbell, 'it [1903] must have been a late season, whereas 1963, in spite of the famous cold spell, had by June become rather an early one.'

A wind from the east coupled with a blanket of cloud gave us conditions certainly cool enough to subdue the birds. It made for thinner pickings than we might have expected at the Keepers Warren, where we set off. It was evidently heathland and not long planted in 1963. Today the well-spaced pines may not yet be tall enough for larger raptors to nest and there is almost no understorey infrastructure of heath or much else, bar bracken. The predated woodpigeon fledgling we found on the track may have been evidence of sparrowhawk, absent 50 years ago. We found some other signs of life, such as the muntjac deer that trotted calmly across the track up ahead of us. The one that Campbell noted in this very part of the estate he described as his first glimpse of the species in the wild. They were no doubt fanning out from Woburn and Whipsnade, where they first went native in the 1920s.

A clear-felled area raised hopes of a point or two, an expanse of colonising foxgloves and other flowering plants among the broadleaf saplings in tubes. We speculated on the species that might have occurred in such a clearing in days gone by – nightjar, woodlark, whinchat, tree pipit – but we found nothing. An isolated shed had the look of a giant bird box in this context, and offered hope, and lured us closer, but we were discouraged by nettles. We did pick up half a white eggshell, which looked good for tawny owl. I popped it in my bag for later analysis.

The 1963 group had gone first to the lake, and enjoyed early success. 'The boathouse gave us our first score, a house sparrow with four eggs on a beam; there were several others to which we did not climb,' Campbell reported.

The boathouse is still here, crowded by trees, but the house sparrows are long gone. The lake covers around 50 acres and remains a place busy with waterfowl and other wetland specialists. Nothing was published at the time of the 1903 visit, but Campbell had his father's diary of the event for reference. In 1963, Campbell recorded that 'herons lumbered off the tall trees on the island. The heronry was not in existence in 1903, so this gave us one species in hand for a start.' A heronry is still present, with up to 40 nests, so we too were able to add grey heron to our list, with well-developed nestlings carrying on a steady simian chatter throughout our observations here.

The 1963 search became 'amphibious' – each of them equipped with gum boots, and between them a mirror on a stick. They found sedge warbler and – curiously – a bullfinch nest in sedges over the water. 'The colony of reed warblers was known to Steele-Elliott but no nests were recorded on the 1903 visit ... we tallied eight reed warblers with eggs.' This seems improbable now, though the reed bed may have been much greater in extent then. We noted just one reed warbler in full song but no nest visible from the shore, to which we confined our search. A reed bunting carrying food was some consolation, and another point for us.

The turtle dove they accidentally flushed from its nest and young as they returned to shore we could only dream of nowadays. They also stumbled on a whitethroat nest nearby. We found a pair not far away, behaving possessively around typical nesting habitat along the margin of neighbouring pasture, grazed by an inquisitive herd of rare breed white cattle. But despite some peering through the mesh of nettle stems and bramble, only derelict nests were apparent.

The lake did, however, provide us with some memorable records. The cold winds had brought more swifts – 80 plus – than we had seen all spring, to hunt insects over the water, circulating like gnats, silent as they cruised. Swallows and house martins had also gathered in impressive numbers. But for all their abundance here we could add no hirundine species to our list of breeders – and my claim that there was a juvenile house martin up there (it had no tail) was met with predictable derision by my fellow surveyors. The carrion crow flying over with the bulging crop we also decided might not be nesting within the Park's boundary and could not therefore be permitted.

The lake gave us a notable record: an Egyptian goose with goslings – only the fourth breeding record for the county. It also gave us some of what our predecessors had noted, but we were unable to find a great crested grebe nest, despite craning to check even the furthest recesses of the shoreline. Mute swan might have been expected to offer an easy score, but despite the presence of one on the water no nest or cygnets were evident.

Things picked up a bit after lunch, as we found a green woodpecker bringing food to a noisy nest hole in a hefty beech, and great spotted woodpeckers doing likewise in a flamboyant London plane. Other highlights were the nuthatches with a boisterous brood of five, which allowed us to count them when they filed out of a spinney and bounded high over a field to an isolated oak. We also encountered family groups of treecreeper and goldcrest ('a rarity in 1963'), with parents feeding downy young, and perhaps best of all were the marsh tits feeding recent fledglings in damp woodland.

The arable fields added little to our list, the winter wheat no doubt too high and dense already for ground-nesters like skylark, lapwing, yellow wagtail and meadow pipit. The lack of hedgerows here ruled out linnet, lesser whitethroat, yellowhammer and corn bunting; a typical modern-day arable scene. Promising cavities in the towering oaks might have given us kestrel and little owl on another day.

One real bonus was our discovery of the return of spotted flycatchers to the vicinity of Gothic Cottage, where the recently retired gamekeeper had told us last year that his nesting pair was no more. We encountered this species at another site, and towards the end of the excursion I braved a thicket of chest-high nettles to check a shed near the cricket pitch in hope of finding perhaps blackbird (which we still hadn't secured), swallow, spotted flycatcher and/ or pied wagtail, all of which were present nearby. My hopes were raised when I was confronted by no fewer than four nests in a row on a ledge at the back, only to find on closer inspection that each looked more likely to have made the '63 list than our own. I felt like

H.G. Wells' time traveller in the future, as the books in the library crumbled to dust in his hands.

Out in the brightening daylight my comrades, meanwhile, were bagging blackbird number 27 by finally tracking down a fledged youngster, making up for my failure to find anything but a wren's nest (contents unexplored) in all the hedgerows into which I peered, each of which remained resolutely nest-free. I had much greater reward with this as a schoolboy, I am sure.

Ten hours in, and flagging, we went in search of what would have been number 26, returning to a stock dove nest hole we'd identified on our recce last year. The bird was *hoo-hoo-hoo*-ing nearby, but we had neither the time nor the patience to stake out the nest hole for long. We looked instead for song thrush, encouraged by one or two being furtive near some ornamental conifers. But although I peered into a dozen such trees, I drew a blank. Instead, we chanced on a chiffchaff gathering tiny prey items from these unlikely trees, and bringing them back to what must have been a nest. Good enough for us.

What was most enjoyable was reflecting, as we strolled between habitats, on what these surroundings might have looked and felt like to our forerunners. Am I right to imagine that what has changed most is the general abundance of life? Is biomass now so shifted to a smaller range of mid-sized generalists? By the end I had estimated 16 woodpigeons clattering off nests, and later upped this figure to 17 when it occurred to me that the predated fledgling we found was admissible as further nesting evidence.

It's tempting to believe that there was just more in the way of life forms present, then. Notwithstanding our competence, there is the definite sense that nests were easier to find back then, presumably because birds were simply much more abundant. Perhaps insects were too. Campbell describes Ferguson-Lees being bothered by midges as he tried to locate willow warblers in a patch of ground elder. I wonder if this snapshot alone reveals a lot about the contrasting world they inhabited. We didn't hear a willow warbler all day, and saw nothing resembling a midge. I don't think we saw more than a single butterfly all day either, even after the sun broke through towards the end. What is perhaps more troubling is that this didn't even occur to me as odd until I thought about it later.

It also then occurred to me that I still had the eggshell in my bag, and towards midnight I checked it against the book. It made a perfect match with the tawny owl egg depicted there. So this gave us number 27, the same score as the class of 1903.

An honourable draw? Hardly. We rewrote the rules, after all. In fact, the only intact eggs we saw all day were those of coot, which would have been impossible to miss. What seems clear is that not only were our predecessors' nest-finding techniques greatly superior to and much less trammelled than ours, but it also seems likely that there were many more nests to find.

So, we can't claim to have emulated the feat, but in any case of course that is not really the point. What is much more instructive is the glimpse the outing gave us of what has changed, and the pleasure of walking this interesting and varied landscape and imagining it five and eleven decades ago, our counterparts in tweeds or khakis, with their basic optics and much closer search focus. The need to prove nesting was novel for us.

'It really changed the way we birdwatched,' Richard later reflected. It also gave us some life firsts – the family parties of some of the species, in particular. The presence today of the red kites, ravens and buzzards that we saw would also gladden our forerunners, I am sure.

So how will it be, 50 years hence, in 2063? One thing's for sure, we won't be the ones doing any ten-hour treks.

THE YEAR THAT WAS

1903

At this time, *British Birds* journal was still three years from its inception, but in spring 1903 the Society for the Protection of Birds (its Royal Charter was still a year away) was launching *Bird Notes and News* – precursor to *Birds* magazine – to provide 'news of the doings of the Society' to its members. Its first issue spoke of the challenges of tackling the 'conspicuous brutality' of the plumage trade – the absence of herons from the 1903 Southill survey may reflect a wider depletion of the birds – and the practices of caging and often blinding songbirds.

1963

In spring 1963 Rachel Carson's *Silent Spring* was published in the UK, as I mentioned earlier. The perils of which it warned were only just dawning on a wider public. And while we have no record of Southill Park being affected, estates not too far away had been reporting dead and dying birds (and other species such as foxes) in great numbers. The RSPB, BTO and Game Research Association had formed an alliance to mobilise volunteer support and quantify the carnage. On top of this, resident species were recovering from one of the harshest winters on record. Barry Nightingale can himself recall field edges littered with woodpigeon corpses. *Bird Notes* was still two years from evolving into *Birds* magazine. It reported that National Nature Week had just been held.

Note

In July 2013, while browsing once again in the file of *Bedfordshire Naturalists' Journals*, I discovered that the 1963 group repeated the survey two years later. It is worth adding this for the record, and to pick out a few of the noteworthy aspects of this visit. They returned on 1 June, a 'dull but promising' day, and the promise was fulfilled as they racked up 100 nests of 35 species, way in excess of their 60/26 score of two years earlier. It supports the theory that there were many more nests to find half a century ago – even more so, perhaps, as bird numbers recovered in the wake of the big freeze of winter 1962/63. There are some other poignant reflections. Bruce Campbell wrote:

> *The muntjac was certainly not dreamed of at Southill in 1903 nor, probably, was the grey squirrel. Another striking change, we reflected, was in the variety of noises which have invaded the countryside. At least during working hours tractors, aircraft, bird-scarers and a power-saw reminded us of the age of technology. Perhaps in another 60 years science will have conquered noise and our successors will not strain to catch the off-nest calls of chiffchaff and willow warbler.*

It may be that there was much more human activity and therefore more noise then than now. But I think Denis Campbell may have been especially surprised to learn that, 48 years on, there are no willow warblers left to hear.

LUGS

I got a rabbit recently. I noticed the droppings first – small round pellets among the red campion below the living-room window, and a little trampled trail leading under the pyracantha or firethorn bush that grows up the front wall of the house.

I've never seen a rabbit in the garden before, front or back, so I was quite excited a day or so later when I caught my first glimpse of this small bunny hopping onto the front lawn. I know it's only a rabbit but, like most mammals, they are indisputably cute at a young age. And, while rabbits are super-abundant not far from here, they almost never turn up in the fields adjacent to the garden. If they do, they soon disappear again. I can only speculate as to why. This visiting bunny is in a sense a refugee, or a pioneer.

The front garden here is around ten metres square, framed by hedgerow, and the lawn I mow in patterns around clumps of first cowslip, in spring, and then ox-eye daisies and vetches in summer. The car is parked elsewhere, now obscured beyond the hedge.

The rabbit evidently likes this arrangement, and browses the long stuff while trying to hide from view of the living room window behind the clumps. It has been in residence for a few weeks. I look out for it most days, and most days it is there. I have given it a name – Lugs (Bunny) – and am growing quite attached. I know that rabbits are the bane of many gardeners' lives. Those of you under siege and considering them vermin will be wondering what my fuss is about. Trouble is, when you have a manageable number of rabbits – such as, um, one – and you get to recognise this individual, day after day, you can't help feeling attached. It also helps that I'm not trying to grow any vegetables or tender young border planting out front. Lugs and I are not at odds.

So, yes, I'm attached. And not a little curious. How does this one rabbit come to end up living here? It has no companions – which seems odd, for a social animal – and no burrow that I can see. It appears to live under the plants at the edge of the lawn, and also to know that, although the house is in close proximity, and the garden path and pavements just behind the hedges are much used, and it remains nervous of noises and people, it is relatively safe here. Bless.

Lugs was also saving me the task of cutting the front lawn, at least for a while. Eventually, however, his (let's call him he) green-keeping skills couldn't keep the sward down fast enough and I had to get the mower out. I'm not sure if the two things were connected but Lugs was then absent for three days. I took it that he must have moved on, to have outgrown this cosy enclave, developed a taste for bigger meals, wider spaces, rabbit company.

And then I glanced out of a side window, and there was Lugs, bold as brass, in the middle of Betty's lawn at 153, two doors down, where the lawns are neat and square, as though ready for bowling. It was a comic moment, so incongruous did he look there, and confounding all my theories about his need for the benefits a wildlife garden – such as mine – provides. He was also appreciably bigger than I remembered him. Betty would get a shock if she looked out now.

As I said above, as little as a mile away, on the meadow by the river, rabbits are present in absurd numbers. I've counted over 100 in one average-sized paddock, of an evening. It's a wonder there's any grass left for the horses. Odd as it may seem, rabbits are another non-native species in these isles. Early settlers, finding the landscape rabbit-free, probably wasted little time in bringing some over: rabbits are such a fast-multiplying source of meat and fur. It is now hard to imagine a UK landscape without them, they are such an integral part of our food chains now, and provide the fuel that fires all manner of carnivores – stoats, foxes, buzzards, eagles.

Lugs made one final appearance back in my mini-wilderness, more alert than before, with age, craning on back legs as I sneaked up to the window to take a photograph of the burgeoning bunny. And then he moved on, up or away.

I'm sure it's for the best. I liked Lugs best when he was titchy, and twitchy of nose. A manageable size. Now he's moved on I am conscious he might now have become someone else's problem. Or dinner. Then again, he might be round the back, discovering the raised beds. Those early settlers have got a lot to answer for.

REFUGEE WILD FLOWERS

It's only a plant and, as such, it might, like other plants, seem a passive bystander as the more apparently dynamic animal kingdom passes it by. But I've come to think of the red campion as a bit of a survivor. It's as though it is determined to hang in there, but not to draw too much attention to itself. It's a familiar and pleasing wild-flower of our margins, more pink than red, to be fair, and turning up in hedge bottoms and often in ditches by roadsides. It offers its modest but attractive flowers as a diversion from the bland uniformity that often surrounds it. It's seldom abundant, but it is widespread.

The patchiness of its distribution isn't easy to explain. It can turn up in most places, but it is pretty sparse here in Bedfordshire, I have found, where it rarely reaches the levels I used to encounter in Scotland. It seems to like damp places – hence the ditches, and Scotland – but not exclusively so. Before we came along and made the landscape cultural this, like a lot of wild flowers, must have been a colonist of woodland clearings and edges, wherever gaps would appear.

And so, to indulge my fondness for it, I introduce this subtle dash of pink to gardens each time I move house. I used to assume it was quite a fussy plant. It wouldn't take to my Cambridge garden at all, where the blue flowers of borage were the ascendant colour. I tried seeds and even seed trays, but my campions never got past seedling stage when liberated. Something about that orchard garden didn't suit it. Plants, even apparently generalist ones, can be picky that way. By and by I moved on, nurturing this campion aspiration, and when the chance came I introduced it here, where I live now. And not only has it hit the ground running, it has practically taken over.

There's a period in June when the wisdom of letting wild flowers have the run of a garden is fully vindicated. It's at this time that the long growing days prompt a surge among the natives, when the plants in the hedge bottoms and around the lawn set their stall out for the nectaring insects. In this case, red campion is now the ringleader. It is rampant.

It takes its scientific name *Silene dioica* from the Greek god Silenica, of drunkenness and forests. It seems fitting here. My red campions grow in hearty clumps, to great heights. I must have more red campion here than does all the rest of the parish put together. And for these several weeks at midsummer it is glorious. Its partner in this is the ox-eye daisy, another favourite, which offsets it pleasingly with its sun-catching gold and white faces.

Quite why this garden should be so ideal for red campion, when the surrounding landscape offers up just the odd plant or patch of these simple wild flowers, isn't obvious to me. Clearly my interventions count for something, but I'm not doing a great deal more than the mowers of the verges out there, beyond the bounds of the garden. I do know that when the red campion tries to spill out and reclaim the street, the men with the boiler suits and tanks of herbicide on their backs aren't far behind it. I think they know better than to spray below my hedge at the front, though. It's probably obvious there's a different code here. I understand the need for order on pavements and roadside verges but, for me, if a wild flower needs pulling, then pull it. I don't use noxious substances. The manual approach is good exercise, apart from anything.

Later in summer I will dead-head now sagging plants, which is easily done, to remove the stems and their pepper-pot seed heads. I will allow these to scatter to produce new plants for next year, alongside the perennial roots of the parents.

It probably goes without saying, but red campion is a magnet for bees and butterflies, and is food plant for the caterpillars of an impressive list of moths – although any list of moths is usually impressive, given the poetry of their names.

There's no culinary use I can find for all this vegetation. It doesn't feature in any recipes I've come across, but I like that, among its medicinal uses, red campion seeds (when ground up) have been thought to be a treatment for snake bites. In fact, one of its local names is 'adder plant' – although you have to think that putting your hand on a ready-made pouch of ground campion seeds in the immediate wake of a snake bite would be a highly fortuitous combination of circumstances, in any era. Notwithstanding, if the adder ever makes what would be a welcome comeback here, I must try to remember to organise a pestle and mortar.

PERSEPHONE

I don't keep lists of things that I've seen, in case the reckless pursuit of bigger and better numbers might start to affect my judgement. I've seen it happen to others. All the same, it is always a significant day when something new turns up. And I've just recorded a new species for the garden – or Jameson Acres as I sometimes think of it, on occasions such as these.

The newcomer doesn't take much finding or identifying, because it is first seen peering in through the back door window, as though intent on identifying us, the occupants. Nor does it retreat much when approached, and even when the door is gently opened. It's a large beast, but at no stage threatening. Peanuts it accepts gratefully. Black sunflower seeds it seems much less keen on, or even to recognise as a foodstuff, curiously.

It is bigger than most of the animals that visit the garden – the recent, unscheduled night-time cow excepted. And it is a bird. A big one, but a young one, and I think a female, so I have to call it a peahen, the female peacock. Not many birds have retained this gender distinction in their common name. But the rules seem to be different for this, the national bird of India.

She lingers for most of the morning, sometimes admiring herself in the window, sometimes resting, lying down but always alert, between peanuts. When she finally stalks off I am left wondering if she might have been checking out some of the more overgrown parts of the 'estate' for a possible nesting site. We christen this bird Percy, quickly adjusted to Persephone when we remember her gender.

I have been surprised at how trusting Persephone is, but I shouldn't be surprised that she has turned up here now. Clive (the farmer down the road) discovered a pair of these birds a few years back. They just turned up, and base themselves around his cattle sheds. They make an interesting, if slightly incongruous, addition to the daily life of the village, with their occasional and always unexpected appearances. It's fair to say they are not popular with everyone, what with their confusing of pet dogs and spooking of cats, and most of all by the crowing of the male, which sounds exotic at a distance (but perhaps no more so than the farmyard cockerel alongside it – another Asiatic import), but which I wouldn't personally welcome at dawn outside the window.

Clive reckons some neighbourly fowl play might explain the vanishing of one or two of the peafowl since their adoption of the farm/parish. With this in mind I wondered whether I'd found the heavily soiled remains of one of the disappeared in a quiet corner of a local wood. But I was able to rule this out after later analysis of the feathers. It seems more likely a fox had dragged a road-killed swan in there, for indeed swan is what it was.

The peafowl pair produced at least one youngster last year. I spotted the peachick with its mother, foraging self-consciously between parked cars on the street. Perhaps our visitor at the door is that peachick, now a year old, exploring our patch. But it's more likely that this is Mrs P. She sometimes appears at the bedroom window at the back, strutting on the flat roof, perhaps checking it out as a fox-free roost site.

There's an unverified story that one day the RSPB took a call from someone offering us – free – a batch of young peafowl that were surplus to the owner's requirements. The caller seemed to think that some resident peafowl would be a welcome addition to the gardens and nature reserve at our Sandy headquarters. We politely declined, explaining that it's not that sort of place. Priority has to go to keeping native species going. The next day we got them anyway. Five young peafledglings were waiting expectantly at the front door. They – and their feathers and droppings – were a conspicuous feature of Lodge life for some weeks afterwards, until they gradually dispersed, or disappeared.

For some years before that, a splendid male peacock was a regular summer visitor, wandering from his base in the garden of a house at the bottom of the hill, amusing/startling staff (depending on proximity) with his shrill foghorn blasts, his optimistic but ultimately forlorn clarion calls to lure females into this apparently suitable breeding environment.

Although I've yet to see my local and Lodge-based birds actually display their tails, I have seen this elsewhere and it's quite something to behold. In one ornamental garden where a small flock of the birds had gathered, it seemed that one particularly reflective window was especially stimulating to the birds, more so even than the attention of rival males and watching females – which may tell us something about narcissism and self-regard.

Two months on from Persephone's visit to Jameson Acres, I have checked with people in my village, and discovered that this year our peafowl have produced three already well-grown young. No one knows where, but it seems to prove that they are capable of doing so. It shows that, like the other pheasants, the peacock can go feral, but will always benefit from and have its chances of surviving tough weather enhanced by hand-outs. I'm sure there are numerous other examples in the British Isles. It's just oddly difficult to find any record of them.

Perhaps it's that we've yet to take the peacock seriously, or accept it, despite (or perhaps because of) its position as arguably the most spectacularly and improbably plumaged bird of all. It may be the logical extreme of avian adornment, which must always be limited by other lifestyle considerations, notably being able to evade predators.

The peacock belongs to the pheasant family. It is invariably omitted from books of British birds in which its smaller relatives, of several species, are routinely described. I wondered why this is, if the species can, like its relatives, breed in our environment. But why wouldn't it? I asked. It is considered naturalised in places beyond its native India, but not yet in these islands, it seems.

I often wonder what effect peacocks must have had on a viewing public when centuries ago they were first imported to new places, such as here, brought back with other trophies from outposts of the British Empire. Landowners, collectors and market-stall holders must have attracted huge crowds to marvel at these marvellous creatures from distant lands. A displaying peacock (if indeed they could entice them to perform) must have been an unforgettable experience for first-time viewers.

I recall as a child being fixated by the first peacocks I saw, in some park or other, and searching for any shed tail feathers I might be able to keep as a souvenir. One peacock, I noticed, had a loose feather protruding from the great swishing tresses, like an armful of rushes, but hard as I tracked him I could never get quite close enough to catch a hold and dislodge the prize.

Male pheasants are armed with spurs, and can be quite handy in a tight corner. Although apparently disinclined to, they are able to fly, although it's rare to see them do much more than flap up a few metres into a roost site. I like that this groundedness makes them too big, too lazy, to shoot. This isn't a game bird.

I've yet to see one fly properly, but I have recently seen photographs of airborne birds. These show them in another light still, revealing the full range of their wing colours, and are as extravagant and breathtaking as anything you might see in a bird of paradise. I shared these pictures with friends, who were delighted. It's like seeing the bird again with that child's eye.

I like pheasants, but I don't like how they are treated, even before they are shot at, and I have no doubt that there are far, far too many of them released into our environment each year, millions of which die on the roads. But if we are going to accept the hapless pheasant as a colourful addition to the warp and weft of wildlife in these isles, perhaps we should also find a place in the bird books for the purely decorative peafowl too. At the very least we shouldn't ignore it, just because it's loud and proud, and usually so close to us it would sometimes seem we don't take it seriously.

Northern Solstice

CHAPTER SEVEN

July

SUMMER BIRD

'Shall I compare thee to a summer's day?' asked Shakespeare, reaching out for a metaphor that might do justice to a lover. This is what occurs to me when I try to define the renowned but little-known turtle dove. Of all the birds, this one can lay claim perhaps most strongly to being the soundtrack for an English summer day in the lowlands. Other birds do continue singing from spring into the warmer months, but if there is a sound that characterises high noon and hazy heat on a midsummer afternoon it is this one. When other birds may start to wilt or relax a little, and when you might feel a slumber in a hammock calling you, the turtle dove should be purring in a near-distant covert.

At least, that's how it should be. I never knew the turtle dove well till I moved south. It was a mythical bird for me in my youth, a bird spoken of in lyrical terms, apparently exchanged in pairs on the second day of Christmas once upon a time, associated with apple trees and honey bees, and teaching the world to sing.

When I got here, and set up home amid the arable lands of eastern Anglia, the turtle dove helped define this dry, flat landscape. Summers were warm then – they really were – and the heaths cooked for long enough to smell differently and appetisingly, of drying pine and box and gorse, and I felt I was abroad, which of course in a sense I was. And I realised that the purring I'd known on the Continent was a sound shared here, and it was the turtle dove. It always struck me as odd that a bird so shy and flighty had such a relaxed vocalisation. You'd struggle to see a turtle dove singing, which added to the seduction effect. It carries a long way, adding to the allure. And so it was the soundtrack to hazy days. If I hear that sound now, which is rarely, it takes me back to then, the way barbecue smoke and the smell of limes do too.

But why is it so unapproachable? The turtle dove's long-distance migratory lifestyle has made it historically a target for hunters. Any that breed in northern Europe must run the gauntlet of guns and nets across the Mediterranean. If they make it back they must have had their fear of humans reinforced en route.

What's curious is how recent and sudden has been the species' decline. A century ago J. Steele-Elliott described or predicted the decline of quite a few species – but not this one. Sixty years later, his nephew was stumbling on their nests in places where today we wouldn't expect to find them. It continued to do well right up to the mid-1970s. Then, if one census site not far from here is representative of the wider picture, it went into freefall. In 1975, 30 pairs were present. In 1992 there was just one remaining. Today, the species looks to be on the brink of total absence from the county.

And I have stopped hearing them from my garden, although they do still seem to be clinging on down and around the old airfield. The group who net and ring birds in the scrub down there even caught a turtle dove one day, much to everyone's surprise and gratification.

My friend Rachel sent me a photo. She'd been pruning the thick thorn scrub at the edge of her garden and had come across a bird on a nest of twigs. In fact, she was practically on top of it before it caught her eye, yet it stayed there, quite motionless.

'What is it?' she wanted to know.

'It's a turtle dove,' I replied. 'Wow! Where is this?' I should point out that, as well as her terraced house in south London, Rachel also has a house she is renovating from an old grain store in south-west France. Needless to say, it's a French bird. The French call it the *tourtourelle*. Like our own received name for the species, this is based on the *turrr-turrr* sound it makes. It is still routinely shot in spring in parts of France, and Spain, where the Europe-wide laws that ought to protect it in spring are openly flouted. In Malta it is the subject of continuing controversy, with the powerful hunting lobby reluctant to give it up as a legal quarry species, and so many other hunters shooting what they like, when they like, anyway.

It's a bit weird and also admirable that the turtle dove is so resolute in protecting its nest. Compare and contrast with the woodpigeon, which clatters out of a nesting tree at the merest approach of human feet, even long before you've any idea there's a bird there.

I advised Rachel to replace some of the trimmed branches as delicately as possible and give the doves a chance to see their project through, and reward her with their therapeutic purring. ·

Outside the European Union, with its hard-won wildlife protection regs, it's still legal to shoot turtle doves (in Morocco, for example, they can be shot in June and July). There was a furore last summer when a London-based agency was advertising trips to do just that, at the same time as media headlines were drawing attention to the plight of the species in the UK and elsewhere in Europe.

Thanks to developments in modern technology, a project has been launched to fit turtle doves with tracking devices. This will help us understand the routes our migrant birds take, and any perils they face along the way. Perhaps we can protect the most important staging posts, while the world around them changes.

While it's clear we don't really know enough yet about the reasons, it's unlikely that hunting has been the main cause of the turtle dove's sad decline. But it has reached the stage where it is unlikely to be sustainable, and on the precautionary principle it seems reasonable for those who enjoy shooting wild birds to find something else to do to amuse themselves on a spring or summer's day.

Apart from anything else, it might make any turtle doves that do survive come a bit closer for the rest of us to be soothed. It's quite difficult to explain what no turtle doves sounds like or why it tarnishes the experience of summer here. Perhaps it's like removing one of the key players from an orchestra or missing out one of the effects from a jazz band performance. If we are not careful, the death of the planet will be measured in such silencings.

THE FORGOTTEN NATIVE

Some years ago I had a week off to explore Wales, and needless to say an important element of that holiday was a pilgrimage to see red kites. As is well recorded, at that time Wales was their last refuge and stronghold. But, at least as memorably, I discovered another refugee species there, although this was altogether unexpected, and the circumstances a little more gory.

I first noticed one on a stretch of road in some pleasant but unspectacular countryside near the border with England. Then another. And another. In fact, I must have counted about ten. Sadly, they were all dead – road-killed – but their size, shape and dark colour were distinctive features in each case. After I'd examined a couple of them, where it was possible to park safely nearby, I worked out what I had suspected: they were polecats. True, wild, native polecats.

Some of our native mammals are so long gone that most of us have forgotten or aren't aware they were ever here. And there are also some that we nearly lost – but not quite – and that are now coming back. If you were to ask your average person to name mammals occurring naturally in the UK, chances are that not many of them would list the polecat.

Like their relatives the pine marten, otter, badger, stoat and weasel, the polecat is a beautiful but not, in the wild state, very cuddly animal, and not an easy one to get to know. It is active mostly at night and doesn't have great eyesight. It seems to be especially vulnerable to traffic, as it bowls along roadsides on its night-time explorations.

I had read about them but mostly forgotten that the remnant population still clung on in this part of the country, where gamekeeping had up till then evidently lacked the comprehensive coverage of the rest of the UK (hence the surviving red kites too). It was tempting to suppose that the ecology and landscape of our isles had changed so much that the polecat would remain confined to this enclave. But they began to fan out again from the safe zone, and there is reason to believe they've reached our eastern counties now too. That's right – more road-kill.

I'd seen one or two possible casualties locally but was taken aback to find a fresh and intact specimen dead on the verge in north Essex. It was a female, about 14 inches long – a long way from Wales.

The polecat is believed to be the wild ancestor of its domesticated cousin, the ferret, which comes in a range of colours. I consulted with Rowena Staff at the Mammal Society for a verdict. She confirmed that:

This is a polecat-ferret and not a pure polecat, but it is never easy to tell. There are a number of characteristics that indicate that this will not be a pure polecat including: body fur paler; dark fur does not reach the top edge of the nose; pale throat patch 50mm or more long; and scattered white guard hairs over the body, especially on hindquarters and tail.

Rowena also told me that there has been 'one verifiable record of a polecat in north Essex. They certainly seem to be spreading east at a healthy rate!' This one was confirmed during a survey carried out by the Vincent Wildlife Trust a few years ago.

And I've now found one within striking distance of The Lodge. It's a hefty specimen, dead by the roadside, face frozen in a defiant snarl. I photographed it, and bagged it up for the County Mammal Recorder, Richard Lawrence. He confirmed it as a 'true polecat'. He has a freezer full of such interesting specimens.

There's an ongoing control campaign against the non-native, escaped American mink at large in the environment. These aliens were once captive-bred for the fur trade, often escaping – sometimes in great numbers – when saboteurs broke in to these fur farms to free them. Mink gone native can be troublesome in the wild, but it is easily forgotten is that once upon a time the related polecat was widespread. There is also a European mink, although there appears to be no proof that it ever lived in the British Isles. Just to confuse matters – but it is worth noting – the European mink is also thought to be more closely related to the polecat than the introduced American mink. It can also hybridise with the polecat. One way or another, whatever the subtle differences in their behaviour and ecology, there is a mink/polecat-shaped niche in the ecosystems of our islands, and it's not the polecat's fault that we've squeezed it to the very edges of acceptability in our lives. We need to find a way of making habitats big and joined up and resilient enough to accommodate the beast, and to make sure we lock up our chickens securely at night.

Consulting more widely, I discover that a polecat – perhaps even the one I found dead – had been seen and even photographed loitering near the rabbit warren on the edge of the reserve here at HQ. They can be active in the daytime. They can even be relatively sociable, unlike some of their relatives. I like the idea of banished wildlife like the polecat reclaiming its birthright. And if it's rabbits – or koi carp – they are after, the chickens can roost easy for now.

A STING IN THE TALE

My friend Martin lives in Hackney, east London, and brought his young son Marco up to visit us, to connect with the countryside. We went for a sunny afternoon walk along the river, which was looking at its best. But the trouble is, each time young Marco connected with nature, he seemed to get stung – by nettles. They do grow in bewildering profusion down there, and are quite hard to avoid. I worried that the experience might put the young Londoner off nature for life.

Safely back in the garden, I was chided for allowing yet more nettles to grow, close to where we were sitting. What Martin didn't realise is that these aren't actually nettles. These are white dead nettle – evolved (I guess) to look very much like their heavily armed neighbours. The ruse is so good that it fools grown men and – apparently – even rabbits.

Marco's tears reminded me of my own formative years getting acquainted with nature in all its benign and sometimes malevolent forms. 'Jaggies', we used to call them, although this catch-all term included brambles too, with would often join forces with nettles in a formidable array of sting and thorn. There was much dock leaf and spit rubbed onto young, inflamed limbs back then, and the same treatment was applied to Marco. It's possibly the only direct herbal remedy our collective cultural memory has retained on a wide scale in the modern era.

This incident left me looking differently at the so-familiar nettle, a species that most people, even now in this much more disconnected age, can name. This visually nondescript plant teaches us its name from a very early age, a lesson reinforced with pain each time.

Nettles are great exploiters of phosphate in soil. They are also fond of nitrogen, which accumulates in streams and rivers, and may account for the proliferation of nettles along river banks. I have found this to my own cost when canoeing along narrow stretches of

Cam tributaries. These are sometimes so narrow the jaggies can't be avoided, as they hang like a surging crowd over barriers, craning to touch the passing canoeist. On sharp bends the current has sometimes threatened to force me right into their clamouring midst.

For all the threats they pose to exposed mammalian flesh and tender spots, this very feature of nettles also provides refuge for many smaller and less sting-prone life forms. Corncrakes seem very appreciative of the early cover that nettles can provide in spring, when, as most gardeners will testify, the emerging plants are often at their most potent. Not many people in history have gone out of their way to encourage the spread of nettles, but the RSPB has done just that at Rathlin Island, off the coast of Northern Ireland. Many tons of nettle roots have been harvested by volunteers and airlifted in to create nettle-beds for the returning migrant birds, in a concerted effort to keep the species going there.

It's not impossible that others have cultivated this plant. Nettles are highly nutritious, and if you ever find yourself having to nourish yourself from fruits of the forest, you could do a lot worse than soak nettles in water to subdue their venom, and cook up something, well, nettly. I probably don't need to mention that they don't taste great – if they did, we'd eat them more often – but there is no harm in using them in a soup, if not as the primary ingredient, or in tea, or even beer.

Nettle potions can also make hair glossy and treat dandruff, I have read, although this fact isn't prominent on the bottle for any leading shampoo brands.

It may be a great wildlife plant but I confess I limit the spread of nettles in the garden. I have to. I feel sure they would take over, otherwise. Perhaps I should eat them more often. I'd feel differently if my nettles ever had caterpillars on them, but I can't remember the last time I saw this locally. It continues to baffle me why once-familiar butterflies like the small tortoiseshell are such a rare event nowadays, when their larval food plant is so super-abundant. Even this year, with the warmest summer in memory and a heartening upsurge in butterfly activity, I've looked in vain for these once conspicuous caterpillar camps, under the webby canopies they weave around the tops of nettles.

Besides the tortoiseshell, nettles also support the larvae of red admiral, comma and peacock butterflies and a few moth species with weird and wonderful caterpillar armoury, here and abroad. The nettle is international in its distribution.

I'm left wondering why more plants don't hurt us, and why nettles haven't taken over entirely. It seems that this may yet happen, at least in this country, such has been the increase of the species in the last few decades. Nettles gather where there is phosphate in the soil, and phosphates gather where there is us – in our waste and in our very bones. For centuries we've been augmenting our local supplies of the stuff with the import of bones and bird droppings from far and near. We have nutrified these islands for years, and the lining of nettles along so many of our lowland waterways now probably reflects this.

On a more local scale, I've often wondered at the clumps of nettles I usually find beside the ruins of long–abandoned farm buildings. In fact, I recently stumbled upon the foundations of a former home in a local woodland thanks to the forest of towering nettles that surrounded it, almost preventing further inspection. Environmental historian Oliver Rackham explains that phosphate can persist in the ground for thousands of years and is present in ash. 'An area of nettles in an otherwise nettle-free wood usually has a story to tell,' he explains. And if there's a sting in these tales, I'll hold on to the old adage: no pain, no gain.

THE SELDOM – AND NOT EVEN VERY – SPOTTED WOODPECKER

The lesser spotted woodpecker sounds like a made-up name for a bird, invented by those heathen types who mock bird lovers, or who have what was once dubbed 'anoraknophobia' – a fear of birdwatchers (or obsessive hobbyists of any kind, perhaps).

'Oooh, it's a lesser spotted whatchamacallit?' they'll remark, scathingly, when a bird enthusiast shows interest in a nearby avian form, and goes into the characteristic stalk mode, eyes fixed on the prize, bumping into chairs and tables, etc.

I wish another common name might have been finally settled on for this enigmatic little bird, which isn't even particularly spotty, and certainly not less so than its more familiar and much 'greater' relative. 'Barred woodpecker' would much more accurately reflect its appearance viewed from behind, which is usually the view you get of a woodpecker, if any. But perhaps by accident the more familiar name does at least reflect how seldom the species is seen now. It certainly isn't spotted very often by me, although I am always conscious of the possibility of it, the plausibility of it. It's a small woodpecker, dammit, it likes trees of many kinds and shapes and extents. *Dendrocopus* (pecker of wood) *minor* (small) doesn't need as much wood to peck as *Dendrocopus major*, which seems to be thriving.

To help me locate one here, I learned its call from cassettes and even heard the real thing in a foreign land. The only time the birds really draw attention to themselves is if and when they utter this cry in spring, before the trees are in leaf. It's odd they don't call loudly more often, as they must also have a bit of difficulty locating each other. The call is a surprisingly falconesque *kek-kek-kek*. It can also be likened to a dabchick's giggle, which is a familiar trill around some lakes and a sound that always transports me back to the campus of Stirling University, which is built around a ribbon of dabchick-infested, Victorian improver-scooped loch.

As it happens, it was while I was taking tea or something stronger in the back garden with some old pals from my student days that a lesser spotted woodpecker decided to drop in at Jameson Acres. Out of the blue, and into the green of the fruit trees at the bottom. Of all the moments to have chosen. I duly did the zombie-like 'staring straight ahead, standing up, tripping over deckchairs, bags and tea cups' thing and began creeping towards the plum tree. This sparrow-sized black-and-white bird was working the ends of the branches, perhaps licking aphids off the developing fruit. You know what comes next...

'Oooh, what is it, Conor? A lesser spotted wotsit?'

'Funnily enough, I think it is...' I mumble back, peering round a perpendicular, vine-supporting railway sleeper at the pied shape appearing and disappearing among the foliage of the low trees.

'This is amazing!' I shout-whisper, singularly failing to convey the momentousness of it all. 'I've never see one anywhere near here before – not definitely, anyway.'

It soon makes off, perhaps even to feed young somewhere, who knows? Lesser spotted woodpecker nests are famously difficult to find, as the birds are so furtive and they can tuck themselves away so easily, drilling a nest hole into soft or dead wood often in high branches, well out of sight.

I think my guests get it, even though there hasn't been much for them to see, from where they are sitting. I resume my deckchair and their thoughts – if not fully mine – soon return to other issues of the day.

I had another very curious encounter with the species a year or so after this. I actually found the nest, several miles from my garden. I'd like to be able to claim this was as a result of intensive effort and expert field-craft, days spent secreted about the woods connecting so closely with nature that I didn't know any longer where it ended and I began. But the truth is I stumbled on it, the pair busily bringing food to the nest hole, and it was right under my nose. When I first noticed them, I wasn't even on foot. I was on my bike. The nest was in a dead tree trunk beside a busy road junction. I braked gently and quietly parked the bike before edging closer to have a closer look, keeping out of sight of the birds and the passing cars.

I didn't have long to wait between feeding visits by the parent birds. What was sweet was the way they would always land on the back of the tree trunk, hidden from view, and then edge round to the front and pop quickly in, feed the young, then pop out again and round the back, and off into the trees behind – a dense conifer plantation. It was pure chance that I happened to be passing on the bike and looking the right way when one of these feeding visits was taking place, otherwise I would have been none the wiser. The birds would have remained under the radar. I didn't even know they were present, never mind breeding. No one did. There had been no local reports all year. No one had heard or seen a thing till now, though when I quietly reported the nest to the appropriate recorders it turned out I wasn't the first to have found it. Cue for some winks and nose-tapping.

Not so long ago, this was thought to be as numerous – if never quite as conspicuous – as the great spotted woodpecker. But while the latter has thrived in twenty-first-century Britain, the little guys have dwindled to the point of widespread disappearance. Exactly why is not fully understood. It has always been confined to southern Britain. When I lived near Stirling they were rumoured to breed in my local patch, and though I only found great spotted woodpeckers breeding there, I always took this to be plausible. Recently it was decided that these rumours were just that. The official records will now show that the lesser spotted woodpecker has never been recorded breeding in Scotland. This has made the appearance of one in Shetland this spring all the more noteworthy and remarkable.

I've had the chance since then to watch them in the ancient forests of Poland and Belarus. Here, there also lives something we call the lesser spotted eagle – and the less said about this indignity for an eagle the better. More importantly, no fewer than eight species of woodpeckers coexist. Nine if you count the wryneck, the woodpecker that has come to resemble a piece of wood. Each occupies a different niche in the forest's many layers and storeys, reflecting a functional native woodland. The great spotted woodpecker is the most generalist of them all, and its predominance in other kinds of modern-day woodland, such as ours, in part reflects the breakdown of this ecological balance; an index of dysfunction, if such an indicator were needed in such an instance. The only place more local that I've been able to study a lesser spot for some minutes was in a carefully managed ancient woodland in Essex, as planes roared into and out of Stansted Airport. Despite the noise, I was able to locate it by call. If there are lesser spots making a noise near me now, I'm confident I'll recognise them.

In places our woods are recovering, with help. It will be a long process. The return of the lesser spotted woodpecker ought to follow such a restoration, given time. And planet Earth has, in the end, all the time in the world. The same may yet be true of us.

BRINGING UP BABY

If you find a fledgling bird, you should leave it alone. That's probably the most important thing to remember from what I'm about to relate. And, yes, I *know* most people probably know this already, and have done ever since they first developed an interest in birds.

I need to stress this point because each spring and summer the RSPB's wildlife advisors field around 10,000 enquiries from people who have found – or, in many cases, 'rescued' – a 'baby bird'. Picking it up is the ultimate act of misplaced kindness. We have to advise each caller to take their refugee back to where they found it, and hope that its parents are still around to resume parental duties. It's either that or rear the bird yourself. This advice can seem uncaring, and people are sometimes surprised to discover that our mission doesn't extend to the rearing of birds: baby, sick, injured or otherwise. We simply aren't set up or equipped to do it.

I hope therefore it won't be too confusing if I go on now to describe how I found a baby bird the other day, and I *didn't* leave it alone.

I was feeling a bit strained most of the evening, and I wasn't really very sure why. It was the last day of a sultry July, and the atmosphere was heavy. Much-needed rain was falling to earth silent and straight; straight down the necks of the plants. You could almost hear them slurping it up. From the moment I got home I was aware of sparrows chirping – it goes on all day, most days, and at this time of year the sparrows are present in boisterous numbers, wheeling between my front-garden hedgerow and the field margins opposite.

But this sounded like a youngster. More *cheerrp* than *chirp*. More insistent. More penetrating. I looked several times in the airing cupboard, the bathroom, the loft, but each time I tried to isolate the source of the sound it seemed to come from another part of the house, to be accessed a different way. I even found myself going outside to check.

By 10 pm, the *cheerrps* had not abated. They were louder, if anything. It was too late and too dusk for nestlings to still be begging for food, in normal circumstances. I knew for sure then that something was amiss, and I worked out, by pressing the base of the airing cupboard (which juts down through the kitchen ceiling) and feeling the tremors, that the bird must be in there.

So I went upstairs with a torch, and by now would have cheerfully removed masonry to find the thing. Luckily I only had to remove carpet and one floorboard. There it was, ensconced among pipes and rafters, wriggling. And *cheerp*ing.

It looked surprisingly underdeveloped, semi-naked, perhaps a week old and only halfway to fledging, with bare patches of skin and rudimentary feathers beginning to show. Nidifugous, they call it. Its bulbous eyes were partially open, glinting between crescent lids. I had to remove my watch and squeeze my hand through a narrow gap, using a screwdriver to manoeuvre the chick into a place from which I could lift it, as gently as possible, between two outstretched fingers.

Here, I had better make clear the difference between a nestling bird and a fledgling bird. I've had fledgling sparrows in the house before, and I put them straight back outside. One I was able to corner on an upstairs windowsill, and simply drop out of the window, to minimise its distress from being handled, and to show its parents where it was and what was happening. As I captured it, I vividly recall a male house sparrow hovering a few inches from the window pane, chirping abuse at me. All the thanks you get for letting them nest in the roof. I dunno...

July

A nestling is a bird that belongs in the nest (there's a clue in the name). It isn't yet ready for life outside the nest, as it doesn't have the muscle development to hold itself upright, or the feather development to keep itself warm. Mine fell (as it were) very definitely into the latter category.

So now what? You've got a ravenous little stomach on your hands, all mouth and naked thighs, it's 10.30 pm, there's no way of popping it back in its nest (trust me on this, I've had a look in the loft). So I soaked some scone and began poking this mush gently into its gullet with the end of a teaspoon. After several dollops, it shuffled around, poked its rear end in the air and offered me a dropping (or faecal sac, as it's known) which my fingers, it turned out, were not delicate enough to transport without splitting. Welcome to parenthood.

Half a dozen dollops of the mush later, the *cheerp*ing subsided and it was time for lights out, shoebox closed.

Cheerps greeted me first thing the next day, a Friday. I had worked out a plan to try putting Cheerps (by now this was his name, and I decided, for the purposes of this narrative, that it was a he) back in a nest, if not *the* nest, but I wasn't going to have time to do the necessary research on this on a workday. I therefore had to take him to work with me, and the box of muffled *cheerps* sat discreetly by my desk. At least, I thought it was discreet, but curious colleagues converged from all corners of the building. One left quickly, saying she might cry… Conservationists really ought not to be so delicate.

I popped to The Lodge shop for mealworms, which I thought would be more nutritious than wet scone – not that Cheerps was showing any sign of losing his appetite for that. He made short work of the mealworms.

I once read a book called *Sold for a Farthing*, the wartime story of Clarence, an adopted house sparrow. I consulted it for some tips on sparrow rearing, and to remind myself of what I might be taking on if I couldn't find more natural foster parents for my lodger. Clarence lived with his owner for 12 years, treated her bed as his, and attacked anyone who came near it.

First thing on Saturday, I began to work out which of the sparrows nesting in my garden and busily feeding young would be the most appropriate fosterers. This involved establishing what stage of development the occupants of the nest boxes were at. Box no. 1 is nailed to a pergola post, seven feet up, garlanded in vine stems. From the side, I could see a head poking out, yelling encouragement at no doubt frazzled parents. The head turned, got me in focus, fell silent, and slowly retracted, almost comically. From the front of the box I could see it, as though at a port-hole, like a Gary Larsson cartoon character, peering at me, wide mouth now firmly shut, head wobbling unsteadily. Anyway, the point is that these nestlings were developed enough to clamber around inside. Too old for Cheerps.

Fortunately, at nest box 2, the parents were still popping inside with their beaks full of aphid paste. Cheerps would have to go in this one.

Before resorting to this course of action, I had also tried to see if the real parents would rediscover Cheerps in a freestanding nest box. This I placed on the flat roof of my outbuildings as near as possible to their nest under the tiles of the gable end. I monitored the situation closely for a couple of hours, feeding Cheerps from time to time but keeping him *cheerp*ing. Unfortunately, no sparrows showed any interest in this or were drawn by any parental pangs of recognition to this displaced source of *cheerp*s. So I placed him into the box housing the younger family. I can't be sure what ensued. I did have a look in the box a few days later, gently lifting the lid, but this sent the occupants scuttling to the back of the box, hidden among straw and chicken feathers.

We know from research that these late broods of sparrows are not very productive. By this time of year the birds often struggle to find enough to eat. It certainly struck me, watching the parents come and go at the nest hole, how infrequently they visited, and how little they appeared to bring, especially compared to how much my foster sparrow had been able to pack away while under my supervision.

I'm hopeful I will still have my unruly band of local sparrows visiting for birdseed and crumbs through the winter. Who knows, maybe Cheerps will be among them. One thing I can be sure of, however, now that I've secured the nest site in the roof, is that there won't be any more like him falling into the house next summer. All being well, my sparrow-feeding duties – and yours – will be 'just for Christmas'. Or a little less hands-on, anyway.

SOARING SPIRITS
I was dismayed to hear of the government's plan to destroy buzzard nests as part of a trial to see if shooting businesses can rear more pheasants to shoot. I find this entirely bizarre.

The buzzard has a special place in my affections, like a first love, ever since I came face to face with my first one, on a fence post, at my eye level, in western Scotland on a family holiday. I've been a fan ever since. And just as I have since followed its fortunes as a recovering species, so it has seemed to follow me, shadowing my movements from west to east, to south. At each of the stop-off points in my life, the buzzard, widely persecuted in the modern age, has been reclaiming former haunts not far behind me, on a roughly north-west to south-east trajectory: from the refuges of the remoter uplands (the Celtic fringes, you could say) to the lowlands, of both Scotland and England.

As a schoolboy, I had witnessed buzzards returning to rural north Ayrshire. I welcomed them back to the foothills of the Ochils while a student in Stirling. And I began to notice the first of them wheeling again over the western fringes of Edinburgh when I moved to find work there in the early nineties. I then moved south, first to Cambridge and then to near Sandy, Beds. And yes, I'm delighted to report that the buzzard has caught up with me again.

On a recent summer evening, I laboured in the back garden over a cabin build. The distant, faintly nasal cries of a bird, almost gull-like, slowly penetrated my conscious mind. I realised that this was probably a young raptor of some kind, either in distress, or simply hungry. And so, I jumped the fence at the bottom of the garden and headed across the pasture and down the hedgerow bordering the corn, in the direction of the sound. I got about 200 yards, halfway to the oaks rising from the hedge line at the far end of the field. An adult buzzard launched forth from the crown of one and glided my way, mewing loudly and anxiously. The hunger cries from the depths of the other oak promptly stopped.

And I did too. I had found out what I needed to know, for now: that there was almost certainly a nest there, and I didn't want to prolong the anxiety of the birds by going any closer. I could do that in a few weeks, if and when the young fledged. The next four days played out to the same 'feeeed meeee' soundtrack, while a parent bird scanned the dry fields below for small movements.

Buzzards are conspicuous birds in flight, so it intrigues me they can nest so close, so unnoticed, at least until the young are near fledging, and get really demanding. I have heard about the buzzard's secretiveness before. I recall about ten years ago, when reports of buzzards locally were rare, but increasing, a local farmer telling me he thought a pair had already bred in a local wood. I thought it unlikely they could have done so without me, or people at the RSPB, knowing about it; even people who lived right beside this wood, and don't miss much. But it couldn't be totally ruled out. At that time, the sighting of a buzzard hereabouts was a noteworthy event; an occasion. Reports would always cause a stir. There is something involuntary about our response to the sight of a buzzard spread out on the sky. It is as though its very wings have your lungs on a string, and pull them upwards as it rises, on fanned feathers. A soaring buzzard often has an entourage of irate crows, flailing in its wake. This serves mainly to emphasise how expert a flier a buzzard is, how much more refined its lines, how dignified its progress. Cool. Chilled out. Effortless. Serene. A ballet within a brawl, protected from the blows of its assailants by some invisible field created by total balance and mastery of the air.

It was just a few years ago I was first able to confirm the successful breeding of buzzards locally. Then, with the permission of the estate and the several tenant farmers in my road, I visited a spinney and found a nest high in the crown of an oak, with young birds calling and adults nearby, clearly none too keen on the idea of me poking about below. I have since seen juveniles nearby, and even found a recently fledged bird dead between the wood and the roadside, probably a road casualty.

All good: but there is something extra heart-warming about seeing these birds from the garden, and even the sofa, or the bed, as they cruise overhead. And to hear them as well now, at the nest, gives me a particular sense of well-being, of inhabiting rural surroundings that are piecing some of their long-missing parts back together. I like that the vexatious mutter of a magpie in the fruit trees tells me there's a buzzard overhead. I like that the mournful *pewww* of the birds themselves makes me look up and see sometimes as many as seven of them 'kettling' high against the clouds, or the blue sky.

My nearest farmer neighbour had noticed the recent hunger calls of our young buzzards. We were chatting about the lack of summer rain. He'd had to move his cattle to another pasture. The wheat, and the beans, were fading in places for want of a decent shower. The persistent pleas of these growing birds made a fitting soundtrack to a parched landscape. He was content to have the buzzards back, though he remarked, as people often will, that it might mean fewer skylarks for us. I told him I thought we could have both. I later dropped him off a leaflet with simple advice on how to make crops extra appealing for nesting larks.

Though you don't often see them doing anything terribly energetic, buzzards will pounce on anything small enough to hold on to easily, and to eat. They are not renowned for their dash or drama as predators. They are as likely to be seen hunting for worms and beetles as anything else, and will tend to tackle only the small and weak where rabbits are concerned, often preferring their meals already dead. No doubt this includes a large proportion of the three million hand-reared and road-killed pheasants provided by the shooting industry every year. Elegant scroungers, you could say.

I often cast my mind back to that first-love moment with the buzzard, on that family holiday. All my siblings and cousins re-member it too, and my parents needed no reminding, though we've debated whether it was Mull or Arisaig, 1972 or 1973. I was the youngest of the troupe, gazing down at the injured rabbit on the roadside. The buzzard that we inadvertently flushed from his catch is watching us back, from the fence post, doe-eyed, soft-feathered. Beautiful, yet quietly lethal.

It's a bird I still associate with holidays, so I think that's part of the special feeling I get when I can enjoy them from my front room or back garden. This used to be strictly a special bird of special places, seen only on special trips. It fair lifts the spirits to have that kind of specialness brought a whole lot closer to home again.

THE POCKET GODDESS

It's evening, and the day birds are getting nervous, as usual, with blackbirds as lead complainants. Even so, my attention is caught by a particular, mounting commotion at the end of the back garden. The blackbirds have escalated the standard fussing and are now erupt-ing. It's much more than the daily neurosis and tantrums of dusk. A song thrush is joining in, and the chaffinches have formed an outer ring of protest. I don't want to interfere or to risk scaring anything off its meal, but my curiosity gets the better of me and, after another minute or so of this disturbance, I edge carefully in that direction to see what's amiss.

At times like these you sense that the birds don't fear humanity, as such, the way they fear those of their fellows that exist to catch them. Or if it is fear of humanity, it is at a quite subordinate level. It's as though they understand or respect our latent capacity to harm them, as though they have been taught this or perhaps witnessed attacks – real or misconstrued – on themselves or other birds. But the fear of those that eat them is the real deal. There is terror here; even hysteria. They may, in a sense, have been calling for my help – or the help of anything else large that might yet disrupt or escalate things further, get the hunter to in turn feel hunted.

But I'm not going any closer. With binoculars I can see the object of their ire in the lower branches of the eucalyptus, part-obscured by the pines. Into focus come the moon-yellow, glaring eyes of a little owl. It has clocked me too – of course it has. Its eyesight is to mine what mine is to the badger's. That's why I'm carrying bins.

I don't know what it's being accused of over there, but it may be nothing more than trespass. It's the first one I've seen in the garden, although I hear them regularly, especially in spring and autumn, calling from the permanent pasture to the east. They *yip* like small dogs as dusk turns to night, complaining in their turn about cats, foxes or larger owls.

Athene noctua wasn't known to me as a species in Scotland. I first got to know the little owl when I was quite young, on a campsite in France. I was exploring the various recesses presented by a pollarded willow: that is, a stump many times wider and much taller than I was then, harvested regularly for the poles it would shoot forth. Within its part-hollow interior I was astonished to come face to face with a row of owlet faces, each gaze fixed firmly on me, impassive yet penetrating. Indifferent, perhaps, or maybe expectant. Who knows what my own countenance looked like to them, these foundlings that had hitherto known only adult little owls bringing comfort and food. Perhaps I might too. With little resistance or difficulty I took one of these furry bundles with the strangely blasé, grown-up expressions onto my forefinger. Here it sat quite calmly, eyes remaining fixed on mine. I found that, irrespective of my hand movement, its gaze didn't shift. In fact, I could turn my wrist through 180 degrees, and its head stayed firmly in place.

The emergence from this delightful fluffball of a huge, parasitic flat-fly was considerably less endearing, but equally memorable, although it scuttled back into its host as quickly as it had sidled on to my hand. Luckily, it didn't sample me. It occurred to me even at that young age that parasites are life forms too, with a right to exist, no matter how ugly their appearance, gait or habits.

The first little owl I met in this country was flying alongside a train, somewhere in the Midlands when I was journeying to visit friends, and – fittingly – the BBC Natural History Unit, in Bristol. I knew then I was in another country.

Little owls are firmly at home here now, but their establishment was not some matter of chance or the odd casual escapee putting down roots. They were regularly imported and sold in London and other markets, and no doubt from there some got away. But today's population stems from a concerted release programme carried out in neighbouring Northamptonshire under the auspices of one Lord Lilford, who had developed a fondness for the birds and wished to see them go native here too. He had to work hard at it for some years before finally, in 1889 (the year the Society for the Protection of Birds was formed, as it happens), a pair was found to be with eggs, in a mature ash tree on the estate.

It was several years later that they seem to have crossed the border into this county. Two birds were shot on an estate south of here. Then, in 1894, in a neighbouring village, the owner of the manor house reported to J. Steele-Elliott, 'This spring I was often startled to hear a peculiar noise in the evening and early morning. After shaking the ivy-covered trees around the house I managed to disturb a very small owl about the size of a thrush, and a stranger to me.'

'Without doubt,' concludes Mr Steele-Elliott, 'it was one of this species.' Perhaps it was a young one, that it needed so much tree-shaking before feeling the need to reveal itself.

I don't think they are short of places to nest nearby, whether the willows or the empty milking sheds across the road, and from which I sometimes on summer nights hear them haranguing cats or foxes. I also see them perched on the gable end of the Dutch barn across the road, curtseying when nervous. I rescued a huge old bird table from a bonfire site when College Farm, just along the road, was being renovated. With little owls in mind I turned it into a bird house, by adding walls and a side entrance, the right size for Athena – the pocket goddess, as I think of them. I've installed it close to where the visitor was, in below the eucalyptus and with some bay tree around it, pointing the entrance hole in the direction of the pasture.

I run into little owls – if I'm lucky – between home and work.

My earliest visit to this road, before I lived here, on a misty winter weekend, involved the discovery of a little owl in the ancient crack willow just along the road. I was looking at it for a while, thinking it is just one more lump of the bark that is regularly shed by the great tree, and had lodged in its lower branches, when it moved, bobbed a few times, looked right and left and then launched off, porpoising across the field to the shelter of another spinney. This incident may just have had a bearing on me ending up living here.

LEAPS OF FAITH

Frogs have always seemed a bit unfeasible to me. I'm not quite sure how they got here, given how tasty they plainly are to a veritable who's who of higher, bigger, quicker and more calculating life forms. I'm talking about crows, cats, foxes, hedgehogs, snakes, rats, otters, herons, certain *bon vivants*... you name it. Even blackbirds eat tadpoles. And then there's the queue of carnivores lurking beneath the pond surface.

No, as a design concept, frogs don't seem viable. Okay, they have a basic strategy of evasion – they jump – but the things that eat them do things like fly, run and, yes, jump too.

Frogs produce huge volumes of spawn, and I know that in the end this is how they have arrived here with us today on the rollercoaster ride of evolution: safety, or continuity, in numbers.

I read a thing in a colour supplement recently where a guru in artificial intelligence (robot–building, to you and I) spoke about the sophistication of a frog. All a frog does, he argues, is jump away from big moving things and jump towards, to eat, small ones. His point being that it ought not to be so hard to replicate this 'intelligence' artificially, in a robot.

Then I saw the winning photographs in the Wildlife Photographer of the Year competition. I was brought up short in the animal behaviour category. Here was a picture of an African bullfrog chomping its way through a small, but significant, in frog terms, mud bank to free its tadpoles from a rapidly dwindling pool.

Blimey.

For my money, that's mind-bogglingly bright, for a frog. That's Champion the Wonderfrog level intelligence. That bullfrog should have a television series of her own, perhaps with an Alsatian in tow to help interface with humanity. The photographer explained that the frog also had a go at him. This is also quite interesting, not to mention brave, for a frog, but not nearly as clever, for me, as (a) understanding the plight of the tadpoles, and (b) having the nous and creativity to put in place a solution. This is more than instinct, is it not, because it's improvisational? I'm inclined to think so. Try emulating that in a robot…

Rightly or wrongly, this has forced me to revise my view of frogs, even though our common frogs are not as big, nor presumably as big-brained, as African bullfrogs.

I have tried to make my garden more frog-friendly, by creating small ponds and damp shady corners. From time to time a frog has taken up residence. One held a constant vigil by the bath pond for two summers, getting steadily bigger, reaching breeding age, always in about the same spot, looking vaguely self-satisfied, ready to plop into the water if I got too friendly. A bit like a robot, really. Then it disappeared.

They've disappeared in quite a few places, apparently. There are fears, which I share without knowing too much about it, that frogs are ultra-sensitive to pollution and climate change. There was a story in the papers in March 2004 about a frog that turned up in a garden centre with three heads and six legs. Another story, from the USA, reported that a herbicide may be causing male frogs to change gender. As if they weren't already unfeasible enough.

I got a sense of frog sensitivity one August evening last summer, when peculiar electrical storm conditions were brewing, and, as the clouds threatened to burst, there was a sudden, coordinated exodus of leaping frogs from my friend Jo's pond. They invaded the patio, where we were having supper, leaping pointlessly hither and yon. They were on the march, it seemed, and something had made them lose all regard for their own safety. Well, we could have been anybody. As it was, we were the sort of people who thought maybe they were hungry, so we flicked some bugs in front of them and, sure enough, these were quickly scoffed. It's the only time I've ever actually seen frogs eat.

On the way home I saw more frogs on the streets, leaping vigor-ously. It was a bizarrely synchronised event, and confirmed my view that frogs are a bit weird, oddly sensitive, and not to be underestimated.

Jo's pond seethes with frogs in the spring. The breeding frenzy can verge on embarrassing, with the males clinging on to anything that moves. I took a few tadpoles for my garden, after the spawn hatched, and they were small but swimming. Maybe doing so will help to plug any holes in that critical mass of frogdom. Mind you, I have had to remind myself, particularly so when I saw one with a koi carp in the grip of a bear hug, that they are not necessarily as daft as they look.

THE BEAST OF BEDS

It seems that every locality in Britain now has a beast. Sightings are all the rage, although hard evidence is usually conspicuous by its absence. I'm pleased to report that my village now has a beast too. It has all the hallmarks: about six feet long, massive canine teeth, big eyes set in a large skull. It is said to consume 10 lb of raw meat a day and is estimated to weigh a couple of hundred kilos.

Far-fetched? Well, we even have admissible evidence. Our beast has been photographed, and turned up in a ditch on an RSPB nature reserve, in a dramatic stand-off with a herd of cattle. Well, it would have been more dramatic had the beast in question been, ooh, a jaguar, say. But in fact, it's a grey seal.

The intrepid animal has ventured inland from the North Sea, navigating many miles of the Great Ouse and about 20 weirs en route. I'm surprised it hasn't had more publicity. I even have a colleague who canoed alongside it in Bedford though I searched in vain in my own canoe.

Of the UK's many fabled big cats, only one has been authenticated in recent years. The Cricklewood lynx was real. We know because they caught it. It seems a touch ironic that the only beast brought back into custody is a species which is native to our isles, and has a right to be out there. I had half a mind to campaign for its release. But perhaps it would be better to reinstate a Eurasian lynx population properly one day. And not, ideally, in a north London suburb.

OUT OF THE WOODS

Have you ever imagined what the world would be like if there were suddenly no human beings in it? I'm not advocating such a measure, of course, frustrated as I might sometimes get with our deleterious effects on Mother Earth. But the scenario does sometimes unfold in my mind.

I can picture it most easily in summer. I'll be in the depths of the garden, in the thick of the action, attempting to restore order to the verdant ranks. While my back has been turned or I've been away, these have advanced on the bits that are supposed to be clear, or tidy – attempting to annexe the lawn or patio, for example. At such moments I can appreciate my garden – and that magical alliance of soil, stem and sunshine – for what it really is: a plot determined to revert to woodland. That is, how it used be before early humans arrived to clear and tame the post-glacial wildwood. A world pre-humanity.

I find myself wondering, if I were to go away indefinitely, along with everyone else – Dorothy from next door with her lawn-edging shears, etc. – how long it would take for the brambles to advance on and envelop our pavements and roads? Actually, I know the answer to this, for brambles at least – at the rate of roughly three centimetres per day at the height of the growing season. Those brambles can shift when they have a mind to, spurred on by a little rainfall. They would be in the vanguard of the assault that covered the tarmac in scrub, creating a nursery and then a soil layer for tree seeds to germinate in, sprout upon, and then begin their concerted surge.

The rate of engorgement of vegetable matter never fails to amaze me, summer after spring, year after year. Nature's powers of recovery too are reassuring, if sometimes a touch overwhelming. Just when you think you've got something under control, back it bounces. It's possible to feel swamped, sometimes, as you struggle to maintain decorum in the borders.

Most of us may not comprehend it this way, but conditions in the British isles are mostly perfect for temperate rainforest. Even here, out in the relatively arid east, the forests would stretch to the skies if we let them. I often contemplate the wet (or riparine) woods that must once have covered my road. Our alluvial soil indicates a former river course and I would guess it is the primary reason why our modern-day settlement is here; the latest in a succession of these, no doubt, since the first human arrivals worked out that it would be an ideal place to clear, grow things and fish from.

Someone else might have been imagining this pre-modern scenario too, looking at my garden, when they decided to push a leaflet through my letterbox offering me 'first aid' for my lawn, in big letters under a large green cross. They had obviously taken the diversity of non-lawn species that I allow to grow in my lawn ('forest clearing' might be more accurate) to be some kind of symptom of sickness. I was almost offended, but mostly disappointed that such a narrow view of what a lawn should be could still prevail in the modern age. Haven't they heard of biodiversity?

So, I ignored this unasked-for diagnosis, this offer of treatment, and gazed fondly at my buttercups, while shredding the leaflet for the compost heap.

With all this wildwood taming, I can be practically self-sufficient in kindling and small logs. There is a eucalyptus at the end of the back garden. In ten years it has doubled in size to 30 feet tall or so. I like the elegance of its limbs, the way the light hits its mottled pale, papery bark. I also like the hint of the Antipodes it gives this corner of rural Bedford-shire (I have been tempted to fix a cuddly koala to its trunk, to entertain the neighbours), the way its foliage swishes, glitters in and harnesses the breeze, the height it gives to the garden and the perching opportunities it presents for birds. But I'd rather it was a native tree species, and less sapping of the moisture in the surrounding soil, which is impeding the progress of the Scots pines alongside it, and the other shrubs that form the garden boundary there.

I've debated with myself and my immediate neighbours about whether I should take it out. I've removed bits of it, to season and then cut for firewood. This has opened its canopy and made its limbs easier to appreciate, and allowed more light on to the pines. These, meanwhile, give me a little hint of Caledonia, to keep me going until my usual yearly fix of north Scotland's Atlantic coast and mountains at new year. This is partly a 'wilderness' fix, but not totally. When I'm there I can detect that something is missing. It's native trees again.

This general absence is brought home when I find stands of native Scots pine, such as those crowded onto the little islets in Loch Maree, like refugees on rafts. There is a craggy outcrop of an island stuffed full of these beautiful trees in the sea loch at Shieldaig, crammed on there, cliff edge to cliff edge, like they are about to be deported, or, more optimistically, reimported. This Highland land-scape looks (and is) ancient, in geological terms, but in an odd way the bits that have Scots pine on them look older still. Primeval, in fact. And definitely pre-human.

Out of reach of the cutter's axe and the browsers' teeth, these trees are lingering, visible reminders that this, like Station Road, Tempsford, was once a dense, thickly forested landscape, up to the mountainside tree lines, with pines in the north and the marginal places, and oaks and other broadleaves prevailing elsewhere.

We are all woodcutters, in the end, and gardeners. That's why, when I look out of my living room window, I can see a garden out there, and not the tree trunks of a temperate rainforest. It may need major surgery, on an ongoing basis, but I think I can live without the first aid.

BIGGER PICTURES

'Hey, small world!' We've all said it. You may therefore be surprised to learn that our planet actually weighs in at 5.972 sextillion tonnes. That's 5,972 followed by 18 zeros. It may have lost weight – this latest estimate is around 10 billion, billion tonnes less than previous ones – but, however else you describe it, this orb we exist upon, this oasis of biology in the solar system, is not small. At least in weight terms.

Yet we never say, 'Hey, *big* world!' on the occasions when we find that our paths *haven't* crossed. Perhaps we should. I've been wondering how often, in this big world, our paths just miss. For all those 'small world' moments – great things we happen to notice, old friends we bump into – how much slips past behind, over or past us, unnoticed?

You get a hint of the answer here at The Lodge, Sandy, Beds. When your back is turned, you find out what is passing you by. Others, you see, notice for you. We have, after all, probably the highest density of ornithologists in the world, not to mention some other kinds of expert. It's one of the many great things about working here. I've said it before: I don't get out much. Not as much as I'd like, at any rate. Mine is mostly a desk job, with occasional forays to the great outdoors to remind myself about – and show supporting organisations – the front-line action.

So, on an average day, while I'm glued to a computer screen, I'm gratified to know that in the world beyond the window behind me my colleagues are noticing all or most of the stuff I'm not. With windows pointing north, south, east and west, not much gets past us, I think, here at The Lodge. It could be a firecrest in a yew, a raven croaking over Sandy, a stoat on the heath, a mandarin duck at the pond, a grass snake in the porch or a four-spotted chaser laying eggs by the canteen, to name, in no particular order, just a few reports that spring to mind. The observations are meticulously compiled by Ian Dawson, our librarian, and he issues them weekly.

When I *do* get out, I have to make the most of it. That's how, in

Inverness, between trains and with an hour to pass, I found myself up by the castle, communing with a black-headed gull. Big deal, you may scoff, but one takes one's encounters where one can get them, in a desk job. We were sharing some shortbread, this gull and I, and I was admiring its chocolate-coloured head, twinkly eye and beautiful blood-red webbed feet and gullet – a straightforward, everyday bird, with an ugly voice – part-Dalek, part-Wicked Witch of the West. It was trusting. I practically had my arm round it on that grassy knoll, under the stony gaze of Flora MacDonald's statue.

And that's why, when the gull suddenly cringed, and changed its tune to a nervous murmur, I knew to look upward. There above us, hanging on the Highland air, was a raptor. Not a hawk, nor a buzzard. Bigger. Much bigger. Long-winged. An osprey. Our fish-catching bird of prey.

Over Inverness city centre? Surely not. But then of course Inverness has a river – the Ness – winding through it, below this castle hillock. And that's where the osprey was heading. It shivered its wings, as though limbering up, like an athlete wobbling a muscular thigh, perhaps to shake off some water. Would it be going back to the high dive? I'd soon find out.

Keeping my eye on the great, bow-winged outline, I moved to a position from which I could watch as it sailed out over the city and the river far below. I pointed it out to a chap sitting on a bench enjoying the scenery.

'You might want to watch this,' I told him, sticking my neck out somewhat. It was quite likely nothing would happen at all and this fast-receding bird shape might soon become no bird shape at all. Then it wheeled and turned. It was now heading back in our direction. Slowly, carefully, it followed the route of the river – I'd guess about 150 feet beneath us. It stalled, spotting something in the shallows (not *too* shallow, I hoped). Down it plummeted, in two stages, with an adjustment halfway. Legs akimbo, talons spread, it crashed into the current.

The wee man on the bench was now a wee man on his feet. We willed the osprey to get clear of the water in one piece, and with a prize. Sure enough, it achieved both, and, with a Herculean effort of flailing wings, it hauled a large trout or salmon clear of the water. It then beat off heavily up-river with its catch, assailed from all sides by irate, or just hungry, gulls. Perhaps the shortbread gull was among them, I don't know; I'd taken my eye off it in my pursuit of bigger thrills. Maybe it had done the same with me.

'Well, I've never seen anything like that round here before,' said the wee man breathlessly, as the osprey disappeared from view. And he told me he spends a lot of time up here, outside what is now the court. I didn't ask how, but he seemed to know quite a lot about the judicial system in Scotland. I explained a bit about the history of ospreys in the UK. About how there were none for a long time after they had been persecuted out of existence. How they made their way back to reclaim their ancestral haunts at Loch Garten in the 1950s. And how from there they have bred and reclaimed the land all the way south now to cross the borders into northern England, north Wales and soon, we hope, Northern Ireland.

I then had to leave for the train, and a further three-hour journey north to Forsinard, our nature reserve there, and a meeting with our site manager Norrie Russell. Next day, in the company of our guests from the Tubney Charitable Trust, we toured the Flow Country – this vast expanse of blanket bog – and learned about what the RSPB and others are doing here to restore these ancient blanket bogs and the unique life system woven into them. With Norrie's local knowledge and keen eye we saw a great many things we would have missed otherwise. He even showed me a couple more ospreys as dusk settled, in addition to all the things you might expect to see in the Flow Country on a good day: scoters, dunlins, hen harriers, black-throated divers, merlins.

I don't know exactly how long it is since society last accommod-ated large birds with hooked beaks living alongside us, but however long it is, it's too long. How fabulous it is that you can now see birds like ospreys in action in built-up areas, sharing the spoils of a health-ier (in places) world, however big or small we perceive it. They may be plunging into a river near you soon – if not already. Believe me, it's not something you want to miss. And if you can't surround yourself with fellow enthusiasts, keep your eye on those gulls, is my advice.

BACK FROM THE DEAD

Can I really have just heard this bird in my village? Before I reveal its identity, I'll give you a few clues. It's been a long time gone. Writing in the early 1920s, shortly before his death, W.H. Hudson thought this species was all but lost to the country. In his book *Rare,*

Vanishing and Lost British Species, he refers to a letter received by the RSPB from a Mr E.S. Dallas, 'who was fortunate enough to hear the bird in Sussex in May 1921'. He writes of listening to its note while on an all-night ramble on the southern slope of the South Downs, near Harting. The letter says: 'We first heard [the bird] at about 11 pm, and after that we heard it with only short intervals throughout the night until about 3.30 am, when we were returning home ... we tracked it to a large field.' The writer sought some corroboration locally, but, 'I could not find anyone in the neighbourhood who knew [the bird] or its note, though I spoke with some who were by no means ignorant on the subject of bird life'.

It's a migrant bird, once found all over these isles, though it is now almost unknown. Mr Hudson refers to another letter received from abroad by the RSPB a few years earlier: 'A letter of protest from a native gentleman in Malta, who wrote of the nets used there: "From this harbour of Valetta alone shiploads of hundreds of thousands of live ... go into Europe, especially England".' He warned that the trade was unsustainable. 'I respectfully suggest that these modes of catching ... only be allowed on the return migration.'

And it seems that, soon after, the few birds now able to reach the British Isles under their own steam may have validated his fears. 'At the present time a single nest would be an event to record,' wrote Hudson. He feared this species might go the same way as the passenger pigeon, once abundant but recently declared extinct in North America.

Reading these notes from almost a century ago reminds me how fortuitous it must be that I've just heard the bird near my home. It's clear from the historic records for Bedfordshire that this once commonly encountered species had become a rarity even by the end of the nineteenth century. A number of local villages have old records of them, including birds nesting, and even birds recovered in winter. It seems they may have been captive-bred at Wilden, which isn't far from here, which might explain this.

There is just one twentieth-century nesting record for the shire mentioned by Dazley and Trodd, at a village just across the river from here: 'a nest with ten eggs found by pea-pickers at Roxton in August 1947.'

And here I should reveal the identity of the bird if it isn't yet apparent, because most people hereabouts are as likely to have eaten it or its eggs as they are to have knowingly seen or heard one. It's the humble quail. Indeed, most people might not even know this is a native British species. Like most game birds, it occupies that slightly uncertain ground between wild bird and domestic, because despite its small size it has always made good eating and it has been easy to breed in captivity, although unlike the others it has migratory instincts and would struggle to survive most winters here, even if it had any inclination to stay.

Our mid- to late-summer quail arrivistes may have already bred in southern Europe by the time they make a second migratory push north to reach the British Isles.

The quail occupies the unusual position of being, on one hand, a species of conservation concern in Europe, due to unfavourable status and depleted population, at the same time as it is one that it is permissible to hunt. The European Union calls on its member states to put in place measures to make sure 'hunting does not affect late breeding birds and birds during spring migration'. It's quite hard to work out the legal status of the quail in the UK. The website of one prominent hunting organisation doesn't mention the bird in its list of what can be hunted when.

Scarcity in recent times seems to have robbed us of our affinity with this appealing species as a part of the make-up of our landscape. This is a shame, because its call is distinctive and easy to remember, once learned. It is said to resemble the words 'wet my lips' – or even, for residents of Oxfordshire – 'quick me dick'. It is a pity that we may be denied this addition to the choir of summer by the interventions of the hunting establishment, whether home or away. I like it that the quail has made it this far, improbable though its success may be. It is still a quarry species in places like Malta, and subject to much debate between hunting lobbies and conservationists as to the timing and duration of open season, and the methods used to trap or otherwise bring them down. They don't always make great sport, as they often fly in the darkness of night, on their improbably long, flickering wings. A century on from that letter to the Edwardian era RSPB, birds are still netted in great numbers.

I'll keep working with my conservation colleagues to try to keep the coast clear for these redoubtable little birds as they navigate the Mediterranean Sea each year. I love the idea of them flying by night, intent on reaching these northern fields to add their upbeat tri-syllabic note to some of our otherwise more featureless landscapes.

CHAPTER EIGHT

August

FREE BIRD

'What's your favourite bird, then?' people have often asked me. It's a question I've usually struggled to answer. Oriole? Peregrine? Nightingale? It's a tough one, right enough. And then one August evening, in the back garden, after getting home from work, I had a moment of lucidity.

I can find August a little dispiriting, on occasion, to be honest. After the highs of midsummer, things can be a little drab, especially if the sun won't shine. When it comes to sunshine I sometimes think I'm no more sophisticated than a geranium. August can be neither one thing (spring) nor the other (autumn) with their defined season-alities, their spirit of change, of renewal and decay.

The lack of moral support from most of our birds doesn't help – they don't *sing*, they don't *show*, you could be forgiven for thinking that they weren't even *there*, most of them. Of course they are just having some time out, at this time of year, recuperating after the excesses of the breeding season; getting mentally and physically prepared for the long journeys or harder, sparser months ahead; shedding one plumage for another, a tarnished set of feathers for a fresh one.

But for swallows, as birds of the air, there can be no such furtive-ness. And in this early evening, in a garden quiet for sober reflection, the approaching, friendly twitter is that of an old summer friend, the swallow, fluttering high over the neighbouring pasture.

For a split second, and despite myself, *I wished I was it*. At that moment it felt like my favourite bird: no contest. Its general exuber-ance, its *joie de vivre*, lust for life, call it what you will, infected me. Lots of birds can make flying look like fun – jackdaws, for example, and of course house martins. Or like a leisure activity – take red kites. But few have the swallow's range of skills, or their grace and intimacy. It isn't a powerful flier, and in strong breezes it can give the impression of swimming against a tide of air, keeping its head clear as it surfs the gusts. But the impression of coping, of exhilaration, is ever present.

Maybe I'm thinking that it's my favourite bird right now because it's the bird I'd most like to be – on the condition I knew it was me, if you see what I mean. Well, you could do a lot worse than stay on a farm and cavort around the English countryside for a summer, then travel abroad with all your mates, destination Africa, for the winter.

In an odd way the swallow isn't photogenic. A photograph rarely – if ever – captures the swallow's movement, the gloss on its blue back, the glint of its red throat and the deep fork of its streamer tail. There is, for example, an often-used photograph of one doing that wonderful drinking thing that they do, when they skim a pond with their beak open, slashing the surface, sipping up a mouthful of wa-ter, and perhaps an insect, as they go. It's a great shot, and who knows what tripwire trickery was employed in snatching it, but frozen in the frame the bird loses some of its essence – at the very least, its motion.

Around where I live, I can watch swallows mixing with house martins and sand martins over the River Ouse – which meets the River Ivel just outside my village – and I can compare and contrast them. Swallows occupy the lower stratum of the three. They are more elegant and streamlined, and have a more articulate twitter (few birds have better claim to *twitter*) – almost a song, really. And they are better at the low-level stuff, skimming the tips of the grass in the flood meadows, picking off horse flies from above the dung.

It's only the third week of August and already I have seen the swallows gathering on the telephone wires opposite my house. Per-haps it was just a couple of families having a passing conference, having bred in one of the local farmyards, but I know that autumn, and their departure for the long swoop south, is beckoning.

One of the most dramatic bird spectacles I ever witnessed was a September gathering of swallows in and around a reed bed that fringed a special place called Ashgrove Loch in north Ayrshire. The sward was thick with daddy long legs that evening, and the swallows were filling up on the blundering beasties in the dairy fields around the loch basin.[3] The reeds seethed and swayed with perching swallows, while other birds zipped and dipped around them before settling: a carnival of wings, for *Hirundo rustica*, a gathering of the clans to banquet, ready for the long march south.

Someone gave me a Woodcrete swallow nest this year, and I have nailed it up above my back door. The outhouse roof juts out a foot or so, which gives the artificial nest a canopy, which swallows need. My local birds should still be able to see the nest as they pass overhead. Where they build their own nests, in open outbuildings, stables and porches, they like cover and a protrusion, such as a nail, to give extra support to the shallow mud tray. They line it with things like grass stems and chicken feathers. They can be very tolerant of humans nearby, as though they quite like having us around.

Chances are they won't need my nest, as long as the local farmers keep their draughty outbuildings in place. But the general loss of such nest sites may partly explain why the swallow is classified as having an 'unfavourable conservation status in Europe'. A lot of farmyards have been tidied up, or aren't like the farmyards of old, with their ponds and muckheaps riddled with insect larvae emerging to take flight into swallow airspace. The livestock, too, have gone from many lowland areas, with the widespread switch from mixed farming to monoculture.

However, swallows are notoriously difficult to census, and where some people report losses, others report gains. It may be that in some cases they just decide to move on to pastures new – if you'll excuse the pun. Swallows like pastures. They like us, or at least they like our dwellings. I'm not certain what they did before we came along. There can't have been that many suitable caves in prehistory.

In my mind's eye swallows were the 'small free birds' of the 'fields

---

3   I spent a lot of time exploring this loch. The 'floating marshes', they are called locally, and in places you did, in fact, get the distinct impression that you were walking on a floating mat of aquatic plants, a sensation not unlike trying to stand up on an airbed. This was, I don't mind admitting, a little disconcerting, especially when you could see the murky depths of the loch's open water ahead of you. But it was really great for birds, with drumming snipe and rails grunting and squealing unseen in the reeds. On one occasion, as recently as 30 years ago, my brother and I even heard the rasping of a corncrake, passing through on its way north.

of Athenry', mythologised in the Irish folk song of the same name, or the 'free bird' that Lynyrd Skynyrd had in mind in their 1970s hippy song of the same name. Nobody ever put one in a cage.

REVERIE

The gleaming rays on the water in my palm hold me for a moment, the touch of the water gives me something from itself. A moment, and the gleam is gone, the water flowing away, but I have had them. Beside the physical water and physical light I have received from them their beauty; they have communicated to me this silent mystery. The pure and beautiful water, the pure, clear and beautiful light: each have given me something of their truth.

Richard Jefferies, *Meadow Thoughts*, 5 April 1884

At the top of an alpine valley close to the town of Madonna di Campiglio in Italy, on the knife-edge of the thing, I have a Richard Jefferies moment. I scribbled some thoughts. I had to. While it is meditative to be alone, and I felt serene, I couldn't help wanting to try to capture something of my mood, to share it.

There are the most breathtaking views in all directions, and the silence and stillness are almost total. The only sounds are my heart beating in my throat – louder when I open my mouth – the fizz of thin air through a swift's scything wings, and the distant croak of a raven. One kilometre away? Two? How, I wonder, can so much of the world be making so little noise, on such a breathless day?

A strong scent of fresh sweat and the zest of orange peel clings to the air around me.

Looking up from the valley floor, I couldn't resist heading for here. The morning sun had thawed my bones, dampened in my tent on a cool, clammy night. The ridge beckoned me to the top tier of this natural amphitheatre. Below it lay grassy meadow slopes, dotted with rock statues, below them forest, and me, sipping cappuccino in the morning sun, which had burned off the mist. I had no map, just a sense of purpose and journey. I wouldn't have done something so reckless in Scotland, with its capricious climate, but here the weather seemed set fair. I was in a warm, bright, pristine room called the world.

The forest and river gully were cool in the shade, but the sweat still soaked me as I picked my way upwards through them. Clear of the trees, the open slopes were grill-pan hot by comparison, and the increasing altitude made breathing more of an effort too. The hay meadows, even in August, still offered a multitude of types of flower, and the seed heads of orchids.

The path was hotching with crickets and grasshoppers, some of them glancing off my forehead. Butterflies danced in front of my boots.

I found a shrine to someone called Paulo where I first reached the ridge. Decoding the plaque using my phrasebook Italian, I took it Paulo was a guide of some kind. Half a million Italians died in these mountains in the Great War, many in the bitter-cold winter of 1916. While so many lives were lost in the mud of Belgium, the snows, avalanches and frostbite of the Alps also claimed their share. A further million Italians were hospitalised. Song lyrics recur in my head – 'And the band played Waltzing Matilda…'

Black redstarts inhabit the shrine. Alpine accentors – dunnocks by an Italian designer – chastise me as I stop to replace some sugar. As I do so, brown butterflies of different species sip at my damp T-shirt. I am pleased to play my part in this symbiosis – they get the minerals and I get the pleasure of their company. When it occurs to me that they often sup on bird droppings, maybe I'm not so flattered.

Cow bells tinkle on the slopes way below. The shepherd passes me on the ridge, with two dogs, more setter than collie. Apart from him I have passed only one other person all day, on a sunny Saturday afternoon in August – the Ferragosto public holiday weekend as well. Where is everyone?

A female hazel hen crouches on the path, thinking maybe I haven't seen her. Anywhere else but there and she would have been fine, she would have pulled off the trick. On the ridge, pine trees grow like groundcover, suppressed by bitter winds.

I hear a warbly call above me. Looking up, I see 150 alpine choughs floating in an otherwise silent squadron. They mingle indecisively overhead, faffing around, as we say, until something, perhaps the warbling leader, pulls them out of the dither and leads them off to a cliff-face roost somewhere.

I realise that I haven't been birdwatching. No, the birds have been watching me.

I often think of Otzi at times like these. Otzi is the Neolithic man they found perfectly preserved by an alpine glacier, until it started to thaw and released him. Otzi is the oldest human being we know any-thing about. He has been dubbed the Iceman.

I know that I had better head down now if I don't want to do an Otzi. The shadows are lengthening. Dusk comes early to half of these valleys (the half that faces east, away from the sinking sun). I'm loath to leave my seat in the sun. I know the forest – the cool of the trees – will chill my damp back and my toes will redden and complain on the descent. But I can't leave it much longer.

Back at the campsite, and serenaded by an oompah band, I am thrilled to discover as I read my *Rough Guide* that the town of Bolzano, one hour north, where Italy meets Germany, has a *museo archaeologia* with a very important resident. Otzi.

He was discovered one unusually mild autumn ten years ago when his head and shoulders appeared from the receding glacier. The discovery has always intrigued me, as the scientists gradually learned more about who Otzi was, and what he revealed about pre-history. I couldn't resist going to see him, even if it means foregoing a day trip to Verona, on the Romeo and Juliet trail.

I travel north the next day full of excitement and anticipation, the way some people feel when going to a movie premiere to ogle the film stars as they arrive. Starstruck.

'The mummy is on the first floor,' one of the museum attendants tells me as I buy my ticket. How does he know that's why I am here? Is it obvious?

The floor is dedicated to reconstructions of the man and his milieu, pieced together from his clothes, equipment, his last meal, his next meal…

He lies as though in state, behind a foot-square glass window, naked, brown and shrivelled, a bit like a sun-dried tomato. He is in an uncomfortable position, the one he died in as the snows of winter covered him and the glacier enveloped him, fingers gnarled in an empty grip. It occurs to me that I'm looking at a dead person, and that this is okay because he's 5,300 years old. Of course he's dead. But who was he? What was his real name? Why was he there? Did any-one miss him?

Perhaps he was birdwatching. Perhaps not. Or not as such. Perhaps the birds were watching *him*. If only he'd scribbled some notes we could decipher. We would feel even more like we'd been with him on his walk.

SCREAMERS

I work in a building that screams as you enter it in the morning. It's quite a nice way to be welcomed to work, all in all, although I have to share this ovation with the colleagues, all 150 of them, with whom I share this two-storey office. It's called the Avocet Building, and it's one of the newer parts of The Lodge at Sandy.

The screams are oddly disembodied. They are actually tape recordings of the raucous yet slightly nasal racket made by swifts, with which some people will be familiar, but which others find surprisingly easy to appear oblivious to, of a summer's day or evening.

Even allowing for the fact that this is 'Bird Central', you might think it a tad eccentric for us to be playing these calls from the rooftops here. But the idea is that these calls will attract real swifts to come and have a look at the des res nest boxes we've installed for them in some recesses near the eves.

We've done it because swifts need help. Despite the fact that these masters of flight hardly ever need to touch the Earth that we walk upon, and do so much to tarnish, they are starting to decline. One of the reasons could be the lack of good places to nest – newish buildings, like the Avocet here, tend to have fewer possible nest sites than old ones. Hence our boxes.

Swifts only really touch down when they come to nest sites, otherwise they do pretty much all their living on the wing – eating, mating, gathering nest material and even sleeping up there; somewhere, somehow. They migrate to southern Africa and back each year, and clock up an extraordinary mileage in the few years that is their average lifespan.

And I'm happy to report that real swifts have started taking notice, and coming in to have a closer listen at our screaming building. It feels like only a matter of time before they take up our offer, and the screams as we arrive for work of a summer morning may soon be for real.

MIXED BLESSINGS

I don't normally go on holiday in August, especially to places like Italy. I prefer spring, when the kids are still at school, the climate's cooler, the crowds smaller and, most importantly, the birds are at their best. But this year I am lucky enough to have a holiday organised for me by friends of a friend, and find myself near Assisi for a week, courtesy of a very wealthy man.

We're in something called *Borgo il Poeta*, which roughly translates as 'the poet's farmhouse'. Which is, well, poetic, I suppose, although the identity of the poet in question has been lost in the rhyming couplets of time. It's in Umbria; north-Umbria, we joke, when it rains, which is occasionally, but still too often, for a joke of this quality. The *borgo* dates from the fifteenth century. Back then it was a tower from which the locals watched for marauding Etruscans, in days when Tuscany was the enemy, and views were needed for staying alive, not gazing at.

It may not be spring but it is hiving, as we say in my house. There are bees on the clover, wasps in the pool, crickets and mantises in the patio shrubs, swallowtails on the borders and moths around the evening candlelight. Lizards streak across the paving, and bats flutter in the dusk. Only the cicadas, like saloon-bar piano players, bother to pause when you approach too close.

I like living cheek by jowl with wildlife, even insects. I don't think my metropolitan friends endorse this view, unfortunately, although I am working on them.

The elder trees are already fruiting here, and there are a few birds around. They don't make themselves easy to see, but some warble loudly from the shrubbery. Cirl buntings flit in the fields beyond, among the frazzled sunflowers. Serins and goldfinches jangle from the tops of thin Tuscan cypresses, with orioles and wrynecks on backing vocals, unseen. Why are birds so shy here? I ask myself. How do they know to be? Surely most birds haven't themselves been shot at, yet they seem to inhabit a culture of fear. Do the young ones learn from watching the older ones? We contemplate these and other questions, by the pool.

The *borgo* is within day-trip distance of Assisi, where St Francis lived. He had no such problems getting close to the birds, back in the late twelfth century. Francis is remembered as the man who, answering a calling to God, renounced war (with Perugia) and all of his worldly possessions. He devoted himself to caring for the sick, and to repairing the church of San Damiano. The giving up of all his possessions included his clothes, to the considerable embarrassment of his prosperous merchant father. Despite being hauled before the bishop, Francis stuck to his cause, and attracted thousands of followers.

He is best known, of course, for preaching to and blessing the birds, and in most of the depictions of the saint in action he is surrounded by birds, listening attentively to him. It is the subject of a famous painting that hangs in the church, not to mention the postcards, statuettes, table mats, dishcloths, paperweights, stationery and key rings on sale throughout Assisi. (No bird baths or bird tables though, I notice, which seems like a missed opportunity to me. I wonder if Lega Italiana Protezione Italiana (LIPU), the Italian version of the RSPB, has considered this…)

We make that day trip, eager to see the church for ourselves. However, we are denied access, as apparently we don't have enough clothes on. The women's shorts are deemed especially unsuitable. I think this a little ironic, considering how much of his best work Francis carried out in the nip. Mind you, I suppose this isn't borne out by the paintings, or the images on the accessories. Anyway, determined to see the church from the inside, we trawl the souvenir shops for something with which to cover up. But there is actually nothing affordable or wearable to be found in any of the souvenir shops. Another gap in the market, I mutter ruefully.

I'm interested in the 'take-home' (since we're on the subject of marketing) message of Francis. Was he a pioneer of sustainability? We ponder how sustainably we are living, back at the *borgo*. The wines flow freely – but they *are* local, we reassure ourselves. I urge my friends to take further solace in the continued presence of birds… and bees, even though one stung Sarah. I have been slightly spooked by an entry in the *borgo* visitors' book, by Bill Oddie, of all people. A modern-day bird man. He has noted that one of their group got stung too.

Perhaps the bee-eaters would come a little bit closer, if we were really, really nice to them.

SITTING PRETTY

I've discovered a way of attracting birds close to the window at home which doesn't involve spending any money. I had seen a spotted flycatcher close to the house, though I'd never seen one actually in the garden. Knowing how much these birds like a prominent perch, from which to study the airborne insect activity of the neighbourhood, I sourced a long thin branch and installed it within the hedge close to the front room window. Its end was in view from the sofa. I promise you that by evening this spotted flycatcher – or one just like it – was sitting proud on the end of that stick.

There are many things we can do for birds and other critters that invoke strong feelings of kinship, but this was a particularly memorable one for me: something about the simplicity of it, the working it out for myself, and the speed with which it was adopted. It made me realise that I hadn't seen a spotted flycatcher in the garden before, not because they aren't around – they are, still hanging on while many other places locally and nationally are losing them – but because I haven't provided the right 'furniture'; both for them to sit on, and for me to witness them doing so.

Since then I've become an enthusiastic provider of perches, and the uptake rate has given me ample encouragement. I've enjoyed similar affirmation from the resident house sparrows by fashioning long, multi-branched stems pruned from shrubs, and placing these in the hedgerows so that the birds have an unobstructed view of both sides, rather than having to scramble about in its midst – which of course they can and still do, after having a good look round.

I've also provided a 'living' perch, while doing a bit of 'surgery' on the ash saplings out front. 'Shaping 'em up a bit,' as a neighbour called it, when he passed by below the ladder, with his Jack Russell giving me a 'what the devil is he up to now?' kind of stare. I have removed all the lower branches bar one, which sticks out over the hedge, about a foot above it, and which I have trimmed of most of its foliage. This is now the point at which many of the birds announce their entrance to the front garden – collared dove, magpie, sparrows, tits, finches, warblers, woodpigeon, wren. They stop here to take stock before descending for seeds or a general poke about. I've even watched a sparrowhawk sitting there with the early-morning sunlight slanting in on it, flaunting translucent wings and tail as it carefully fanned and preened each in turn. It was definitely the most relaxed I've ever seen the normally restless raptor appear; and all within ten metres of me, propped up in bed.

Perches don't have to be sticks (or branches, I should add). I've also discovered that ripened and withered teasels can be easily uprooted from out-of-sight spots and propped up in the hedge at the front, adding architecture to the row and bringing goldfinches into view to pick at them. The sparrows perch on them too, despite lacking the mandibles and dexterity needed to get at the seeds within.

But my biggest bird perch of all is the eucalyptus at the end of the back garden. It has died back now, through a combination of severe winter weather and me ringing its bark at the base, I think, although it has taken several years to succumb. I liked it for its year-round swish and its sinewy limbs, but it was hampering the growth of the native trees around and under it, and was hell-bent on getting out of proportion to its surroundings.

Some eucalypts grow – rapidly – to be among the tallest trees on the planet. It has always been a magnet for perching and singing birds, and it will remain so, and they will be more visible than ever, while it slowly disintegrates, and provides kindling and small logs for the fireplace, and infrastructure for woodpeckers. And it will continue to catch the sun on its ivory and now drying sapwood, as it sheds its bark casings like a giant, moulting reptile. There is beauty and of course renewal in decay. The pines and fruit trees and rowan beneath it are perking up already.

Perch provision needn't just be a domestic endeavour. I've found that strategically-placed props near tents or holiday cottage verandas can also help make contact with the locals. A site which catches the morning sun can be appealing for birds getting charged up in the early hours of the day. More than once I've seen even the dowdiest sparrows glow like baubles in the dawn sunbeams, as they fluff up and nibble themselves in preparation for the day ahead. And it isn't just birds that can be brought in. Dragonflies are also keen on sunny vantage points. Butterflies too, on occasion. And a perch under cover can be equally appealing for birds roosting or sheltering from a downpour.

It's always worth thinking about rearranging some of the furniture in the garden, or outside any convenient window. We're not the only ones who appreciate a good sit down and a view. And if my flycatcher is anything to go by, it may not be long before the guests start to arrive.

Batman and woman

Tiny bats that I've always assumed are pipistrelles have been a familiar feature of my garden airspace and its surroundings since I got here. They emerge from some secret crevice in the evening and have a favoured beat between this house and next door. On calm nights I can sometimes hear their flickering wings. In case they need it, I've put up a bat box on that side of the house, west-facing, where it might get some warming sunshine later in the day, while avoiding the more intense heat that can hit a south-facing wall.

I can sometimes watch these diminutive bats after dark, as they try to intercept moths, midges and mossies by the light of the street-lamp at the front. I found one in the house once, after I'd been away. I don't know how it got indoors, perhaps via the chimney, but I was too late to rescue it. The guidance I've had, for any future rescues, is to give a moribund bat water, and somewhere quiet to recuperate.

I've started noticing a much larger bat in the half-light of dusk. It flies lower, and appears to brush the foliage of the hedge, shrubs and trees in the back garden as it goes, I assume to dislodge insects that might be lurking there. Keen to identify it, I've consulted books and colleagues. It could be a brown long-eared bat, from this behaviour. It might even be a natterer's bat – but this is an elusive species, with few roost sites discovered, and a preference for caves, which we're not known for, locally. Or maybe it's a noctule. The latter are sometimes seen by day, flying high, and fairly direct. I've had them pointed out to me in some places, so I know what to look out for. Their echolocation 'clicks' are sometimes audible to the human ear.

Some of my colleagues are bat experts and have the kit needed for bat detecting, which can help identify what kind of bats are present, when of course it's too dark to tell by eye alone. There are 18 species in the UK, a quarter of all our mammals, and each calls at a different frequency, which the bat detector picks up. My friend Marcus Kohler came around to help ID this mystery bat out the back. At that time he was running his own ecological consultancy, and doing a lot of this kind of survey work. Bats are fully protected and many building renovations cannot take place without a survey having been completed and the needs of any resident bats assessed.

Unfortunately his visit coincided with a no-show by the bat. It might have been too cold for it on this night, or Marcus might have turned up too late. It seems that the likely species does its best work before complete nightfall, and may have packed up before we got Marcus in position and the gadget poised.

We made good use of the time remaining and checked out the empty farm outbuildings just across the road and down a bit. Marcus also checked out my attic, and though we didn't find any bats or bat droppings, he did pronounce it the ideal kind of roof space for long-eared bats – airy and spacious, with the sort of rafters they like to hang from.

We have brown long-eared bats at RSPB HQ. These are also

pretty tiny but have the most enormous ears, almost as long as their bodies. I've held a dead one in my hand, and marvelled at how light it was. On another occasion a roosting bat chose an unusual place to spend the day and dangled from the frame of a window, allowing a procession of staff to admire it.

I made a chance discovery of a bat roost in an oak tree on the nature reserve at The Lodge. I was actually investigating the source of a stock dove, which had flown out from the other side of this tree close to the footpath. High on the trunk were a couple of large holes, in which the doves were evidently nesting. The presence of bats was betrayed by the trail of brown staining from the holes, caused by bat droppings. I earned some stripes for this two-in-one nest hole discovery.

I've recently helped one of our local farmers to check out his old outbuildings. He was concerned that bat needs be considered if renovations had to be carried out. This time my colleague Sarah Richards came and led the survey, and we spent several hours pointing the gadget in different directions and peering at the dust of the floors of the old barns for bat droppings. You have to get your eye in, and my eye was too easily distracted by the evidence of birds – feathers, pellets, droppings, bones. But I did absorb some bat-detecting discipline, and we did find some pipistrelles, of which there are several different varieties.

Perhaps my most memorable bat encounter of all was indoors, as I watched a dramatised concert within the spectacular arena of Ely Cathedral. Diverting though the performance was, the show was stolen by the bats illuminated from the stage below, and flitting between the cloisters, bright against the gloom, high over the performers and audience far below. I'm not sure what they were doing inside, but perhaps they were disoriented by the acoustics, and I'm sure once the din had died down they'd be savvy enough to find their way out, like the rest of us.

POND-GAZING

The garden pond has sagged somewhat, like a deflated soufflé, under the lukewarm, moistened air of an eastern August. Four inches of mucky plastic liner are exposed. The soft crust of the pond is composed mainly of the bright lime green of duckweed, the lentil-sized disks sitting two or three deep in places. They jockey for position with the emergent stems of elodea, and the relatively large pads of frogbit.

Pond skaters cannot skate in these days. Instead, they tiptoe across the floating terrain. A garden pond is a volatile thing; always, in the warmer months, threatening to breathe – or transpire – itself to arid oblivion.

Mysteriously, within this low forest of dense floating plants there is a window on to the water beneath. It is a clear circle of seven inches diameter; below it are the radiating swords of a water soldier. Somehow, this jagged plant, like the top of a submerged pineapple, keeps the surface discs of the competition at bay. How it does this, I have yet to discover. I can't find anyone else who has noticed the phenomenon.

The water soldier looks a little alien but it is a native, once common in the waterways of East Anglia. Not so nowadays. Garden ponds are its main refuge. As the water cools towards winter, the plant sinks, to lie dormant in the depths of a pond, only to rise again in the spring.

Oberon the cat pushes in front of me and from the pond rim cranes his neck down to drink. He cannot reach the clear surface above the water soldier, so he lightly dabs the vegetated surface with his rough tongue. He is trusting. My boot toe, after all, is just off his rear end. I could tip him gently in. That might help clear some more pond surface and allow extra light to the life beneath. Ponds need interventions, after all, partly to save them from themselves. Water soldiers are fighting only their own small battles. Of course I let Obe drink unmolested. Both cat and pond can breathe easy, for now.

THE CARMEN BIRD

As time passes, voices are disappearing from the choir of singers in the landscape around us, not all of them birds. But two out of five bird species here aren't doing too badly, numbers-wise, and there's one in particular that seems to be trying solo to make up for some of the mounting silence in our lives. It's been bucking the general trend of declines, and moving steadily north since *Silent Spring*. And what a soloist. I have one now, perched on the top of the bird cherry at the back, rattling off its joyous, exuberant medley of trills and jingles. The fact that this is now early August, and many of the birds are lying low and long gone quiet after the toil and territory marking of spring, makes it all the more welcome. It sings for much of the year, I've noticed, but right now this is the song of summer in the garden, and it's from a bird that is at the height of its own brood-rearing activity.

It's a visually beautiful bird too. Mine has now flown to the apple tree, then done a display flight to the roof of the house. Robert Burns called it the gowdspink, 'music's gayest child'. Elsewhere it's been known as petaldick, King Harry redcap and the seven-coloured linnet. In Gaelic it's the *las air-choille*, which means 'flame of the wood', and the Anglo-Saxons knew it as *thisteltuige* – the thistle-tweaker. All this lyricism has been filtered down over time to leave us with the common name goldfinch, which isn't such a bad outcome, reflecting the value of the bird and the sparkle it brings into our lives. The actual 'gold' on its plumage isn't properly appreciated till the wings are spread to reveal bold, lemon-yellow bars that help to distinguish it in flight. It seems unable to fly very far without feeling the need to announce the fact with its excited twittering, a constant chatter with its fellows, a commentary on what it's doing and where it's going by a bird that likes company.

I'm sure a pair is nesting up there in the flimsy upper stems of the cherry, but I can't pick out the nest among the mass of shimmering leaves. To be fair I'm not busting a gut, here in my deckchair. It calls to mind my first encounter with goldfinches as a boy. There was a bay tree in the back yard of the cottage we lived in, regularly raided for soup seasoning, close to the back door. I used to climb up through it on to a wall, as a route to the roof of the garage and outhouses. On this occasion I reached the top and found my nose within inches of a cup of what seemed like cotton wool and feathers, embedded in thin shoots. I think there was a goldfinch somewhere else within the tree, and when I gently pulled the foliage towards me I could see tiny eggs within the tiny bowl. I climbed down again promptly, carefully, knowing to leave it well alone, to respect the birds and their secret. I didn't even know we had goldfinches in the garden. It was an early glimpse of how nature can be resident right under your nose and you not even know it.

Forty years on, the nest above me remains secret, out of reach, as it should be. Come the winter, I'll be able to see it up there, surprisingly tiny, swaying in the now bare twigs, holding fast against the elements for a few weeks at least. The goldfinch didn't used to be a bird you saw at the bird table, but that appears to have changed. Nowadays goldfinches will visit feeding stations for nyger seed, of which they seem especially fond, and the teasels I place strategically for optimal views from the window as the birds work the spiny cones to ease out the slender seeds within. The bright red face of the gold-finch could be taken for blood, as though the thistles were extracting something in exchange.

And this explains its important place in devotional art, and Christ's crown of thorns. It is said to be the bird most frequently rep-resented in paintings, especially religious art, after the white dove of peace. The goldfinch symbolises resurrection, fertility and healing. Although familiar all year round, most of these goldfinches fly to southern Europe for winter to find food and milder weather.

Goldfinch song often reminds me of French towns. Visiting *centre villes* as a child I would often hear this charming twittering, even in the narrowest of streets, and look up to see a cage on a balcony. I could sometimes make out the singer within. Finch trap-ping and keeping was – until not so long ago – widespread in Britain too, before the law changed in 1954 to make trapping for personal use illegal. Trapping for sale had been banned in 1933. Freeing the goldfinch was one of the RSPB's first missions, and like most cultural shifts it took time. I can well understand people wanting some of this natural music in their lives, especially back then when people were more likely to be stuck themselves in urban confines. But what I think the fullness of time has shown is that the goldfinch, freed from trapping and fear of people, has come close to even our most urban settings for us to hear it sing while independent.

A group of goldfinches has come to be known as a charm. Francesca Greenoak (in *All the Birds of the Air*) notes that this means 'a blended sound of many voices', and also the Latin *carmen*, mean-ing a magic song or spell. It feels good to have the many-voiced carmen bird above me in the garden now, irrepressible on a sum-mer's day while all around has already gone quiet. It was the French actor himself Eric Cantona who asked, 'Does a bird in a cage sing as sweetly as a bird that is free?' He isn't crying out for an answer.

WHO WILL GATHER FOR THE DYING VULTURES?
'It's the most interesting reason I've heard of yet for anyone visiting Harrow,' said my friend Judith, who lives there. My RSPB colleague Chris Bowden and I were attending and speaking at a gathering of Parsi and Irani Zoroastrians at their headquarters for Europe.

To explain why, I have to start at the beginning. As a bird conser-vationist, I often try to persuade people that we should save birds for our own sakes; as well as for the birds' sake, of course. Birds, gener-ally speaking, are nice; some more so than others, perhaps, but in the main they enrich our lives. But when the aesthetic arguments don't wash, I bring in utilitarian ones. Birds are useful. More than that, they may even hold the whole ecological deal – of which we are an ever larger and more dominant part – together.

No example better illustrates this than the demise of vultures in Asia. You have no doubt heard about this, but I'll give a short sum-mary. Until the mid-1990s, vultures in Asia were present in tens of millions. They were the most abundant and widespread large raptors on the planet. If you visited India or thereabouts up to this time you can't have failed to notice them.

Since then, they have disappeared to the point of extinction. A staggering 99 per cent of them have gone. This is vultures we are talking about – widespread, generalist scavengers. Cleaner-uppers of all our mess. Removers of livestock carcasses. Preventers, by dint of their habits, of infection, decay, disease, too many rats and feral dogs, rabies, bad smells and polluted water courses. But not so much now.

So how did this happen? By the tragic accident of secondary poisoning. Livestock in India, especially cows, are routinely given an anti-inflammatory drug called diclofenac. It relieves rheumatic pains and the like. It is similar to drugs humans take for back pain. Present in carcasses of these livestock (and it doesn't need to be many) it kills the vultures that are clearing them up, causing visceral gout and kidney failure. It's a cruel quirk of vulture physiology, and the drug appears not to have this effect on other scavengers. And so the vultures have disappeared from entire regions.

The economic impacts of missing vultures on India, Pakistan and Nepal are demonstrable, now that someone else has to do their job, or pick up the tab if it isn't done. Vultures, more plainly than other threatened or already extinct bird species, really are useful.

For the Zoroastrian/Parsi community, vultures have performed an additional role. You may have seen towers of silence in India. Tra-ditionally, the Parsi community places their dead on these towers for the vultures to consume and take to the next life. No vultures means no more of this tradition. Hence Chris and I are in Harrow on a Sunday evening, talking about what we are trying to do with our partners in India, Nepal and Pakistan to put this right.

We are holding safe populations of vultures in captivity, and trying to breed them, until the coast is clear – that is, diclofenac-laced livestock offal is removed from the environment. There has been progress. Licences to produce the drug for veterinary use in the three countries have been withdrawn. And we have three vulture centres up and running, though not yet at full capacity. We need to do more, to prevent one of the biggest extinction disasters yet witnessed.

Even the helpless dodo took longer to be wiped out when its island home Mauritius was colonised by European sailors. It is to be hoped that humanity is in a better position to intervene on behalf of the vultures than we were for the dodo in the seventeenth century.

A NIGHT IN THE WOODS

I've been wanting to spend a night in the wood for a while. The RSPB's Big Wild Sleepout event has given me the impetus I needed. And while it would be intriguing to stay out communing with nocturnal forest creatures, I have a particular search focus. I've not yet proved that the goshawk is in that wood. I and others have seen one around, on widely spaced occasions, but I have no idea if it is a permanent fixture, or where it might be based if in fact it is resident.

The goshawk is a lone hunter, a stealth predator. The male forages while the female protects the nest. He will move from wood to wood, hiding, waiting, attacking. When the young are grown, she goes hunting too. Imagine a buzzard with muscle, after-burners, balls.

I'd be astonished if they nest here. But I'd be much less surprised if it's on their regular hunting routes, or somewhere a juvenile might find refuge in early life.

I have a theory that goshawks do most of their best work long before any of us are normally out of bed. Their vision is beyond our imagination. I reckon it's pretty good in near-darkness too. I'm sure they use the half-light of dawn and dusk for most of their ambushes, perhaps on drowsy woodpigeons or inattentive, myopic grey squirrels. I've also heard that goshawks call to each other in a wood, just before dawn. Perhaps if I am somewhere in its midst, I might hear them – if indeed there are any to hear. At this time of year, young goshawks have jumped from the nest and are dispersing, though not yet far. They can be noisy and gauche at this stage, and there's no risk of me disrupting the breeding cycle. All in all, the Sleepout is timely.

And the weather is fine too. I head down there early evening, to select a site for my hammock. I've decided that I need to be open to the elements, off the ground, inconspicuous, but I want to be able to see and hear around me. The hammock seems perfect, apart from its rainbow of eye-catching stripes.

Selecting a spot takes a little while. There's the practical consideration of two trees the right distance apart with branches the right height for tying the ropes. There's also striking a balance between a discreet site, but one with a reasonable view. In the end I plump for a berth between an ash and a hawthorn, on the eastern edge of the wood. Looking left I can see out over ripened wheat to an isolated oak. Beyond that is a neighbouring wood, where I once saw what I'm sure was a goshawk menacing the resident buzzards. To the right is a wall of trees.

The ash tree creaks in the breeze as I set up. A scraggy robin in moult follows me, hoping for collateral. At dusk I return from a walk in the fields and discover it to be almost dark in the wood. I creep as quietly as possible over dry debris, to minimise disruption to the local routine. Despite my efforts, there is much scuttling and scuffling around me. A large bird flaps clumsily into the canopy high above – a young raptor, I am guessing. I climb into the hammock, which I've slung a good four feet off the ground. I'd like any passing badgers and other animals to be unobstructed.

By now it's so calm I can hear the flitter of wings as a bat patrols the woodland edge. The creaky tree is now stilled and the many rustlings in the wood are mammalian. I can hear something approaching, and a face appears above the undergrowth below the bat's flight path. Ears twitch, and I squint to identify this beast. It turns tail and bounces off, barking. Muntjac: flouncing its white scut at me like a rude gesture. Another one answers its bark from the murk of the wood to my right. They carry on this conversation for ten minutes, as though debating what to do about me. It reminds me why they are known as barking deer in China, from whence they were imported. You wouldn't want to be woken at close range by this voice, in a hammock, in a darkened wood. I try to put this prospect out of my mind.

I lie awake till midnight and beyond. The muntjacs seem to have got used to me, and most of the noise is now coming from a pair of tawny owls, corresponding between the two woods, and the oak in between. After that the wind picks up gently. I doze off for longer than I realise, sleeping in fits and starts in synch with the movement of air across the canopy from the west, approaching like a ripple of sustained applause, sometimes like waves, and sometimes sounding like rain. I realise I've chosen a good spot, sheltered from this prevailing flow, but occasionally a breeze slips through and moves refreshingly across me, like breath. The creaking tree is back, at the tail end of the stronger surges of air. Perhaps the hammock influences this impression, but these are like the creaks of a galleon rolling gently on a heaving ocean. If it rains at all I feel only one drop on a cheek.

For me, 3 am brings the first hint of returning daylight. The owls have been quiet for a while when there comes a new cry: not close, and not loud either. A one-syllable 'kek', repeated at intervals. I might have thought little of it, but oddly, the roosting woodpigeons above my head clatter out of there – this in near total darkness, remember.

There is another reason I wanted to do this. In his cult book *The Goshawk*, written in the 1930s, T.H. White described spending the night in a local wood. He was also trying to be up before the hawk – sparrowhawk, in his case. The goshawk was extinct in Britain at that time, and he'd lost the one he brought from Germany. He disguised himself under a blanket of cress. The camo must have been good, as the closest encounter he had was with a poacher, whose ankle he might have grabbed as he passed. But White never got close to catching a hawk, as one local man bet him 33-1 he wouldn't. Because, he was advised, a hawk can see through walls.

This morning, the robins and wrens come back to life after 5 am, the latter even mustering a blast of song in this otherwise quiet time for birds. By now the wood is swishing vigorously in the gathering wind. A banner of low cloud across the eastern horizon has delayed the burning sunrise. If there's a goshawk in here, it's way ahead of me again. Good luck to it.

CHAPTER NINE

September

A SONG FOR ALL SEASONS

Robins are different. They're *strange*. They like people, for one thing. Well, perhaps I'm jumping to conclusions here. But they are definitely *interested* in people. They approach and scrutinise you with their deep, dark eye, head tilted inquisitively, perhaps suspiciously, perhaps intrigued. What *are* you doing?

The other odd thing that robins do is sing again as summer ends. Their autumn song, though, has a sadder quality. All has been quiet for most of August. The birds are sulking, skulking, regrouping after the frenzy of the breeding season, changing their costumes, scratching around for stuff to eat, out of sight, out of earshot, moving on.

It was 20 August when I heard my first autumn robin this year. It was about 5 am, Monday morning, first light. I was easily roused, waiting to go to hospital to have a damaged knee examined. The robin's song is a lament for the passing of summer. This robin's song, at that melancholy hour, felt like a lament for my passing.

The song is perfectly pitched for the time of year: sombre, soulful, an expression of solemn duty. Almost a requiem. *Sorry folks, but this is my patch, and I'll be defending it to the death from here on in.*

I heard the song again early the next morning, from a hospital bed. It was coming clearly through windows that had been left open on a stuffy night. This was a familiar, friendly voice in an alien world of humming electrics, muffled moans from other wards, shadowy night nurses swishing across the polished floor.

I shared my ward with 95-year-old Ernie, and Harry, in his eighties, and a younger chap recovering from multiple injuries. How much like injured birds we seemed, crouching in corners, quiet and withdrawn, tattoos faded like plumage (for some of us), waiting. Presented with food, or some attention, we flickered to life. And of course we dreamed of being free, of being fully mobile again, like the robin outside. He was challenging us to defy the onset of autumn, to dispute his theme that something has ended. To dare to re-enter the world outdoors that is his.

I was lucky: I got out of hospital the next day, after saying farewell to my fellow inmates. Back home, convalescing, I dragged my leg to the end of the garden to sit down. One of my robins played that song again as I picked plums, relieving the tree of the sweet-fleshed and bitter-skinned fruit under the weight of which its limbs were dragging on the ground.

Robins like my garden, I'm pleased to say. They like most gardens. I have done a few optimistic things to offer them a choice of nest sites – the re-purposed pots, drainpipe, footballs, etc. Robins like their nests to be tucked away under cover. They like a roof, but don't make one for themselves.

My robins have their own ideas. In late March I had noticed dead leaves accumulating in my porch, and then caught glimpses of a small bird flitting away when I opened the front door. I assumed at first it was a wren. Male wrens are hyperactive in spring, building several nest structures and then allowing their mate to choose the one she likes best. I thought that this wren was just showing off, building in a semi-circular pot of ivy I had attached to the wall of my porch, only two feet from the regularly slamming front door. Daring, but impractical. Mrs Wren – her outdoors – would never choose it.

I then discovered that it was actually the robins building it. I did what I could to minimise the disturbance caused by my comings and goings, especially in the early stages of their occupancy, when they would be most likely to desert. Later, once or twice I was unable to resist the temptation to stand on tiptoe and peer in. Usually those dark eyes would be staring straight back at me down the barrel of a beak, chin resting on the lip of the nest. If no parent was sitting, I would carefully check the contents. Four warm eggs soon became four bristly nestlings, craning their gaping yellow flanges, heads lolling on the end of scrawny necks, eyes managing to be both goggly and closed at the same time.

I was amazed and delighted to discover that another pair of robins had all the while been raising a brood in the broken earthenware jar in the back garden. I paced it out and this nest was no more than 30 metres from the porch nesters, which seemed a bit close for birds so territorial. But I think that the house forms the boundary of their territories, their Berlin Wall. They are near, yet far enough away.

My friend Giovanna couldn't believe it when I showed her the nests. 'I was sure you were making this up, just like you make up all your other stories,' she said.

'Listen, Gio,' I replied. 'Conservation isn't just a day job for me.'

'No,' she said, quick as a flash. 'It's a day*dream*…'

About a month later the nests were empty and fledgling robins were hanging around the garden, both front and back. On one occasion I found a speckly youngster exploring the house. It allowed me to catch it without too much fuss, and when I took it outside and gently opened my hand to release it, it sat there clutching my finger for a few minutes, head turned through 180 degrees to stare at me, caught between fear and fascination, before it took flight. It's just as well I'm not superstitious. At one time a robin in the house was taken as a warning that someone was going to die. Now, if they'd said 'leg injury', rather than death, that would have been spooky.

Robins gone, I was once again able to water the ivy pot in the porch. Or so I thought. Picture me tipping water in, when out shoots the robin again, brushing my ear as it passes. They obviously liked this site so much they came back for a second brood. Fortunately, the sitting robin survived the trauma of a light dousing. I watched from the window as it made its way back to the eggs.

Unfortunately, the second brood was not successful. The nestlings died at an early stage. Perhaps a dry period had made food scarce, or one of the adults had succumbed to an accident or predation. Still, one successful brood of four young is pretty good going, and only one adult and one chick needs to survive till the following spring to sustain the population.

For most people the robin is a symbol not of autumn, but of winter, of snow, of Christmas. It's many children's favourite bird;

friendly and familiar. As a woodland species, by origin, rather than a species of open field, the robin has not been so vulnerable to agricultural changes. Our recent milder winters have doubtless also been a factor in keeping its population stable.

In cold snaps their boldness helps to see them through. One ice-cold winter morning I was carrying a huge bowl of crumbs out to my bird table. Halfway there a robin intercepted me, landing not on the bowl but right on top of the mound of crumbs. It began tucking in greedily, throwing crumbs all round itself and over me.

They are bold with people and belligerent with each other. A couple I know put a lovely Christmas wreath on their front door, with a particularly lifelike model robin as its centrepiece. Before long the resident *real* robin was inspecting this closely, and, finding its songs falling on apparently deaf ears, tore it to pieces. So much for Christmas spirit. (And then he had the brass neck to turn up at the back door looking for crumbs, as if butter – or, better still, suet – wouldn't melt…). Robins may look demure and confiding, but they are nature red in tooth – or should that be breast? – and claw. And that's another reason to like them.

Winter will follow, and on the brighter days the robins will still be singing. Not long after that their tune will change again, and other birds will join the chorus, announcing the start of something new.

THE POET IN THE PORCH

I've been getting more and more interested in the life of poet John Clare. Clare was born in 1793 and lived at Helpston, near Stamford. Clare's parents couldn't read or write, but from an early age he developed a love of books and reading, and then of writing about the landscape and rural life around him. Discovered by literary London, he found sudden fame as a young man. Visiting the city, he rubbed shoulders with agents and other famous poets and writers of the day. The culture shock he felt is evident in his own accounts of the time.

Clare wrote of his remorse at the changing rural landscape, following the Enclosure Acts of 1836. We know from his writings that he was upset and disoriented by the drastic changes happening in the environment around him, the clutter and geometry of ownership rules and exclusion.

For reasons we can only speculate about, he went into a steep psychological decline, and was taken to an asylum in Epping Forest.

It was by no means a high-security or oppressive institution, by the standards of the time, and he was free to wander locally, observing life in the forest and meeting local people, including gypsies, whose freedom he envied. But he came to describe his lot as 'cooped up in this Hell of a Madhouse'. And after four years there, he'd had enough. One night in late July 1841 he absconded, and set off to walk the 80 miles home.

I have often wondered at the route he might have taken. I ordered Jonathan Bate's biography of Clare, and the prologue reveals all. A man is described waiting by the Old York Road, something I can readily imagine as I do this often myself, and it passes my village not far from the precise spot Clare was resting, smoking a pipe, making notes. Because, despite his confusion and delusional state, he kept notes of his journey. He seemed to believe by turns that he was Byron, that his daughter was the Queen of England, that he was a prize-fighter so feared that none would challenge him. Most tragically, he believed his childhood sweetheart Mary was waiting for him at Helpston, though she had died in a fire a year after his incarceration at Epping, and since then he had married and had seven children.

It is intriguing to follow this account of the route he took. Approaching Sandy at the end of a day on the road, he headed into Potton to seek a bed for the night. He knocked on a door, and was directed to a public house called the Ram, which stood out on the heath, towards Gamlingay.

Clare found the pub (the house is still there today), but thought better of going in. He had no money. Pressing on, he walked for another five miles or more, despite being lame, and exhausted, and unsure of his way in the darkness. Eventually, he saw a light, 'bright as the moon'. It was hanging over a tollgate. The watchman there informed him he had reached 'Temsford'. The course of the road – and the river – has shifted since then, but I'm fairly sure it is pretty close to here.

Reoriented, he bedded down for the night in the 'porch of a big house'. Perhaps this was in what is now my road or perhaps it was a tiny hamlet two miles further on. Either way, it's oddly pleasing to find a link to the Clare legend this close to home. And I think of him often, and the changing scene of rural England as witnessed by users of this road, as I watch the traffic roar by today.

Clare's cottage has been opened to the public. It makes an evocative and thought-provoking day out. When I visited, my favourite moment was inside the restored dovecote, with messages to the poet from visiting children slotted into the pigeon-holes. I loved this one and made a note of it: 'John should have been allowed in the fields,' wrote Phoebe, 'but he shouldn't have drunk so much.'

RINGS THAT TELL STORIES

I have mixed feelings when I find a dead bird. My first thought of course is remorse that it has died. Then my rational self kicks in and I think to myself, well, it died anyway and in a sense maybe it's lucky that I found it. For one thing, it means I can get a closer look. My non-birdy friends – and some of my birdy ones too – think me a bit macabre for this. I've even stopped the car – carefully, of course – to see what the unusual-looking road-kill is.

Besides identifying the bird, I can also check its legs for any rings it may be wearing. I've had quite a high success rate with retrieving leg rings from dead birds in recent years, and although removing the rings can be a slightly yucky business, it is, in the end, why the bird ringers put rings on the birds in the first place.

Ringing is done by people who are fully trained and licensed to catch birds in controlled conditions, using mist nets. They catch birds both to ring them and to record the details if they are already ringed. This includes weighing and measuring. It's a skilled business, and the birds must be very carefully and briefly handled to ensure that they are not damaged or distressed by the experience.

The first ring I recovered was from a blue tit, which I found dead, and rather flattened, on the drive here at The Lodge. The date was 6 April 1997. I carefully removed the ring and made a note of the number. Each ring has an address on it – British Museum, London SW9 – and a unique number code, in this case J13 5543. When I submitted my report by telephone I was asked a few questions, such as exactly where I had found the bird. This is the most important thing. The point of ringing is to establish something about birds' movements and longevity, and cause of death.

'So it was a road casualty, then?' I was asked.

'Not necessarily,' I replied, and not just because I didn't care much for the idea of this wee bird having been killed by someone driving a car at the HQ of Europe's largest wildlife conservation charity. I *happened* to find it on the road. It might, theoretically, have died there of old age. Well, we're supposed to be scientific, aren't we?

It's quite exciting waiting for your report to come back, even though this can take some months. Where was it ringed? Russia? Peru? Would my find reveal some remarkable feat of hitherto unsuspected endurance on the part of this species? In due course my blue tit letter arrived, from the British Trust for Ornithology.

It turned out that the bird had been ringed two and a half years earlier, aged one, sex unknown, on 14 October 1994, zero kilometres from where I had found it, by a man I know, Andy Evans, of our Conservation Science department. Oh well, no globe-trotting blue tit this, but it *was* almost noteworthy how little it had travelled, and how old it was (three and a half years is a good age for a tiny bird) and great to know something of this particular bird's past, no matter how narrow its horizons. Blue tits must like it here.

In the end every little bit of information is useful: even the mundane helps us to build pictures and patterns of bird behaviour. And who's to say it hadn't been to Peru and back in the interim?

My next find definitely had done some travelling. I couldn't identify it, another road squash, this time at Dunwich on the Suffolk coast, on 7 June 1997. I assumed it was a sparrow, but when my report came back it revealed to me that I'd actually found a whitethroat, sex unknown, ringed on 11 May 1994, aged one year plus, again zero kilometres from where it was squashed. However, whitethroats being migratory, I could be reasonably certain that it had been to and from central Africa three times in that period. Just think, surviving all that perilous migration just to be hit by a car in Dunwich. Assuming it *was* hit by a car, of course…

Then there was my dead sparrowhawk, found beside Pitsford Reservoir in Northamptonshire. I was intrigued by this one, as it seemed to have been predated, and the plucking seemed to have been done by another bird, as the feathers were intact – plucked, not bitten. I thought it might have been a juvenile bird, recently ringed in the nest and killed soon after fledging. The report from the BTO told me it had been ringed nearby just over a year earlier, a mature male, two years plus.

And then there was the song thrush that I found, again on a road, near where I live. This was a female, ringed four years earlier: an impressive age for a thrush in the wild.

Besides all the important data that is analysed, there are great stories that emerge from recovered rings. There is the occasional remarkable example of the widely travelled wren or the inexhaustible blackbird. But what's amazing is how long-lived some birds turn out to be, like the 35-year-old oystercatcher (born in the same year as me, ringed at Snettisham that August, and recovered in Norway), the 12-year-old swift (flying non-stop to and from Africa since 1990) and the gannet aged 60. Imagine: 60 years old and still plummeting head first into the North Sea from a great height. Finding out these things has to be worth examining a dead bird's leg for a ring.

RETURN OF THE EXILE

I've just seen a bird that's been missing from most of lowland Britain for about 150 years. Despite this physical absence, I would guess you are familiar with this bird if you are over the age of eight. It's a large bird too, though not a bird of prey. You may have encountered it in fairy tales, fables, Greek mythology, Roman art, the Koran, the Old Testament, Arthurian legend, Shakespeare (he was always on about them), *Don Quixote* or Harry Potter.

Besides our own uplands and cliffs, it is found all around the northern half of the globe, from arid deserts to snow-packed Himalayan peaks, in major cities and quiet rural villages. But it hasn't been found in Tempsford, Beds (for example) since probably 1845. I'm estimating this from the recorded dates of its disappearance from London (1830) – 50 miles south of here – and Northants (1850) – 30 miles north-west. It is to the north and west that this species retreated, under a sustained Victorian-era onslaught of guns and traps.

If you haven't worked out what it is yet, this is probably because, like me, you haven't fully grasped that it's even missing. The good news is that it looks as if it is coming back.

And I've just seen one. I'm still slightly disoriented by this. Improbably, I saw it first thing in the morning, while still in bed. My bed is by the window and, propped on an elbow, I can admire the view from here. I can see across to Esme Wood, about a half mile away. And there, on this morning, a large bird took to the sky. It circled, and began to head in my direction. I took it at first to be a buzzard, but it made a sudden and dramatic tumble earthward, before rising again and continuing my way.

As it got closer, I could see that it was a crow. Not the usual carrion crow or rook or jackdaw, though. Bigger. Much bigger. Bigger still. Materialising overhead, as I craned to the pane, was a raven, of all things. The long-lost raven. Two feet long, four feet across its spread wings. Shaggy-necked, sword-tailed. And not a mountain refuge for 200 miles. Blimey.

Perhaps the first raven seen in Tempsford for 163 years? That's a long time gone. No question: this was a moment, in more ways than one. My excitement was tinged with intrigue, and a little apprehension. This is a bird with a longer history of association with people than almost any other, but we have totally lost touch with it, us lowland Britons. It's fair to say we've been bewitched by it, even in its absence, but are we ready to have it back? How will reality compare with the lore?

The raven has provoked fear, respect and awe in equal measure. It is a bird of portent and omen; sometimes good, sometimes ill. Try to imagine how its carrion-eating habits might have appeared to our medieval ancestors. Helpful, in most instances, grotesque and macabre in others, not least at the hangman's gibbet and on the battlefield.

Ravens cleared up a lot of our medieval mess, not least in major cities. They sustained a reputation for having supernatural power, which endured even through the Victorian era, when the gun was turned against them. Many landowners were content to see them exterminated, though they would not do the deed themselves for fear of the likely curse that would result.

London, of course, held on to a few ravens – the pinioned birds in the Tower. The consequences for the nation of losing these, of course, are too dire to contemplate. We won't be repeating the mistake made by the Hapsburg dynasty.

Aside from its less appealing habits, the raven is renowned for its intelligence, for its spectacular display flights, and for its sense of play. It is, to some who know it, the bird that is most like us. It will be good to have around. It may present some challenges – crows usually do – but finding room for all our birds, even the large and predatory, is part of sustaining a balanced and well-ordered environment, complete with the streaks of wildness that help to keep us properly oriented.

The bird I saw was probably a prospector from a family known to be breeding near Woburn safari park, not far south of here. It remains to be seen how widely they will return. Persecution will no doubt remain an issue. Only recently, a gamekeeper convicted of killing protected species in Shropshire had recorded 40 ravens in his 'Diary of death'.

Some people might find ravens a little spooky, but I'm hoping for more raven moments. Back in the day, ravens were widely taken for 'earthly agents of the supernatural forces that were presumed to run the show'.[4] I'm not so sure we need to think of them very much differently today.

LEAVE IT OUT

Recently, there was a low-speed drama in our road, and I was at the centre of it. In scenes reminiscent of an incident in the sitcom *Father Ted*, when Dougal is stuck behind the wheel of a milk float running out of control at four miles per hour, I found myself desperately shovelling piles of mushy leaves into garden sacks at the roadside, while a leaf-sucking council lorry bore down on me. The lorry may not have been moving as fast as Dougal's milk float, but nevertheless...

So how did such a scenario come about, you may – if you are still reading – be wondering? Well, the end of our road is overhung by mature deciduous trees, mainly sycamore and chestnut. Each autumn, the fallen leaves bank up against a roadside brick wall. A thick, damp mound of leaves had been building up over time, encroaching onto the tarmac. I had already been down there on a couple of trips to bag up the leaves, to use as garden compost or mulch.

Back home, I'd been piling it up around the base of my yet-to-mature hedge plants – beech, hawthorn, holly, hornbeam, guilder rose and the like – to give them a bit of nourishment and to suppress weed growth. This is very important in the early development of a hedge, and particularly so in dry weather, like recently, when moisture is at a premium. Leaves add to the organic content of soil, boosting its moisture-retaining properties and the activities of important soil-conditioning organisms such as earthworms.

My beech trees in particular haven't been growing so well. I had protected them from weed competition with plastic sheeting, but this can create the dry soil to which beeches are vulnerable. Even

---

4   In the words of Derek Ratcliffe, author of *The Raven*.

mature beeches are vulnerable to drying out – making them one of the trees we can expect to see fewer of if climate disruption results in drier weather all round, and drier soils, impervious to irregular downpours.

Anyway. Back to the drama. I had taken a day off and was making an early-morning foray to the station when I noticed that a council team had arrived and men were raking the leaves into lines for the sweeper. I rolled my window down.

'Do you do anything with the leaves?' I called over to one of the rakers, thinking they might be going to some community recycling scheme.

'No, we just take 'em down the tip,' he replied.

'Would it be okay if I had some of them for compost then, please?' I asked.

'Sure – help yourself,' he told me, adding, somewhat melodramatically, I thought, 'As long as you can get here before the lorry sweeps 'em up...'

I was home and back in no time, armed with my shovel and a pile of sacks. The lorry was just getting into position for the remorseless, steady, sweep and suck. I couldn't expect them to hold back, drive more slowly, say, or leave any leaves. They had a job to do and probably other leaf piles to hoover up, after all.

So this is how I came to be there, frantically bagging up in the path of the lorry. I hate to see waste, even if it's only waste that's being wasted. I got two boots-full of leaves in the end, about ten sacks in all, before the rest was sucked to oblivion. As I'm sure you've guessed, I managed to roll out of the path of the vast wheels just in time before the machine swept past. I can't be sure, but at that moment I probably looked like Bruce Willis, or some other action hero. Or perhaps I looked more like Dougal from *Father Ted*.

CREEPING REALISATIONS

I like spiders but they do creep me out a bit. My head says 'cool', my heart (or wherever mild phobias lurk) says 'eek'. That said, I don't have arachnophobia anywhere near as seriously as some people I know. In fact, I'm much better these days. I had it pretty badly as a child, not helped by that unforgettable scene in *The Incredible Shrinking Man* when the incredibly shrunk man in question is chased by a giant house spider, which by this stage of the narrative is the size of a garage in relation to our hero. That has to be an arachnophobe's worst nightmare: shrinking, and being lost in the cellar. Luckily TISM has the presence of mind to fight off his assailant with a pin.

Of course I'm much too grown up and brave nowadays to worry about getting in a tangle with invertebrates, but I do like spiders to stay where I can keep an eye on them; especially the big ones that invite themselves indoors in late summer.

It's not obvious why spiders have this additional spook factor. I'm deeply appreciative and not a bit worried about other crawly things, even the ones that can deliver a painful sting. Six legs, or even 26, I am fine with. But I'm sure it's not about the numbers. Perhaps it's the movement. Spiders have a kind of tickling gait, and I am avowedly ticklish.

I can live with that, and spiders, and with the ever-present threat of being woken in the night by one trotting across my forehead. It's a small risk, and I might not even wake up if it does happen, but the chances of it occurring are greatly increased at this time of year.

To limit the chances of it happening I usually scoop up visiting spiders in a jar and put them out in the garden, though I know that the bright lights and warmth of the house will probably draw them close again, to burgle their way back in by whatever cunning route they have mapped.

Human beings are by no means the only danger lurking within. There are spiders in this house, of a type that inhabit the ceiling, where they set their delicate but deadly traps – intended in part for other spiders. These ones are known as *Pholcus phalangioides* and they are slow, measured, balletic in their movements, and can knit a deadly mesh around any unsuspecting fellow invertebrate that wanders within range, before the hapless victim knows what is happening.

There are more spiders around than might be immediately obvious to the untrained observer. I know one spider aficionado who counted over 100 species in and around his house and garden, not too far from here. He told me he discourages the spider-eating varieties, lest they limit the appeal of his house to new and interesting arachnids. I attended a spider awareness session he ran one day, and we collected specimens that we shook gently out of the foliage of shrubs and low branches. What was oddly thrilling was not just their abundance, but also their variety. I was left thinking of them as a kind of safety net – web, if you prefer – under-hanging the ecosystem around them. Mostly unseen, but no less vital for that.

And the fear factor of our massive, hairy house spiders was finally put in perspective and laid to rest by an experience I had in Amazonia. I went on a night-time walk into the swamp forest, wearing a head torch. I was part of a group of Earthwatch volunteers, and we had local guides to help us stick to the paths and avoid getting lost. Our guide explained to us through an interpreter that if you aren't careful the spirits of the forest will try to trick you, to get you lost, and that the jaguar is out there, waiting patiently for this to happen. It was a hair-raising excursion, in places, and one of the highlights was the discovery of a tarantula, emerging agonisingly slowly from a crevice in a path-side tree, a metre or so above our heads.

On the way back we stopped again at this place, so that 'Flashbulb' – as we had dubbed him; a man who had to photograph everything, a lot – could get the shot he'd missed on the outward traipse. By the time the tarantula had obliged, and the necessary picture been secured, we realised that our small group had become detached from the rest of the party. This was mildly perturbing, but became more so a short time later when we arrived at a fork in the track. We hadn't anticipated there would be a choice to make. One way pointed to safety, the other, presumably, to the waiting jaguar. Our thoughts quickly returned to our guide's advice about the spirits of the forest and their tricks to get you lost, and to the waving forelimbs of that very shaggy spider in the tree, teasing Flashbulb and undoubtedly luring him, and us, into this trap.

There was a rustling just up ahead, on one of the tracks. Imagine our relief when its source was traced to our guide, a tiny man with a large machete and what looked, at that moment, like an even wider grin.

DARK ANGEL

The RSPB takes hundreds of calls in late summer from people troubled by an apparent absence of birds. It is true that this time of year can seem eerily quiet, and painfully lacking in avian action. Not to play down the disturbing and ongoing declines of many species, but 'twas probably ever thus, where our birdlife is concerned. There are still birds around, mercifully, but they tend to hide. Late summer is a time of relative inertia, and birds can afford to loaf around under cover. Energy requirements are lower, and plumage is being moulted, making them less mobile. It is a good decision to sit tight in these circumstances.

You have, therefore, to look a bit harder for the ones that are still active. I am scanning the damp stubbles of the blue-clay plain near my home. There is not a lark in sight, nor a pipit. I am lucky enough to pick up on the dashing flight of a falcon, which is zipping low over the bristling stems. I would have assumed it a kestrel, but I can see the blue-grey back and the 'moustachial' stripes of a hobby. *Arriba!* It is in view for several seconds, but I lose it against a distant hedgerow, as a pair of skittish woodpigeons rise in its path and decoy my eye away.

Perhaps the rapid raptor was looking for larks and pipits too, hoping to flush a skulking part-feathered juvenile from within the dampened stalks; or to chance on a big insect, like a dragonfly. It may have been heading south for the winter.

Further on I flush a wheatear from the field margin, right under the flight path taken by the hobby. Its white rear, from which the bird derives its current common name, flashes tellingly as it dances away to perch on a stalk, to better regard me and the plains around. This bird is definitely just passing through, another little gem to make up for the general absence of more familiar birds, and some consolation for what feels like the slightly premature onset of autumn.

To the migratory bird, the A1 – the Great North Road – here at our village, as at any point between London and Scotland, might look like an obvious route-finder south, come autumn. The swallows and martins are gathering over Lammie's Farm to the east. Its deep grass, mucky yard and mature broadleaves are all issuing insect fuel for the birds' imminent journey.

Further east again is Tempsford's secret World War II airfield (which I mentioned earlier), scene of night-time missions to the Low Countries of north Europe. Beyond that, at the National Trust's Wimpole Hall, the other day I found a pageant of 500 house martins gathered around the chimneys, adding to the sense of the long, grassy avenue in front of the house as a runway pointing south. I later found out that it has actually served this purpose in times of need.

Another hobby comes through: a streak of ochre and avian elasticity announced to me by one of the swallows – perhaps a civic voice of some kind – issuing an anxious *pleep pleep pleep*, interrupting the relaxed community twittering.

And so I have ten minutes with my eyes glued to this fizzing, athletic little falcon, as do the hirundines between me and it. It makes one pass quite low, the smaller birds making way like iron filings repelled by this larger but otherwise similar scimitar shape, with the deep beating wings. There's a breathless drama that seems to envelop hobbies, a thrilling-ness to their dexterity, that raises the pulse. I've seen them over the farmyard along the road, slicing through the air, as though fencing somehow with the juvenile swallows, swiping and missing, swiping again, and missing again. I've seen one chase a martin to an ever greater height, looping to get above it, and stooping, over and over again, as though darning the wind, until both were out of sight, I imagine exhausted. And sometimes groups of hobbies hawk for chafers on set-aside fields near The Lodge, putting on an evening air show low over the weedy fields, the air singing sometimes through their feathers.

Today's bird drifts upwards on September's rising, rain-flecked winds, then banks, dips, cruises overhead. The flock below gives a collective shiver. But *Falco subbuteo* does not attack. It climbs higher in wide circles, against a pile of blue-black cumulus. I sense it is surveying, like a cheetah on the plains, for any signs of weakness in the herd below. Then finally it is lost from sight in the heavens, epic as a John Martin cloudscape, like an angel of hirundine doom, making itself known, and that it will be back – whether here or further south, or somewhere beyond on the annual pilgrimage to Africa. A shepherd of a kind, on an ancient odyssey, rounding up the hunger-weakened strays, for which there may be no further chances and for which this might be – if they straggle – the final voyage.

THE SECRET NEIGHBOUR

Sometimes, it takes a bird to die before you know it's there. This happened recently in my neighbourhood. I think I know my patch quite well. I survey it quite regularly, after all, and I live in it, of course. But this species hasn't been on my radar, let alone my records, until now.

It was discovered by someone who lives along the road from me. She sent me a message at work, headed 'Dead bird at Tempsford'. There were photos attached, showing a headless sprawl at the laneside, of mostly brown and black-barred feathers. My immediate thought was owl, presumably tawny owl. Tawnies are present, and vocal, and very much on the resident list. But a closer inspection revealed longer wing (primary) feathers, and a warmer orange-brown colouring. It was a long-eared owl. Definitely a noteworthy record. It would have been preferable alive, of course, but then alive long-eared owls are notoriously difficult to see – on which I say more shortly.

Fortunately, the remains are still there. It might yet be possible to establish a cause of death. A fox may have eaten part of it. But was a fox the cause of death? An X-ray at the vet might tell us more.

Needless to say, the find got me delving in the library for more information on long-eared owls. Now that I know they may be present locally, I am going to need a bit more knowhow to increase my chances of finding or watching one. What is immediately confirmed by the books is that long-eared owls are elusive and evasive creatures. They are the least researched of all our birds of prey, and as exclusively nocturnal as any of the owls. They are also less distinctively audible than most, and nomadic. Unlike the tawny, which is a familiar bird to many people, if only by call, long-eared owls are adapted to sustained hunting in flight and cover impressive distances. Tawny owls never made it across the Irish Sea, for example. Long-eareds, meanwhile, are widespread in Ireland. They are long-winged and lightweight, a bit like barn owls.

On the positive side, as far as finding them is concerned, they can turn up pretty much anywhere. They don't share the tawny's reliance on mature woodland trees. A celebrated example of this was the one that appeared in the lower branches of a birch tree that stands outside our post room here at The Lodge. Undeterred by the passing staff, or the groups that gathered regularly to admire it, it used this daytime roost site for a number of days. In due course it vanished again, no doubt off on its wanderings, perhaps back to northern continental Europe.

They are hunters of the margins of things, and they go where the food is. They nest in relatively flimsy trees, including tall hedges, and they like to use the derelict nests of crows and pigeons. Small rodents are their main prey, and they have exceptionally well-developed hearing. Ironically, the 'ears' that give them their name are not connected to this hearing faculty at all. At almost two inches long, these tufts are impressive, but perhaps 'horns' would be a better name for them. Their exact purpose is debated, but they probably serve the birds well as decoration, and for impressing each other, or would-be assailants.

The young birds might be even more likely to spook you, if you encounter one in a darkened shrubbery. They also make particularly eerie creaking noises. It is not hard to see why our ancestors were often deeply superstitious of owls, even if the harshness with which owls have often been treated is a little harder to understand, in these more enlightened times.

For obvious reasons, the exact numbers of long-eared owls in this country are difficult to estimate. Populations ebb and flow according to prey numbers, especially voles. Intriguingly, our UK owls can sometimes be joined in winter by a huge and mostly unseen influx of continental birds. Fishermen and oil rig workers are sometimes surprised to find these wide-eyed stowaways on board storm-lashed rigs and vessels out at sea. The vagrants will pause to rest mid-voyage, before rejoining the invasion force that crosses the North Sea and slips into our culverts, spinneys, gardens and who knows where else, from suburbia to upland conifer forests. Wandering long-eared owls are happy to form loose colonies, and very occasionally they will hunt in winter daylight.

My search for a live one is ongoing. I've been looking more closely in local copses and tall hedges. I am alert now to the possibility that the owl shape that passes over the road ahead, on a murky night, might just be one of these enigmatic wanderers. I like very much the idea of these intriguing birds living secretly in our midst and around us. I'd love to meet the orange-orbed gaze of one, some day, in a familiar place, but I won't be too disappointed if the secret neighbour continues to evade me. That, in the end, is what most wild birds are good at, and few more so than the night owl with the horns.

FIRECREST

I saw a tree fall the other day. I reported my observation, as it seemed to be quite a thing to have witnessed; especially considering there wasn't a breath of wind at the time. What are the chances of that? I asked. This was quite a big tree – a Scots pine. It had probably been standing for 120 years, since the Peels owned the estate and planted it with a variety of trees. 'Depends how long you spend looking out of the window,' they replied. 'Typical scientists,' I muttered, 'answering questions with more questions.'

I honestly hadn't been looking for long. And I don't say this just because I was at work at the time. Our department looks out over the woods of The Lodge nature reserve. We have a cedar that brushes the window, and when parties of tits and their friends pass through its branches I have to make sure that the goldcrests aren't firecrests. We have firecrests round here, and I have yet to see one. That's why I was looking out of the window. Briefly.

I popped out – at lunchtime – to make sure the tree hadn't fallen on anyone, or anything. I couldn't see any collateral damage – of course, there could have been a woodpecker under there, I suppose. But hey. They know the occupational hazards.

Two days later these same scientists staged a ringing demonstration in The Lodge garden. They put up a mist net, and soon word was spreading that they'd caught something properly interesting. That's right – a firecrest. I and many others took the opportunity to go out and find out more about ringing, and to see a firecrest up close. In the end they caught three different firecrests that day, making a total of six ever caught in Bedfordshire, five of them right here.

I've only ever seen one abroad, where they are far from scarce. It is what you might call my bogey bird. I'll see one off my own bat one day; and for now I will console myself that at least I've seen a tree fall over, unassisted.

Southward Equinox

CHAPTER TEN

October

THE REFUGE OF NO RETURN

As September became October, I went south with the birds. I made landfall on the starkly beautiful island of Cyprus, in the eastern Mediterranean, to meet colleagues working to protect the birds that choose Cyprus as their migration route to Africa. Millions of birds do this each autumn, funnelling down the eastern edge of the island. They come to rest and refuel, building up their energy reserves for the final push south. It is a long and hazardous journey, made more so by the illegal trapping activities that await them here.

In 2001, it was estimated that up to 12 million birds were killed each year at the hands of Cypriot trappers. Bird trapping is big business and, although many of the birds are tiny, in the volumes they are caught their market value is high. Most end up in local restaurants, where they are served up as a speciality dish called *ambelopoulia*, behind closed doors.

The trapping and trade make some people very wealthy. The trappers use mist nets and limesticks, which birds perch on and stick to: 150 species have been recorded, including the rare and threatened. Action must be taken to stem the supply from the trappers, to stop the demand from the restaurants, to encourage the authorities to make law enforcement a priority, and to change attitudes.

The odds have seemed overwhelming, but the RSPB and BirdLife Cyprus have stepped up the action in the last three years. After just three days with our team, I have seen for myself the difference we have been able to make.

Autumnal Cyprus is parched pale, a landscape of rocky hillsides, dry salt lakes and scattered scrub, etched with white tracks. Most of the illegal trapping is in the south-east corner of the island, including the eastern Sovereign Base Area (SBA) administered by the UK authorities. We are working with the SBA Police here, and elsewhere with the Game Fund Service, the Cypriot government department responsible for wildlife protection.

RSPB Investigations staff have filmed illegal trapping activity on Sovereign Base land. Soon after, the SBA Police arrested trappers and seized hundreds of mist nets, attracting a lot of publicity to reinforce the message that illegal trapping would not be tolerated. We then turned our attention to the restaurants, and with an undercover BBC camera crew we filmed *ambelopoulia* being served.

Cypriot conservation societies and BirdLife had made an official complaint that Cyprus was failing in its duty to protect migratory birds under the Bern Convention. Hundreds of people, many of them RSPB members, wrote to the Cypriot authorities to register their disgust at this annual massacre. The Cypriot government promised to do more to prevent it.

In the autumn we employed two project officers to monitor 60 survey squares, so that trapping activity could be measured year on year, working closely with the SBA Police and the Game Fund Service. The authorities also came down hard on restaurants still serving *ambelopoulia*, and high-profile raids were carried out in busy restaurants, again amid a blaze of publicity. A marked reduction in trapping – and therefore bird deaths – resulted. At the time of writing, there was also much less evidence of *ambelopoulia* being served openly in Cypriot restaurants.

The following autumn we employed two project officers again.

One was seconded from his job as an RSPB warden, the other lived in Cyprus (they cannot be named for security reasons). I was impressed by their familiarity with the landscape and their ability to spot a limestick or netting pole at 500 metres.

On the morning of my first day, we met two animal rights activists, in Cyprus to take direct action against trappers. Our advice was not to interfere with trappers' equipment, where they found it, but to notify the authorities. We learned later that day that they had ignored this advice and had been caught by some trappers in the act of removing nets. One of them had been assaulted.

The committee of BirdLife Cyprus met that evening. It is made up of Cypriots and UK expatriates, and at the time was under the chairmanship of the charismatic Melis Charalambides. Melis has been busy. He reported on meetings with the Minister of the Interior, the Assistant Chief of Police, the District Commander of the SBA Police, three MPs, three other government ministers and the Attorney General. These high-ranking officials are demanding tougher action from their staff.

Melis accompanied us the following morning. It was a typical day for the team, not exactly my normal day job, scouring the rocky capes for signs of illegal activity. I learned to recognise telltale stands of acacia, planted in a characteristic pattern, creating 'net rides', or channels, across which mist nets are slung in order to trap birds. These groves are irrigated to produce fresh growth, creating oases of greenery in the dusty landscape.

Birds moved all around us – swallows were constantly overhead, sweeping seawards in steady flocks, while chats, wheatears and warblers flitted from rock to bush to wire, their colours vibrant in the crisp autumn light. I have a picture etched on my retinas of a male redstart, glowing against the azure Mediterranean.

We entered the acacia grove to discover the evidence of a night's trapping. The mist nets had been removed, but the base poles remained, embedded in concrete. Trampled earth was spattered with blood and sprinkled with feathers from turtle doves, cuckoos, orioles… I found the remains of two long-eared owls, killed and discarded, face down in the dirt. Not on the menu. Speaker wires trailed in the dirt, leading to audio equipment in the trees used to issue a constant stream of bird calls through the night, to lure passing migrants.

The seduction is complete. Little wonder these groves are such a magnet, an apparent sanctuary, from which millions of birds find no way out. A refuge of no return. The mist nets are virtually transparent and soon fill with the shapes of struggling songbirds.

'What we have seen this morning is crazy,' said Melis, leaving the net rides, his mobile phone pressed to his ear as he called the authorities. Our dismay was compounded by the fact that our field workers had reported this trapping site some days ago. The authorities had not yet taken the chance to seize the equipment, never mind attempted a raid to catch the trappers in the act.

Later, we called two Game Fund officers to the site where the animal rights activist had been assaulted. The trappers were still active. Our arrival was enough to scare them off, although we would have preferred the officers to have attempted an arrest.

We brought up key issues with the SBA Police when we visited them on the morning of my last day. District Commander Jim Guy left us in no doubt that he and his officers were fully committed. He told us:

> We've seen a substantial reduction in trapping activity. We've probably deterred about 90 per cent of the casual poachers, but the business element is still active and no doubt still making big money out there. Make no mistake, these are highly skilled and devious people, with a system of lookouts and mobile phones that makes our job much more difficult. My officers aren't armed and we are often dealing with people who are. But we will find a way. If you flew over the Pyla range three years ago, you would have seen netting activity everywhere. That has changed now. I'm satisfied there are no restaurants on SBA land selling ambelopoulia now. There's a greater political will now, too.

At the time of my visit there had been three arrests, compared with nine the previous year.

'What we need are arrests with a heavy sentence,' Jim Guy told us. 'It would help if we increased the fines, but that's in the hands of the judge. A prison sentence would be a great deterrent too.'

Encouraged, we left to visit another of the survey squares, just north of the popular resort of Ayia Napa. We parked in the shade of a chapel. A storm was brewing to the north, hills looming bright against the darkening sky. Hundreds of swallows, martins and bee-eaters called overhead, surfing the currents high above the pomegranate orchard near where we searched for limesticks, finding little but a dead sparrow with glue- and dust-encrusted feet.

We were set to leave when we saw the unmistakable fluttering wings of trapped birds. We called the Game Service. The urge to rush to the aid of the trapped birds was powerful, but we needed authorisation. This was granted, as long as it was 'safe'. We hurried to assist the birds, just as a rainstorm reached us. I've seen plenty of pictures of birds in this predicament, but until I saw it for myself I hadn't fully grasped how squalid limesticks are. As we got closer, we could see two birds on the first stick – a yellow wagtail and a fan-tailed warbler. In their distress, their instinct had been to peck each other, as though each was the agent of the other's misfortune. Fresh blood on the tiny warbler's face contrasted vividly with the lemon-yellow breast of the wagtail, their delicate feathers equally incongruous on the gunge-covered stick.

A particular brand of spray-on fabric conditioner is effective in loosening the hold of glue on the birds' feet and plumage. Using this, we soon freed these first two casualties, but spotted more dangling pathetically in other bushes. Working quickly, we found and removed 21 sticks, freeing 17 birds, some stuck by the feet, others by the tail, a wing, or the face. Each quivering bird felt hot to hold, its liquid black eyes wide and penetrating.

We unstuck a Cyprus pied wheatear (a species found nowhere else), a tree pipit, a whinchat, eight yellow wagtails, two fan-tailed warblers and four willow warblers. Each fluttered and clambered to the undergrowth, in varying states of shock and debilitation.

'Welcome to Cyprus,' my colleague muttered bitterly. He loves most things about his beautiful island, but not this. As we worked, we saw the pick-up truck that had rolled slowly to a halt at the far end of the field, joined soon afterwards by another vehicle. Our action was not going unnoticed.

There's a lot of job satisfaction in freeing wild birds from such a fate, although I know in my heart of hearts that this was a token effort. The tasks of protecting birds in the long term – of keeping all those others we won't be able to rescue out of nets and off limesticks – are in the main done by people behind desks, in the corridors of decision-making power and in the courts. But for today we could see the product of our labour: we had held the birds in our hands, and we had released them.

We loaded the clump of sticks into the boot of the car, and headed back to dry off, update our charts, file our reports, tell our story to anyone who would listen, and keep the pressure on.

PIER PRESSURE

Even in decline, and depopulated, piers retain their allure. Stages over the waves. Little promontories over the edge of the world. Visiting Brighton, I find myself more intrigued by – more drawn to – the part-crumpled, part-skeletal remains of the West Pier than the still-glowing neon strip of its eastern counterpart, a mile along the strand. These days, mind you, it is birds that take the stage.

The West Pier was closed in 1975. After this, it withstood the waves for years, including the drama of 1987's great storm, which knocked over so many trees, and left starlings without roost sites. Their vast, spiralling flocks moved to the crumbling pier and began roosting there instead as it slowly disintegrated around them.

Peregrines returned in the 1990s, taking a box on Sussex Heights, a residential apartment block in central Brighton. The starling flocks would have been, for peregrines, one of the attractions of the place. In late 2002 a large part of the pier finally sagged into the sea. The following spring, fire ripped through it, leaving the skeleton of girders we see today.

I had been at a wedding at Alfresco's on the seafront all day, enjoying my place in this human flock, but all the while with one eye on this quiet seaward pier, beyond the heaped pebbles. A sense of quiet drama settled on the pier, especially when a near full moon began to arc across the evening sky. There was an Edward Hopper atmosphere, as couples strolled past the lamp-lit security guard.

The gulls had not yet tucked themselves away for the night. They still cruised overhead, their calls reminding us repeatedly that this is both the seaside, and a city. Even then, in the gloom, I hadn't given up on seeing one of Brighton's peregrine falcons. Urban peregrines can hunt by night. The partial darkness can give them an added advantage, as if they needed it.

I was rewarded by seeing a falcon on Sunday morning. It circled tightly, against a glaze of clouds, like a Spitfire among the lumbering bombers, the gulls. It was supervising the pier far below, and anything that might use it as a departure point for migration abroad. The stage, though buckled and rusting, was still set.

A TASTE OF HONEY

The word on the streets – or country lanes – of north Bedfordshire is that there are honey buzzards passing over, in unprecedented numbers. I should look out for them. It's an odd collision of words: 'honey' and 'buzzard'. It could be a character from a children's story. I am intrigued by the implausibility of this species: a bird of prey – a raptor – with a taste for raiding bee and wasp nests. It's so unlike what other birds of prey – common buzzards, for example – do that it is worthy of a raised eyebrow. And a delve into the literature.

I find it intriguing that they have learned to specialise in finding – and raiding – these hives, and that they can eat the contents without being stung to, um, buzzardry. I have conservation colleagues who saw one in action recently, in India, where we are captive-breeding vultures that are threatened with extinction (see page 197). A honey buzzard attacked a beehive in a tree near the vulture enclosure. Having knocked it down, the buzzard made off, and the apoplectic bees went looking for a scapegoat. Staff at the centre had to flee.

So what are they doing over here in October? There has hardly been a wasp in evidence this autumn, compared to most years. The pickings cannot currently be rich for such specialist birds. But they are just passing through; migrating from northern Europe to Africa.

I think (and hope) I may just have seen two of them. I have been watching the sky for parts of the day, but it is the calling – an almost wader-like, two-syllable whistle, from high overhead – that captures my attention. There are two buzzard-sized raptors heading due south. Too high to make out any plumage details, but the call is not one I recognise – and definitely not the almost feline mew of a common buzzard.

There are a few honey buzzards breeding in the UK, in widely scattered locations, from the New Forest to Speyside. They feed the contents of hives to their growing young. This includes honeycombs and larvae, which they will dig out of the ground, seemingly blasé about the attention of the irate occupants. Besides this, they take the usual range of buzzard food – small things and dead things. Nothing too challenging.

Word has been reaching us from the 'raptor camp' conservation volunteers in Malta that migrating honey buzzards are still being shot down illegally by groups of hunters. Perhaps some of our own, or perhaps Sweden's breeding birds. One was taken in for veterinary treatment, but couldn't be saved: a sad and wasteful end to an intriguing bird on an already improbable journey.

THE FORT

The Lodge, Sandy, Beds. As well as being quite possibly one of the UK's best known addresses, it is also a great place to work. It's not just me who thinks so. The RSPB has scored high marks in polls to find the UK's top employer. We were 37th at the last count – the highest position for a charity. Not that the wages are great, as you might expect. But if you care about conservation, working for the RSPB has a lot to recommend it. And we are driven on by our loyal membership.

I'm pleased to report that The Lodge is getting even better. The nature reserve that surrounds us here has been undergoing some changes. It's fair to say that we are now, on our own doorstep, here at the RSPB's HQ, doing habitat restoration on a landscape scale. We are in the process of turning The Lodge from somewhere that is nice to work, and quite good for wildlife, into a place that is of real conservation significance, and a flagship site of which we can all be very proud, and delighted to show to visitors.

I'll rewind this story to the early Noughties. After a period of negotiation, we had finally reached agreement with neighbouring landowners to buy large areas of the maturing forestry plantation by which we were partially surrounded. Grant aid had also been painstakingly secured, a membership appeal prepared, and we were poised to treble the size of the RSPB's nature reserve here. Our modest scrap of relic heathland could now be envisaged as something large enough to provide an honest living for a number of rare species long lost to the area, and lost to large parts of the country where heathlands have also been sacrificed to other types of land use.

Purchase secured, the long-awaited day arrived when I'd get my first glimpse of this new land. Odd as it may seem, given its proximity, this was a largely uncharted area to us: private, dense with conifers, impenetrable to the eye. So one moment I was in the office, as usual, the next I was in a plantation, walking along a ride, with Corsican pines and Douglas firs towering around me, along with the odd sycamore, oak and birch. The ground was damp and mossy. Spindly nettle stems brushed inertly against my trousers. If I'd been dropped here blindfold I'd certainly never have imagined I was a mere five-minute walk from my desk.

I was with a small group of colleagues. We were just getting a feel for the lie of the land, so we could tell people about it, people who might help us to purchase it. And we asked the site manager lots of questions about the species we could expect to attract back here when the trees were thinned, the grazing reintroduced, the soil structure improved.

One of these species is the nightjar – which last bred here around the time when the trees were first planted. Another is the tree pipit – which used to sing on the edge of open fields opposite The Lodge entrance, within my memory, but hasn't been seen or heard for a couple of years. And there is the woodlark, which has recently passed through, pausing for a few days to sing, but without lingering to breed.

It's not all birds. The natterjack toad could benefit too, spreading from the population we have established already at The Lodge. Rare acid heathland flora could recolonise, and views would be reopened to the Ivel Valley below. We'd also be restoring scenery. There is a branching, periglacial river valley that has been buried from view within the plantations all these years.

I'd heard there was an Iron Age fort hidden somewhere within the plantation, and when it appeared to us through the trees I was taken aback by its scale. A special place, for sure, and a Scheduled Ancient Monument, which had been kept mostly clear of plantation trees, bar a few pioneer birches. It was ringed, like a huge open-air theatre, with dense conifers closing it in on all sides. It sits on the shoulder of the sandy ridge, with an earth bank still very distinct around it. The views it must have commanded to the south and west are now screened by the trees. The A1 and the north-east rail line are audible on the plain below. It made for a wonderfully atmospheric setting that day, with dragonflies enjoying the late October sunshine, after the first serious overnight frost of the autumn.

If they made a film of the history of this site, I could see this as one of the scenes: us walking into this clearing, AD 2002, where once a tribe had sat around fires with their livestock, keeping watch over the valley below, perhaps returning from the river with fish; a little soiled, clad in skins, wielding flint tools and arrows and spears, tattooed.

Seven years on, another scene from the film: back on the site, on another clear autumn day, with copper butterflies on the wing, and buzzards crying overhead. Most of the dense plantations have been removed. The landscape is reopened, the heathland exposed to the sky, with heather and gorse poised to regenerate. A flock of primitive-looking, four-horned and faintly devilish Manx Loaghtan rare breed sheep tiptoes among crumpled bracken. it is a place in transition, from timber crop to living landscape.

I have been part of a work party to clear scrub from the public paths we are opening to the public. We are now able to reveal this piece of history, the full human historic significance of the site, to local people and all visitors. We can now link the past to the present, telling a story of history, of natural history, and the relationship between people and the land: why this spot was special to them, and to the Romans, and to the previous owners of the estate, and now to us.

At RSPB headquarters you do a lot of the theory, while staff in regional offices, country offices and nature reserves tend to do more of the practical, front-line stuff. Now we are getting a real sense of that too, with our own issues to tackle, communications with neighbours to get right, management of visitors and balancing their needs with those of the wildlife – some of which is here already, and some which may yet come back.

OLD FRANK DROPS IN

The field opposite my house has recently been harvested. A muck heap in the middle distance has been spread across a portion of it, a black stain on the damp stubble. It has attracted a lot of bird activity. I can see magpies and jackdaws behaving excitably at the field margin, hanging and swooping in the stiff breeze over the hedgerow. A larger shape moves into view. I think it might be a cat, but a quick squint through binoculars reveals a heron.

It is standing, straight-necked and angled over the long grass of the field margin – a strip of uncut vegetation which harbours life and which has been a steady source of bird activity all summer. That's why agri-environment schemes promote them. The heron is hunting, I would guess, for rodents – voles, mice, even rats. It looks a little gawky beside the partridges, pheasants, woodpigeons and crows of different kinds that are picking around the muck, and working the margin for titbits. Margins – edges – are always good places for life to gather, as well as harbouring the potential for ambush.

Rodents aren't what you think of first and foremost as heron food, but a sequence of photographs by a Dutch photographer shows a heron catching a rabbit, dunking it in water, and gulping it down.

This prompted a debate about whether predatory birds drown prey on purpose. I checked some records and found plenty of examples of herons taking mammal prey – and dousing it. But do they knowingly drown it? Or is this dunking just to add lubricant? In any event, you'd want a strong stomach before swallowing a live, kicking rabbit.

I also found an old reference to a heron that was found on its back, incapacitated. When rescued, it promptly regurgitated a 25-inch eel – which was still alive – whereupon the bird recovered quickly and took flight.

The drowning question has been settled by YouTube. There I found some footage shot in Germany, of a sparrowhawk foreshortening a death struggle with a magpie by dragging its opponent several metres to a garden pond, and unceremoniously shoving it under the water. Learned behaviour, instinctive or reasoned? They say it's probably the former, but perhaps this will never be known.

On Crane Hill

One of my favourite places within easy reach of my house is a perch on the crest of the greensand ridge, towards its northern end. I can reach it on foot or by bike, via footpaths and a former Roman road known as Hazell's Hedge. The ascent is long and gradual and, this being Bedfordshire, the summit nothing spectacular, but the view from up there is surprising in its breadth. It helps too that the ground is reverting to low scrub and wild flowers. Sitting there, I can see across to the west, and view where I live from a different, slightly disorienting angle. From here Bedfordshire starts to look like a wooded county, although the impression is distorted.

I'd visited this place more than once before I noticed on an old map that it was – and still is – called Crane Hill, although it's nowadays so off the beaten track and little visited that only the very local would need to call it anything. It reminds me that the huge arable fields stretching south below this vantage point were once a very watery place, and scrubby too, I'm sure, with clumps of willow and alder and thorns. The name Crane Hill probably reflects how this must have been a magnet for flocks of these tall, eye-catching and often highly vocal birds.

There are other local clues, I discover when I consult with local historian Stephen Coleman, who tells me:

Just over one kilometre to the south-west of Crane Hill and immediately south of Hill's Farm in Tempsford parish, adjacent to the duck decoy, are the historic field names of Cran Close and Cran Green, referred to in 1825 and 1829. Other associated documentary references include a 1776 mention of a Manor of Cran or Crandon. A twelfth-century grant refers to land at Crandon.

The 'Crane' part seems to apply only to this particular bit, as nearby the slope has a different name – Hungry Hill. This tells us something about the low fertility of this low hilltop, and may even explain why today it is being allowed to revert to scrub.

I hadn't realised I had such a connection to cranes right on my doorstep, even though I've been well aware of other places with historical connections to these 'birds of heaven'. As many as 300 place names in the UK derive from the presence of cranes in centuries past. So conspicuous and vocal were these flocks of birds that local people would choose this rather than any other local feature or association as the defining characteristic of the area. The words cran, carn and tran are all usually derived from cranes, the last of these being ancient Norse. Places like Cranfield, Carnforth and Tranmere are examples. Cranes have also been long revered in the Far East, and have religious significance there. They have also, like storks, been associated with fertility.

In W.H. Hudson's day, a century ago, the crane was long gone as a breeder, and was already just an occasional visitor.

The birds are always shot on appearance [he wrote, fearing it was gone for good as a resident]. *The resonant, far-sounding cry of this noble bird – one of the most fascinating sounds of wild nature, especially when several individuals, as their custom is, unite their voices in a chorus – will probably never be heard again in England, except from rare stragglers or from captives in an enclosure.*

I'm delighted to report that we're putting things right for Mr Hudson. Four centuries have passed since the common crane became extinct as a resident of these islands. One of the many important projects I'm lucky to have been involved with at the RSPB has been the reintroduction of cranes. I've also been proud to play a minor part alongside colleagues in the nurturing of a few more which have returned of their own volition to the Norfolk Broads. The generosity of the public, supporters and grant-making bodies enabled the purchase of a place called Sutton Fen there, with nesting cranes the centrepiece of one of the most diverse ecosystems anywhere in Britain. Cranes have also visited the RSPB's Loch of Strathbeg nature reserve in north-east Scotland, and wonderful, unexpected news was released recently that the birds have raised a chick at an undisclosed site thereabouts for two successive years.

As ground-nesters, they can be vulnerable to predators foraging at night, and to disturbance generally. But cranes will put up brave resistance if their nest is threatened. They are our tallest breeding birds, armed with a long stabbing beak, kicking legs and a broad wingspan, which makes them nimble in combat as well as elegant in display. They are tenacious survivors, which bodes well for further future successes.

The great marsh that once covered much of the landscape south of my village, marked on seventeenth-century maps at a time when the area was known as Wixamtree, isn't likely to be restored any time soon, so the crane will live on in the name of the hill only, and the occasional glimpse reported of birds passing high overhead, necks and legs outstretched. Perhaps one day there will be more of this commuting, with strongholds re-established at Norfolk to the north-east of here and Somerset to the south-west.

And I've had a glimpse of what those fields near my home might have looked like once. That was on the edge of the great fen mires of Poland and Belarus, where cranes nest in flooded, stunted woodland groves. And I've seen what hundreds of cranes look like in a winter flock, on the frost-bound plateau of Gallocanta in Spain. Their bugling calls carry for miles across that beautiful, apparently inhospitable wintry landscape. I've heard these pipers now in this country, distant in the mist in Sussex. They could, in theory, turn up anywhere, gleaning the bare soil and stubbles of the winter landscape. I'll be holding on to that thought this winter whenever I return to those gentle, sunlit uplands just along the way.

CHAPTER ELEVEN

November

WILD AND PEACEFUL

Aloof upon the day's immeasured dome,
He holds unshared the silence of the sky.
George Sterling, from *The Black Vulture*

A dead sheep is pulled from the back of the jeep. As it slumps on the stony ground it emits a low, growling belch for several seconds, causing Tommy to recoil and Bo the dog to approach curiously. But by the looks of things even Bo is a little overpowered.

The sheep died of natural causes some days ago. Its delivery here was delayed by the checks for scrapie required by government vets. I am grateful for the small mercy that the sheep didn't belch on the journey up here, to this vulture-feeding station, even though I already had my head partially out of the open window to evade the worst of its ambience.

We are in a beautiful Mallorcan valley, which rings with the sub-songs of autumn migrant birds, mainly thrushes and their relatives. I cannot say exactly where, as the resident black vultures, which have benefited from occasional supplementary feeding in the past, are sensitive beasts. That they can have recovered from just one breeding pair in the 1980s to 110 birds now seems extraordinary on an island as popular as Mallorca. It is a tribute to the conservationists who have been protecting them.

No one deliberately harms vultures, as a rule, but (as mentioned earlier; see page 197) they are among the collateral damage of the illegal poisoning war waged by some against other wildlife and feral animals. But vultures are also vulnerable to disturbance, and to starvation, when there is not enough large carrion around.

My visit here has coincided with the unprecedented arrival in the Balearic islands of up to 100 griffon vultures. It is quite likely that these birds have wandered here in a desperate search for food. A year or so ago, a similar number travelled from Spain as far north as Belgium, on a foraging mission. Changes in European Union livestock hygiene regulations have reduced the availability of animal carcasses. We are working with our BirdLife partners to try to balance the needs of the birds with the need for sensible control in livestock disposal.

There are worse places for a lost griffon to land than Mallorca, given the island's track record in vulture conservation. There is food, which brings me back to why I am here in this valley with the Black Vulture Conservation Foundation team, putting out a dead sheep. The griffons are exhausted and hungry, and have fallen on this offering ravenously, bringing the resident and much more timid black vultures in with them, to strip the carcass in a matter of hours.

By another happy coincidence, my holiday here has also coincided with the Foundation's AGM. I was invited in to have a tour of their HQ. This was my chance to see black vultures up close. The Foundation has several injured birds in captivity that are healthy enough to be pairing up for breeding. It is only November, but this is when the giant stick nests are assembled.

They are massive birds – at 8 kg the largest and heaviest birds of prey in Europe – and remain very wary of humans. They have room to manoeuvre within their large enclosures. You cannot fail to be impressed by their obvious power, the noise generated by the beating of their three-metre-wide wings, and the thump they make as they land on the floor of their pens. The centre also has three juvenile griffons, sourced from buoyant populations in Spain, and awaiting release in the Balkans.

After meeting the captive vultures, I gave a presentation on the work the RSPB is doing with our partners in Asia to save vultures there. An estimated 40 million vultures have died in Asia in little more than a decade. It is small consolation that the poisoning of the birds there, by the veterinary drug diclofenac, present in just a small number of livestock carcasses, has been accidental rather than deliberate. Here in Europe, conservationists have been trying to put our own vulture species back in the wilder parts of our continent for the last 20 years. Lammergeiers (also known as bearded vultures) and Egyptian vultures have also been the subject of intensive reintroduction schemes. We are hopeful that the expertise that the Foundation has developed may be useful to our colleagues in Asia, and all concerned are making efforts to build conservation links.

Meanwhile, back in the high peaks, the lost griffons seem to be recovering their strength and their bearings, and are now capable of catching a thermal off the spectacular Sierra Tramuntana mountains to gain the height they need to make their way south to Africa. A dozen or so remain, for now. We can see five of them, circling beatifically with several of their darker relatives over the jagged crests of the valley.

'It is green Helvetia under a Calabrian sky,' wrote George Sand of a Mallorcan winter, 150 years ago. 'With the solemnity and silence of the East.' The vultures add greatly to that sense of the serene and the *sauvage*, the wild and the peaceful, that makes Mallorca so special.

THE UNDERWORLD BIRD

There's a bird you're never very far from, although you see peculiarly little of it. It inhabits the shadows – a kind of underworld, if you like. A hidden world of dark recesses, cobwebby corners, murky depths.

Within the cast of birds that strut the stage of our gardens, parks and woods, and although it's never far away, this bird isn't one of the main players. It barely lays claim to a supporting part. It lives offstage, behind the scenes; a skulking presence, occasionally visible, often narky, but apparently much too busy and preoccupied for attention-seeking, theatricals, squabbles, limelight-grabbing.

From time to time it emerges from the wings, from the midst of an untidy back room, or as though from the very earth itself. And when it does, it sometimes opens it lungs, and pours forth a song-explosion, an improbable spark from a mouldy woodpile.

'Here! Have some of that!' it seems to yell.

And it proceeds to show the upper world, in all its vanity and ostentation, that in fact here too is a formidable voice. The prodigious aria reverberates from the rafters, from a forest canopy, from a gully's walls, from a city street at dawn. It may be repeated several times, and on any day of the year, as though season is no object. And then – silence. It is gone again, slipping noiselessly under cover once more, back to the underworld, to the subterranean life that gives it its scientific name of *Troglodytes troglodytes* – the cave dweller. Ladies and gentlemen, meet the wren.

I have journeyed to this underworld recently, or so it feels. I don't have to go far. I've brought that world to my back door, by a channel of tangled hedgerow, and along it has ventured the wren, building a nest right next to my back door, just beyond the window.

It's a male wren. The male builds the nests. Occasionally he notices me, seems to register me in some slightly disconnected way, a wee bit perturbed but mainly distracted by foraging, firtling, feeding, fetching, carrying. His movements are staccato, impish, all flicks, ticks, twitches, shuffling, bowing, here a curtsey, there a half-turn. I watch him build one nest, but by some alchemy a male wren builds a number of these tiny, perfect domes with ways-in at the side, all moulded into nooks. He is a hyperactive craftsman.

His partner chooses and provides soft furnishings for the one she likes best. Whichever nest my underworld neighbours go with, it isn't the one I know. Perhaps she has noticed me hanging around. Quite likely the wren I met wasn't always him. We lose touch. A wren can no longer be relied upon to pop up in this quiet corner.

Our acquaintance is soon to be renewed. I stumble on an active nest, seamlessly integrated below a pot in a plant hanger. The pair are feeding young. I take some time on a Sunday morning to watch them at work. And *how* they work. The pace they set is fierce. It is impossible to imagine them finding a higher gear, ferrying insects and spiders back and forth.

And then, an odd thing. I witness one of these wrens suddenly off-duty, having what can best be described as a break. It is clinging to a wire just a few feet from me, and appears to go into a trance, eyelids narrowing. A wren power nap. After a few drowsy minutes it reignites and resumes its duties.

A few days on, the hyperactivity has ceased. All is tranquil again. I stumble across some of the offspring making their first cautious steps between this world and theirs. Four of these even-tinier-than-usual wrens are venturing forth, a nervous scouting party. I crouch down close to them, as they flutter and crash-land in clumsy sorties.

And that's when I have a rare one-to-one with a wren: one of these feathered ping-pong balls with the wide stripe of mouth clambers onto a twig an arm's length in front of my face, unsteady but undaunted, meeting my gaze with its own level stare, eyes bright. It is leaning closer. It dawns on me that what might be attracting it is not so much my benign, Dolittle-esque natural magnetism for forest creatures as my open mouth. Not wishing to become over-acquainted, I pop it shut.

You can take underworld exploration too far, in the end. The tiny wren expedition is soon safely absorbed by more appropriate recesses.

Winter comes, as winter must. In a sharp December dusk I notice another small party of wrens near the unused nest from spring, by the back window. They are lined up on the fence, and I watch them carefully to see if they might lead me to their roost site. There is a record of more than 60 wrens jemmying themselves into a Norfolk nest box to see out a frosty night. Tiny birds like this have to know how to keep warm. I don't in the end see where they go. But I do note them climbing on top of each other, in some wren law, pre-roost ritual, perhaps arranged to work out the sleeping arrangements to come.

Who knows how they organise their secret society, how 60-plus wrens have a sleepover together at short notice. But what is clear is that the wren has long intrigued us. In various historic times and places it has been caught and sacrificed in midwinter, to confirm the retreat of darkness and the renewal of light and life. It is not hard to see how the enchanting little wren might come to represent the spirit of the winter netherworld in Europe, surviving against the odds in conditions that force most birds with a wren's metabolism to clear out and head south. In other times and places we have been more suitably protective. There is an old Scots rhyme that warns of 'Malaisons, malaisons (curses) mair than ten, That harry our Lady of Heaven's wren.'

If you haven't been there already, I can recommend the wren's world to you. And if you do find it, here's a wee tip: best remain tight-lipped.

RED-LETTER DAYS

I thought of the cartoon adventurer Mr Benn the other day. I popped to the shop in a neighbouring village, and had a bit of an adventure of my own. You may recall watching Mr Benn on TV in the 1970s. He lived in an ordinary little street called Festive Road. For recreation, he simply visited the local tailor, donned a costume, was led through a curtain, and an improbable escapade would ensue, with Mr B as pirate, native American, astronaut... At some crunch moment, the shopkeeper would appear again, and our hero would make a sharp exit. He would return to Festive Road and find it just as he'd left it. His neighbours would be none the wiser.

Unlike Mr Benn, I was visiting a newsagent, and I didn't have to don a special costume. But something happened that took me out of the everyday, a happening slightly at odds with the sleepy familiarity of the village, with its neat house fronts and tidy gardens. My eye was drawn to a large shape passing overhead. To my surprise and delight I realised we were being visited by a red kite.[5]

Now, I've seen quite a few red kites in recent years. I've seen them from the garden of a village pub in the Chilterns. I've driven under one circling over the A1 at Peterborough, and seen another from a train near Inverness. I've visited the feeding stations we've set up for them in south Scotland and Wales, and I've seen one over a gentle glen near Stirling, close to another of the reintroduction sites. I've even seen one passing low over The Lodge, as though to pay the RSPB HQ a special visit, to acknowledge the role we've played, with others, in bringing them back to these different parts of lowland Britain.

But there is something about seeing one over my own patch, in my daily life, like this that stands apart from all of these sightings, that puts the seal on what I already hoped – that the red kite really is back, reclaiming its rightful place in the landscape. A little taste of adventure, of discovery, close to home.

I followed the progress of this kite as it drifted back and forth over the back gardens and fields beyond. I wasn't the only one, as it was harangued by vexatious jackdaws and rooks. Red kites have great presence and apparent bulk, and their appearance in unfamiliar places is guaranteed to noise up the local corvids. But they are mostly unaggressive, carrion-feeding birds, and don't carry a lot of muscle. It would impede their effortless flying technique. They are searchers more than hunters.

---

5   Red kites were formerly widespread in the UK, but were persecuted to extinction, except in mid-Wales. They have been reintroduced in a number of locations since the mid-1990s. The population is now growing, although the incidence of illegal poisoning of kites was higher in 2007 than for many years.

I suppose I hoped someone else would appear so I could show them what I was watching, this languid raptor, draped on the breeze, but the few streets remained quiet. Festive Road slumbered on.

From a very early, Mr Benn-watching age, I have known that red kites are rare and special birds. I'm not completely sure how I first knew, but I think it was a card game, or maybe the Young Ornithologists' Club magazine of the period. These showed the red kite alongside the other birds that were clinging to existence in these islands at that time, birds like the marsh harrier, the Dartford warbler, snowy owl, red-backed shrike – some now gone, others revived.

I can remember very clearly the moment when I actually saw one of those few remaining red kites. It was high in mid-Wales, the only place it could have been at that time. It was drifting along the crest of a hillside, showing clearly its forked tail. My sister Brigid saw it as well, which helped to overcome the scepticism of my mum when we relayed the news of our find. She was right to be dubious: red kites were really very scarce indeed at that time, and we were only young, with imaginations fed by Mr Benn and his contemporaries.

That moment, on a short family holiday, defined Wales for me. Well, that and the moment when we discovered a grass snake trying to swallow a plump toad by a woodland river. These two incidents became the sum of Wales in my young mind. What a place. Wales had red kites. More precisely, the upland oak woods of central Wales had red kites, and nowhere else did. It was easy to assume at that time that nowhere else would ever have red kites again, as the Welsh population seemed very stuck on its upland oak woods, and wouldn't be likely to find or move to any similar places any time soon. Then conservationists intervened. Red kites, it seems, can thrive in 'ordinary' landscapes too, if allowed.

Thirty years on from that first kite encounter, I'm pleased that such adventures have been brought closer to home, for the residents of Festive Road – or the next village – to share in, if they wish. And you don't have to dress up as a hill climber, or even a birdwatcher, to join in. Red kites are easy to get excited about. They exemplify what so much of conservation – of putting the life back – is about.

Back home, Mr Benn would always find a memento in his suit pocket, to show that his adventure had been real. I found my pocket empty this time – but the rosy glow of seeing a red kite will do just fine.

THE REALITY OF DREAMS

In 2010, I escaped a rainswept November to join Earthwatch's expedition to the upper reaches of the Peruvian Amazon. It is a glimpse of paradise. It is also a taste of our planet's distant past. The river boat *Ayapua* that I travelled on with my fellow volunteers is itself like a time capsule, locked in the year 1906, when it rolled out of a Hamburg shipyard. The landscape we moved gently through can have looked little different when the first conquistadors began their tentative explorations 500 years ago.

Not many of those intrepid Europeans got as far upstream as we did, to the Pacaya-Samiria National Reserve. Writing now, a few days after arriving back in the UK's sub-zero temperatures, to our comparatively colourless winter, the contrast with where I've been could not be starker. Forest people in Amazonia say that everyday life is merely an illusion, behind which lies the reality of dreams. I feel like I have woken from a dream of Arcadia.

Our group of 19 assembled in the friendly, frenetic city of Iquitos (population 422,000), the largest human settlement in the world that has no road links other than a two-hour stretch of road leading to Nauta, where we board the *Ayapua*. The boat is beautiful, lovingly restored after years of dereliction, with original features salvaged from scrapyards and the carcasses of other riverboats beyond redemption.

The boat was re-floated in 2006, on her 100th anniversary, upgraded for the modern traveller, the pioneering conservationist. The *Marañón River* here at Nauta is a mile wide, coffee-coloured and surging, flecked with flotsam, some from the Andes, several hundred miles upstream.

Restoring the *Ayapua*, and the Casa Morey Hotel in which we gathered the night before embarking, has been part of the dream of Richard Bodmer, the expedition leader here. Conservation extends beyond the natural environment to encompass cultural and historic elements like these and the lifestyles of the local people. The dream is sustainability, the preservation of this earthly paradise and its people.

In a series of short presentations in the main dining room on board, Richard sketched out the ecology of Amazonia. He emphasised the importance of our expedition. Our surveys will inform understanding of the impacts of recent climate changes here. The wettest year on record has been followed by the driest. Impacts on river dolphins have already been noted, and the flood forests that make the Pacaya-Samiria National Reserve so special have entered uncertain times.

We rely on Amazonia to air-condition our planet. There may be evidence now that the Amazon itself is malfunctioning in a world changing too rapidly for it to cope. The results of our work will add to that evidence base.

Richard also set out his vision: community-based conservation, working with people locally on management plans that incorporate their needs. This approach has resolved conflicts, and Earthwatch surveys indicate it is helping species to recover.

Our final destination lay two days upstream, after we left the churning silt- and debris-laden waters of the Marañón River and forked left into the tannin-rich 'café negro' waters of the Samiria River. Here the channels narrow, the water reflects bright sky, scattered canopies of cumulus clouds and looming trees, and ripples with the curved spines of dolphins, fishing languidly around us. We moored by a forest ranger station.

Most days began at 5 am, with sunrise, and the firing up of the generator, replacing the night-time chorus of frogs, crickets and owls. With the moon receding, and butterflies taking wing, we sat quietly in open boats, recording macaws. Between macaws, ornithologist Alfredo confirmed the identity of the many other bird species calling, flitting and swooping around us.

We surveyed dolphins every day, drifting with these gentle animals for several hours, noting all we saw. We also helped set up a study of white-winged swallows. We installed around 50 nest boxes at the edge of the lake and river channels. And we released baby turtles as part of a scheme to help them recover in this part of the reserve.

We studied fish in the river and in the vast ox-bow lake a few kilometres upstream, a place I grew to love. We caught, weighed and measured piranhas and primitive fish species. In the forest, we walked long transects, noting the primate species and other larger animals we encountered.

After dinner each evening a boat was despatched to survey three species of caiman. I'll never forget spotting them under the glare of a fizzingly intense full moon, complete with halo covering half the sky, as we scanned the shorelines for eye-flash. Our biologists on the prow would gently noose these great reptiles, haul them aboard, tape their smiling jaws, restrain their thrashing tails, and take the necessary weights and measurements.

Moving back down river on our final days we visited the Cocoma people of the village of Bolivar and the larger settlement of San Martin. We gathered at Bolivar's schoolhouse, with most of the village joining us to share brief words of welcome and thanks. We were tested by local children on our knowledge of the local wildlife we had been studying. To round things off, three musicians struck up some vibrant drum and flute music, and we danced away the final hour of a Saturday morning with the children, a touching and memorable finale.

It was an honour to be part of this Earthwatch project. The group, the scientists and the crew were all hard-working, good-humoured people I am glad to have met.

Anyone choosing to join this project can make a direct contribution to Amazonia's conservation. As conservationists we dream of a world that protects forests like this, that recognises their reciprocal value to people who live in and with them, and to all of us. The dream of a sustainable Amazonia, and planet Earth secured for the future, has to become a reality. A dream like this is, in the end, the only future reality that we have.

A KESTREL FOR A NEIGHBOUR

Kestrels are regular inhabitants of the view I enjoy from bed, where I often sit with pen poised, and cup of tea. Of all the visitors to the airspace outside, kestrels are perhaps my favourite. They usually put on a show, and I particularly like the elegant parabola they describe in the sky as they swoop upwards to apparently perch in mid-air, balancing there on waggling wings to scrutinise the field margins below.

The garden birds below me seem to regard the kestrel with a wary tolerance. It's as though some kind of unwritten agreement is in place that the kestrel hunts the landscape across the road and beyond, but doesn't venture to hunt over or into the garden itself, front or back. I've simply never seen one any closer, in search mode, even when the grass needs cut. This is in sharp contrast to the sparrowhawk, of course, which mounts sporadic but repeated steeplechasing garden raids.

Not that the kestrel doesn't catch sparrows and the like, of course. It may be doe-eyed of expression and balletic in movement, but it is wide-ranging in its tastes, and not shy of tussling with hawks and barn owls over captured prey. And yet, unlike the hawk, it seems everyone loves the kestrel and the barn owl. I've heard hawks described as the most bloodthirsty of raptors, and I've wondered what the other raptors are thought to be eating when the hawks are being more bloodthirsty than them. Salad?

I sometimes count road-hugging kestrels when I make the journey north to Scotland, and invariably count more in the southern lowlands. Kestrels took better than most raptors to the landscape we've created since the dawn of agriculture, although there are signs of recent decline. You can get quite philosophical on a Sunday morning with a cuppa in your hand. I find myself wondering at the ungraspable timescales across which birds like these have drifted in pursuit of their prey. The longevity of species like these can be counted in the millions of years. *Homo sapiens* has been around for a mere 200,000 years. Go far enough back in time, to the dawn of modern kestrels, say, and look around for us. You wouldn't see a human form you recognised, never mind agriculture – or culture of any kind. It's hard to begrudge a hawk a sparrow, in this context.

Talking of primitive humans, I came into possession of an old wooden commode and, having little practical need for it in an age of inside loos and modern plumbing, I stood back, chin between fingers, to consider new uses for it. It didn't take long to take on the appearance in my mind of a kestrel nest box. And after a few minor modifications (I put an additional board behind the lower half of the seat to make the entrance smaller, and better for perching on) and screws, the old lav had been re-purposed. I donated it to Clive the farmer and he wasted no time in installing it high on one of the legs of his open-sided barn.

I found a natural kestrel nest site on the edge of the village, where an isolated ash tree, snapped in a gale but still holding on to the broken bit, like Anne Boleyn's ghost with her head under her arm, has created a handy cavity. The birds are particularly regular round there, hunting the roadside verges. I often think of the book and film *Kes* (the book was originally called *A Kestrel for a Knave*) when watching these birds, and how the book's young hero, Billy Casper, is smitten by the birds, and compelled to somehow raise and train a young one.

Kes captured perhaps most vividly of all the way birds like these offer inspiration and escape, and sometimes companionship with nature. I used to wonder what would have become of Billy, in any sequel. But I am pretty sure his love of the eponymous falcon Kes, and his experience of flying with the bird, would have served him well in later life.

HOMECOMING

There are two reasons why I can't let myself believe that the large, bow-winged bird beating languidly north, way overhead against the darkening November sky, is an osprey. For one thing, this is pretty late in the year – ospreys should be well south by now, to winter in Africa – and for another I am on the platform at Sandy rail station. I have to let this possibility go.

But the next day I notice reports that an osprey *has* been seen over and around The Lodge nature reserve. Life is breathed back into my faint hope of having seen one in such an improbable time and place. In fact, as winter approaches, and the days shorten still further, it becomes clear that this dilatory bird has adopted the Scots pines that stand dark against the reddening western sky at the heathland plateau edge here as its preferred roosting site. The spot it has chosen has an Iron Age fort behind it, and a grandstand view out over the gravel pits and wetland below.

We've been doing a *lot* of habitat restoration work at The Lodge, to attract back some lost species, some of them long lost. They're heathland specialists, mainly, and there have been a few encouraging early signs. But we have to confess that we weren't expecting to welcome back an osprey, also long lost. So long, in fact, that it would be hard to say exactly when one last spent any significant amount of time around here. There have been increasingly regular sightings of ospreys in recent years, as they have recolonised Scotland and now begun to spill into England and Wales, and hopefully Ireland again soon.

In the days that follow, reports of our unexpected guest are regular, if sporadic, and I have kept my eyes on the sky in hope of another view of our lodger. I have a chance early on a bright, blowy Sunday morning to visit those gravel pit lakes. One is apparently heavily stocked with rainbow trout, to which the osprey may be particularly attracted. I ask the first fishermen I pass if they have seen it, and they point me towards the lake in question, though they aren't sure if the bird has been seen for a while. I head in the direction they suggest, although a river channel and high fence and 'Keep Out' signs block access to the other pits. As it turns out, I don't need to get any further. Beyond the fence and a bank of trees, into view comes the large, arched profile of the osprey, wings lazily beating, with gulls for company and comparison. It is clearly on the hunt for those trout, and I watch it for several minutes, at a distance, until it drops out of sight beyond the screen of willows.

I return to the car and head down the A1 to try to relocate it at closer range. No sooner have I stepped into the car park than it is there again, right overhead, as close as any osprey I've encountered. The fishermen with their windbreaks by the water's edge have their noses pointed to the sky in admiration, tinged with envy.

'What's it been catching?' I call over to them.

'More than we have!' comes the resigned response.

We watch it cruise, imperious in the icy air. The gull entourage follows in its wake as they might a fishing vessel: patiently expectant. The osprey oozes insouciance. I can't help thinking of former foot-baller turned actor Eric Cantona's enigmatic statement to a bemused assemblage of journalists, before he walked out of that infamous press conference: 'When the seagulls follow the trawler, it is because they think sardines will be thrown into the sea...'

The gulls are obviously by now as familiar with and adjusted to the unusual visitor as the fishermen below. Sooner or later there will be action, perhaps some trout scraps. We are able to watch the loom-ing raptor for several minutes at a time, on and off, playing hide and seek with us around and behind the rows of poplars between the different pits.

The clear impression is of a hungry bird, bold and inexperienced; perhaps also, like the anglers, by now finding fish less easy to locate, less active near the surface of the cooling water, lapsing into winter torpor at last.

Finally there is a commotion of gulls, distant and unseen. But for us the osprey is gone. I find out later that this is the last anyone saw of it. Sunday 27 November 2011: the latest date any osprey is known to have lingered in our islands, which probably tells us something about a changing climate as well as a more osprey-friendly world, and a local glut of trout.

It is fitting that a bird which is worthy of the much-used term 'iconic', one woven tightly into the very history of conservation and the RSPB, came to stay. It's a milestone moment in conservation, the day – the four weeks, in fact – that this six-month-old osprey came home to RSPB HQ, almost 60 years after we stayed up all night, night after night, to first help the species regain a toehold at Loch Garten in the Highlands of Scotland, after decades of absence. I wasn't there for the Loch Garten all-nighters in the 1950s, to be fair, but I'm proud to have been here to greet the first osprey to find sanctuary at RSPB HQ.

CHAPTER TWELVE

December

My journal for December begins with a couple of despatches I sent from New Zealand, where I spent time with 'activists' (as they call themselves) of Forest and Bird, the RSPB's partner organisation there.

WALKABOUT

I've always loved the film *Walkabout*, which is partly about conservation and our relationship with wild nature. You may know the story: a teenage schoolgirl and her young brother are lost in the Australian outback, and probably doomed, until an aboriginal boy finds and befriends them, shows them how an apparently forbidding and hostile place can sustain life – their lives – and leads them ultimately to safety.

My RSPB sabbatical feels a bit like a walkabout, the year-long rite of passage young aboriginal boys must undertake, alone. Of course my 'walkabout' differs in some important respects. For one thing, I'm Scots-Irish. For another it is only a month long, plus some annual leave tacked on. Also, I am not doing it in Australia (although in flying across Australia I was able to take a long, long, long look at its empty miles of red desert, with John Barry's epic score echoing in my head), but in New Zealand, and I realise there is a big difference.

And in the end I'm not doing it alone, as I have a guide and

mentor in the shape of Jo-Anne Vaughan, a full-time environment-
alist with Forest and Bird.

Having said all that, when she brought me to this 'rilly spishal'
place called Mangarakau Swamp, part of Westhaven (Te Tai Tapu)
Marine Reserve and the Westhaven (Whanganui Inlet) Wildlife
Management Reserve a remote corner of South Island, she *was* leaving me here alone for a time (almost a week). I'm here to get to know
the place and to write a management plan. And I'm armed only with
a notebook, a hamper and a pair of secateurs, in a rather fetching tan
leather holster. The swamp (in the UK we'd call it a wetland) has just
become a nature reserve. We want the public to visit and enjoy it,
without compromising the wildlife values of the place or intruding
on the peaceful lives of the very few people who live locally. The man
I saw first thing this morning carrying a machete, for example.

It's almost Christmas, and by day the birds are singing in the
intense sunshine, a medley of the familiar – blackbirds and yellow-
hammers, for example – and the exotic – tuis and bellbirds. By day
and night bitterns 'boom' and frogs belch from the reed and raupo
beds below the wooden hut that is my temporary home. The swamp
is special because, unlike 90 per cent of New Zealand's wetlands, it
has defied every attempt made to drain it. It has lain here while the
gold prospectors, the coal miners, the timber cutters, the flax millers
and the farmers have come and gone. Communities have lived and
died, flourished and withered. Gaps in the hillsides up to dramatic
limestone crags have appeared and disappeared too, some reclaimed
by bush, some halfway there, currently scrub.

Well, they *call* it bush, but jungle would be more like it – a benign
jungle, without thorns (although imported gorse and bramble do exploit any openings), but often dense and tangled. I know, I've been in
there, seeking a passage to the crags and caves above.

The people may have come and gone, leaving only photos and
folklore, but the signs of many of the other mammals they brought
here remain. The tracks of feral pigs, for example, make my progress
through the jungle in places a little easier than it ought to be. I see
sheep in there too, 'gone bush', their fleeces trailing on the ground.
There are deer droppings on the paths and goat droppings in the
caves, where once there were bats, laughing owls and *harpigornis*,
the biggest eagle that ever lived. The growth and regrowth of these
wonderful cabbage trees (they look like tall yukkas but they taste,

apparently, of cabbage), tree ferns and vines must battle the on-slaught of the mammals left behind in a previously mammal-free world, where birds ruled. Perhaps the worst offender of all is the possum, a rampant defoliator which strips and kills mature trees, supplementing this with the eggs and nestlings of birds it finds as it does so.

A ring of traps is aimed at protecting the swamp and its ground-nesting birds, rare plants and vulnerable frogs and mudfish from these and other threats lurking in the bush (mainly rats and stoats). At least the wetland creatures can rest easily, cradled among these hills. That's the theory, anyway...

The sun dips behind the crags and darkness gathers. Owls call 'more pork' from the direction of the old mine entrance in the bush. I read a book about the early settlers, as the house timbers creak and crack as they shrink in the cool of night (my rational self explains to me). But that cannot account for the loud clunking noise outside my window. It sounds like a club being dragged across the wooden balcony. And again. I roll quietly out of bed and turn out the light to peer through the curtain. My eyes gradually adjust to the diffuse moonlight. The wooden planks of the balcony are pale, right-angled against the house. Lumps of driftwood and logs for the stove sit dark against them. Nothing stirs, except my heart.

At last the source of the noise reveals itself, as one of the lumps comes to life. It bounds darkly up to the living room window. A second, much larger – cat-sized – one enters ponderously, stage left, and sits down stiffly as though being forced to observe the antics of the first. It looks slightly groggy. I feel immediately like a witness if not quite to a crime, then at least to the fugitives in hiding. I confess also to feeling intrigued – and relieved – having identified the source of the noise. They are brush-tailed possums.

I slip through to the next room to flick a light switch, to illumin-ate the stage. They are unperturbed by the limelight. I return to the audience, and the performance continues, stooge and clog-dancing clown. The clown makes mock charges, and jumps on its parent's back. It then shins up one of the roof supports, hangs there, comes down head first and jumps on the parent again. It is the final act. I go back to bed.

What I've witnessed is a female possum encouraging a juvenile to become independent. She has brought it here to get used to new surroundings, before she leaves it behind to begin its own journey in the world.

The walkabout theme recurs. If this were Australia, where these critters have a place in the natural order of things, I could have found this piece of marsupial cabaret quite charming. But it's not. The introduction of possums to New Zealand has been a tragedy, not a comedy. There is, alas, no place for them in New Zealand's already beleaguered environment, least of all in a nature reserve.

New Zealand is, in the end, not the right place for a walkabout. I regret that this young possum's walkabout is likely to be even briefer than mine.

TROUBLE IN PARADISE

Kapiti Island is five kilometres (a little further than a stoat can swim) from New Zealand's North Island. It is uncannily similar in shape to South Island, and, at ten kilometres by two kilometres, it is like the old New Zealand in microcosm, because conservationists have managed to clear it of all introduced predators. This was finally achieved, after years of effort, in the mid-1990s. Since then, the forest has been regenerating madly and the birds are responding in kind. I've been privileged enough to see this for myself.

Not many people get to stay overnight, as I did. Some conservationists are opposed to visitors being allowed to do any more than day trips, because of the risk of them bringing stowaway mice in their backpacks. Anyway, I was thoroughly frisked and found to be rodent-free. I was looked after by John Barrett, whose extended family still owns land in the north of Kapiti. The rest of the island is managed by the government's Department of Conservation (Te Papa Atawhai), who organise the day trips.

Kapiti redefines the term 'bird sanctuary'. The birds are everywhere. Wekas (like ancestral corncrakes) came to greet me as I disembarked on a narrow strand of boulders. Kakas (a kind of parrot) congregated noisily around the deck and roof of the house where I was taken for the introductory talk. Kererus (large pigeons) slapped each other with their wings, and gazed at me expectantly, chins resting on puffed bellies with bibs. Takahes, like prehistoric moorhens, high-stepped deliberately across the short grass. A large male called Mr Green came to introduce himself. He had a beak like a bolt cutter, but he wielded it gently. There are only about 220 of these birds left in New Zealand, and therefore the world, yet their needs don't seem so exacting – here they happily graze the introduced grasses of the former pasture.

These are all A-list celebs in the bird world, but very down to earth, even vulgar, when you get to know them. It's a bit like *I'm A Celebrity Bird, Get Me Out of Here* (the 'reality' TV show set on a tropical island) around the house, in fact, or a safe house for refugees, in keeping with the role that New Zealand has played for many humans.

Call me obvious, but for me the big prize was to see – or rather meet – a kiwi, most famous of all, most eccentric (which, by New Zealand standards, is saying something) and most intriguing. The national bird of New Zealand. A bird that lives in a burrow and sleeps on its back with its legs in the air. And this is how it happened…

Evening came as I sat counting tui after tui (blackbird-sized honey-eaters, with cloak-like wings) that have flown across the pasture to roost in the trees of the south-facing valley side. The wekas squawked their goodnights – neurotic, even here, where the biggest risk to them is someone treading on their toe. The time came for the kiwis to rouse. Kapiti has 1,400 little spotted kiwis, which could be capacity, and which, incredibly, is almost the entire world population. They are almost extinct on the mainland, having no defence whatsoever against introduced predators. There are six territories around the little valley I am staying in, but kiwis are unpredictable, so experiencing them is far from guaranteed.

My fellow overnighters – Jeff, a bird photographer from Montana, and Catriona and David, a young couple from just across the water – and I wait expectantly on the porch. Before long the first kiwi call – the male's – issues from the dark, like a long blast on a referee's whistle. I half-expect the *Match of the Day* theme to ensue. The female replies, slightly less shrill. It can be described as ululating. The four of us go quietly with a red-tinted torch to see if we can trace the source of the calls. It is a perfectly still night, and a crescent moon has risen. Visibility is quite good. After 20 minutes or so of waiting, we finally hear an approaching rustle from the dark wall of bush. It gets louder, coming through the undergrowth towards our clearing. We hold our breaths as not one but *three* little dark shapes emerge, and scuttle into the open, right towards our feet. When they get really close we can see them quite clearly. Ducks.

I laugh aloud, despite myself. But what I don't realise until later is that we have just seen brown teal, another endemic species that is actually even scarcer than (though not as famous as) the kiwi, with only five pairs or so here: a really noteworthy discovery. Captive-bred brown teal were introduced on Kapiti back in 1968.

The others call it a night soon after that, but I am happy to stay outside. I explore in the direction of some other calls, prepared for and familiar with disappointment, having recently spent three fruit-less days searching in the high mountains for rock wrens, so I could do something towards their conservation. I know well now what the 'presence of absence' means, the feeling of looking so hard for something you don't see what *is* there any more, only what isn't. And then I realise that this shape, the one that has materialised on the path in front of me, is a kiwi. Not a duck, or weka, or a rabbit, but a little spotted kiwi. Not quite as the picture in my head depicts it, but nonetheless a kiwi. Bold as brass, in the middle of a grassy, pebbly path just above the boulder beach, within hearing range of the occa-sional lapping wave.

'Hello there,' I may have whispered. I stop where I am and it strides over to me, stretching its neck upwards like a puppet and sniffing audibly – the first time I ever heard a bird sniff – either because I smell (the backpacker's prerogative) or because my torch looks like a glow-worm, which kiwis like to eat. It trots and snuffles off into the longer grass, much as a hedgehog might have done.

Seeing a kiwi was beyond my wildest expectations when I came to New Zealand, and I regaled my cabin mates with the exact details of the encounter well into the small hours. The next day, on our way back to the boat, I reconstructed the event for them. I think they were still paying attention.

Back in Wellington I have gone to meet up with Jeff for an espresso, and to show him some pictures I've had developed. 'ECO TERROR POSSUM PLOT' scream the newsagent billboards and headlines in the *Dominion Post*, Wellington's daily broadsheet. The story has also been on national TV and radio, apparently. All are leading with a story about Kapiti, and anonymous 'terrorist' messages sent to Forest and Bird saying that possums have been smuggled onto Kapiti Island and let loose. Forest and Bird's cam-paign manager Eric Pyle is quoted, and I realise that when I go to meet him this afternoon, as per an earlier arrangement, he is likely to be a little preoccupied.

He honours the arrangement, although he tells me he's never before experienced this level of media interest. We chat about all the issues conservationists face here – intensive dairying, albatrosses and longlining, the struggle against introduced species – between him jumping up to give telephone interviews to Australian journalists and taking calls from hunting organisations anxious to distance themselves from the alleged act of sabotage.

So who would sabotage such an island sanctuary, or even consider doing such a thing? Apparently, some hunting interests who are opposed to conservationists removing 'game' animals that do serious damage to native forest.

We won't know if it's a hoax or not until the Department of Conservation has taken the possum dogs over for a sniff around, which they can't do yet because the wind has picked up today, which prevents sailing. As the story develops, it emerges that the threat extends to other offshore wildlife havens – Stewart Island and Codfish Island. This time stoats are mentioned. And I find myself wondering if someone would really contemplate that if they'd ever been sniffed by moonlight by a little spotted kiwi.

THERE *MIGHT* BE GIANTS

Family business was the perfect excuse for a midwinter visit to Northern Ireland. There was time for a bit of sight-seeing too.

The Giant's Causeway in County Antrim is an extraordinary place. A *quare* place, they might say, locally. And a quare thing happened to me there between Christmas and New Year. I saw a giant.

A friend and I are sitting on a bench high above the foaming bay, wind whipping and wintry sunshine glaring off the waves, people congregating tinily on the causeway way below, their cries and laughter fluctuating on the onshore breeze.

Sitting there you feel you're in a cathedral. The so-called causeway is made of columnar paving slabs of basalt, in a honeycomb pattern, and in places these columns are varyingly tall, like the pipes on a cathedral organ. If you know it, it's hard not to hear Mendelssohn's *Fingal's Cave* booming in your head in symphony with the sound of the elements, the chacking of ticker-tape jackdaw flocks and the polite sneezing of choughs (presumably to draw attention to their specialness) above you.

Fingal's mythical cave is actually some distance away on the tiny isle of Staffa, just off Mull, in Scotland's Inner Hebrides. Any giant would get his troosers wet if he walked to that end of the causeway.

But at this end you are on the north coast of Northern Ireland, in the care of the National Trust. The RSPB's Rathlin Island nature reserve, with its recently imported tonnage of nettle roots for corncrake cover, is just round the corner. Donegal's beautifully-named Inishowen Peninsula lines the horizon to the west.

And so to the quare thing – as if the setting weren't enough in itself. Enter the Giant.

'What's that?' My friend nudges me and points down towards the sea. There's a bit of a stramash going on.

Phases of the following incident will take much longer to write about than they took to occur, so for seconds read split-seconds (but remember that time stretches in your mind when you are excited...).

At first I think we are looking at pigeons skimming in off the sea – one normal one, one large and very white. The first lands on the rocky shoreline, and immediately crashes into a crevice between the wet boulders. The second lands nearby. It sits there for a short while, taking stock, confused, or knackered, or both.

'That looks like a gyrfalcon...' I venture, thinking, Nah, it can't be a gyrfalcon. Perhaps it's just a huge dove. Nah, it can't be a huge dove. No such thing. Perhaps it's a large, albino peregrine. Nah... etc., etc. I think it is while the bird is taking off again, beating along the shoreline below us and then climbing on an updraft along the curve of the causeway, that I realise we *are*, in fact, looking at a gyrfalcon.

It is soon overhead, stout and ivory against the sky. And, as though for reference, a peregrine falcon appears, even higher, and launches a jealous tilt at the glamorous interloper. A brief dogfight ensues. Hyper-real.

And then they are gone. Open-mouthed and giddy, I think there has to be a sobering explanation... It's an escaped bird, perhaps (although I saw its undercarriage and there were clearly no telltale jesses dangling from its legs), or it's about to fly onto its owner's wrist somewhere on the cliff-top. And would anyone believe me anyway?

I report the sighting at the National Trust Visitor Centre. The information person isn't an ornithologist, but I think she can tell something exciting has occurred. Maybe it is because my commentary is slightly falsetto in pitch.

Gyrfalcons come in a range of colours, from snowy white to

chocolatey black. This one was the Greenland race – at the paler end of the spectrum. Gyrs (as you are allowed to call them when familiar) are seen about twice a year in Ireland, and little more often than that in the British Isles as a whole. And we got incredible, close-up views of one. What are the chances of that? No, really. What are the chances of that? Of all the pairs of eyes, in all the bays, in all the stretches of coastline, in all of Ireland, in all of the British Isles... It was a once-in-a-lifetime bird experience. Some birders never get to see one at all. Even Mike Everett, long-serving RSPB spokesman, tells me he's never seen one in 50 years of birdwatching.

I have established that no one is sure how to pronounce 'gyr'. This species is so seldom seen here, and its name so seldom therefore uttered, I suppose, that opinions vary as to how you actually say the name. Gear? Gire? Jur? Jir? Jeer? Jire? Gur? And what does gyr actually mean? Nobody's very sure. Or, if they are sure, they shouldn't be.

In case you hadn't guessed, I have dined out on tales of this adventure, here at The Lodge, and by email with colleagues in Ireland – including some, I heard, who had travelled from as far afield as Cork, on the south coast, just for a glimpse of the arctic vagrant. They didn't get one.

A colleague in Belfast told me the bird, presumably the same one, had been seen at Runkerry earlier in December. Liam McFaul, our man on Rathlin Island, saw it in the first week of January too. The fruitless search by the Cork party took place the weekend after. I heard that Giles Knight, the RSPB's agri-environment project officer in Northern Ireland, was one of their number. I couldn't resist emailing him to ask if he thought my observation noteworthy.

'Noteworthy is right, Conor,' he replied. 'Elusive too. Twenty-five bearded types went to Rathlin on Sunday and didn't see a sausage. I was among the birdy throng for my first ever twitch (I forgot my beard in the rush to catch the ferry). Some boys on the boat were from Cork – a seven-hour drive. Extraordinary. Happy new year. Giles.'

'Don't worry, Giles,' I consoled him. 'It was a brave attempt. If it's any consolation, the views I got were good enough for both of us. Imagine, a bird all the way from Greenland stopping off for a pigeon supper and getting hassle from the local peregrines right in front of me.'

I've always had a reverence for peregrine falcons. Lots of people do. But the gyr is a souped-up, turbo-charged version of the peregrine

– the peregrine on steroids, perhaps. Everyone knows peregrines are fast when hunting, particularly so in a stoop. But they can look stiff and muscle-bound in level flight, more *potentially* explosive than actually so. The gyrfalcon takes this theme to another plane. The one I saw looked laboured on take-off (it might have been entitled to, being a thousand miles or more from Greenland), and it climbed heavily from the base of the cliffs before catching an updraft to engage the peregrine 'buzzing' it – my kind of air show.

I have a lot of sympathy for the twitchers who missed out on this extraordinary bird. But nothing beats finding such a quare thing by chance.

AN AMERICAN GOSHAWK IN VICTORIAN SCOTLAND

It has some of the hallmarks of a Conan Doyle murder mystery, complete with period costume, a shooting, a body, a fairytale Victorian Highland setting, suspects, big city and small town locations, journeys in between, and – for good measure and Hollywood appeal – a strong American angle. In fact, the central character is a 'Yank' in birder parlance – *Accipiter gentilis atricapillus*, to be precise – the fabled northern goshawk.

Plot summary: it is spring 1869. There is unrest in the British Empire – Canada, this time. The finishing touches are being put to the *Cutty Sark* in a Glasgow shipyard. She will be one of the last of the tea clippers built, as the age of sail gives way to the age of steam. The journal *Nature* is also launched, and the *People's Friend*. A gamekeeper called Stewart is patrolling the slopes of Schiehallion – the 'hill of the fairies', some say – in Perthshire. Spying a bird of prey, in the tradition of the day he shoots it dead.

By and by, he gets into conversation with a road-surveyor called Menzies, who relieves the keeper of the bird, which has been crudely gutted. Menzies takes it to the town of Brechin, on the east coast, to a shop owner there called Lyster. Lyster can turn his hand to taxidermy, and sells many things, chief among which are fishing lures, for which red kite feathers are particularly suited. But the skin he is presented with, he can see, is no kite (or gled, as they were then known in Scotland). In any event, he has better things to work with, and puts it aside.

Some time later a man called Gray drops in. He's a keen ornithologist in his spare time, and an inspector of banks by day. It's not in great nick by this time, but he recognises the bird skin as that of a goshawk. He takes ownership of the specimen, and arranges for it to be sent on to Glasgow. There, he has another taxidermist clean, stuff and mount it. Goshawks were by this time rare, even in Scotland. It would be extinct as a breeder in Britain in little more than a decade. Having collected his order from the stuffer, it is only now that Gray realises there is something particularly unusual about this goshawk. It is of the North American race *atricapillus*. This seems to be the first specimen of its kind for Britain. The record is generally accepted. Gray becomes a respected ornithologist and author of books on the subject.

Fast-forwarding a century, and cutting a long story short, this American gos is dropped from the Scottish list. No one seems very sure why. By this time there are several records of American gos in Ireland, and one in England (the Scilly Isles). In each instance the birds were evidently shot, enabling close inspection.

Forwarding again to the present day, the Perthshire record is reviewed once more, and officially rejected. Over at the National Museum of Scotland in Edinburgh, experts are once again peering at the corpse. The identity of the bird is not in dispute, but there is apparently sufficient doubt over its provenance, with the possibility that a different American gos skin was stuffed in Glasgow.

The verdict suggests a general doubt about the American goshawk's ability to cross 3,300 miles of ocean, a doubt which it is easy to share. Even with a hurricane at its tail (there was such a weather event and a major southward movement of gos in the US in the late 1860s) and/or with the help of a boat, believing the gos can achieve this feat assumes a voyage of weeks or even months rather than days, and a diet of seabirds caught on the wing, over the waves, en route – unless Roger the cabin boy had taken pity on the stowaway in the rigging, and was bringing it ship's rations, or rats.

Some ornithologists I've spoken to have shrugged their shoulders at the idea of *atricapillus* being capable of crossing the Atlantic. 'Northern harrier and American kestrel can do it,' they'll say. But this is to equate the talents of Mo Farah with those of Usain Bolt. The gos, we know, is a bird that will spend most of an average day loafing, waiting for prey to come within ambush range. A sprinter, not a distance runner. They are three times as heavy as harriers. We know they can cross the North Sea, but show a peculiar reluctance to do so, if the low number of records for Shetland, the oil rigs and the east coast are anything to go by (there has been one Scand-inavian ring recovered from a goshawk here, ever: a Norwegian bird that turned up in Lincolnshire).

But is it any more feasible that a Victorian trader would import such a specimen, and not label or market it for maximum value as an exotic? That it would be so casually or carelessly switched by a professional taxidermist for no apparent additional fee?

In the end, we can only speculate. Despite some of the finest minds having been trained on it, the Perthshire goshawk saga will probably remain one of the great unsolved mysteries of ornithology, and just one of the many riddles surrounding the enigmatic, spectral, much-studied (abroad) yet barely understood and often overlooked northern goshawk.[6]

THE POSTMODERN BIRD

There's a common or garden bird that lives among us, pretty much everywhere in Britain. It's not the first garden bird that comes to mind. It's not even the fifth bird that comes to mind. Trust me: I've done a straw poll. I asked 30 people to name five garden birds, and only one person included this species.

It's as though this bird is so close to us we don't really see it. Or we don't take it seriously as a wild bird. Or maybe it's too plain. Too unassuming. It is a bit like the shy, awkward kid in the play-ground: doesn't quite fit in, somehow. Not one of the boys, or girls. Self-conscious. Gauche. Wearing the wrong uniform. I wonder if it is somehow apparent that it's the new kid in town.

It may also be that we think of it as semi-feral, perhaps, or even semi-domestic. But it is neither of these things. It is definitely urban, when it wants to be. And modern. Postmodern, even. Another clue, if you need it: this bird is the colour of a classical temple, and also the colour of inner-city concrete. It is a bit conspicuous on a lawn.

It actually hasn't been with us very long at all. Perhaps that's the issue, whether we are conscious of it or not. It doesn't feature in bird

---

6   The Irish goshawk records are also currently under review. The fact that two of the Irish records occurred within days of each other (both birds shot), and within weeks of the Perthshire goshawk, merely adds further intrigue to the overall tale.

lore. We haven't inherited tales about it, or images. Few people photograph it, or publish photographs of it. John Clare did not know this bird. I had this thought while visiting his cottage recently, and two of these birds landed on the thatched roof. I almost didn't register them. But the poet would have been amazed, and moved to verse, I am sure.

Its mild-mannered demeanour belies at least one truly remarkable fact about this bird. In a world in which we have become wearily accustomed to reports of wildlife in retreat, this species has bucked the overall trend. In the post-war period through which so many other birds' ranges have receded, this bird decided it was going to colonise an entire sub-continent: Western Europe.

In the 1930s, to find the nearest of these birds you would have had to travel to Turkey or the Balkans. By 1955, it had spread west and was poised to cross the English Channel, and begin its colonisation of the British Isles. The first of them nested at Cromer, in Norfolk, where enthusiasts were waiting to greet the avian expeditionary force. I know people who travelled quite a way just to be there, odd as that now seems today.

Since then, it has moved into almost all our lives: our farms, villages, towns, cities and open, rural landscapes. But it has perhaps not yet moved fully into our imaginations. I was watching a pair of them recently, closely, in case I was missing something. As I watched, they mated. Nothing too odd in that, until you consider it was Christmas Day: a wintry one at that, in the middle of our hardest winter for many years. There is some clue here to the secret of their success, perhaps. In late October, a pair had attempted to nest on our bedroom windowsill, under the gutter. They failed, sadly: two bristly dough-ball squabs succumbing to a northerly gale. Another pair built a nest in spring on the wires that radiate from a telegraph pole above our street. They failed too. And I watched a pair building their nest in early February on a satellite dish, above the pavement and a busy road in central Sandy. They may have had more luck.

I was reminded of the nest I found while climbing a tree near the railway station in my home town, 30 years ago. It was built entirely out of wires, neatly bent into a shallow saucer. It was a fittingly post-industrial installation close to a scrapyard and derelict foundry.

A picture starts to build of a twenty-first-century species. It appears to have torn up the rule book on annual breeding cycles (one pair has been recorded nesting up to nine times in a year) and ecological niches. It is just getting on with the business of reproducing and making the best of our postmodern world (it was barely here for modernism). A bit like us, perhaps; which is no reason for ignoring it.

I got very close to one recently, as I walked home in the dwindling light of dusk. It was crouching quietly, against a wall. Kneeling to look more closely, I was disturbed to discover it was weeping a thick tear of vivid, crimson blood. It appeared otherwise unharmed, but its appearance was ominous, ghoulish, even. I would guess it had collided with a car. I reached out to pick it up, in a plastic bag, expecting little resistance. As my hands approached it suddenly exploded into life, shooting upwards, brushing past my face as it beat off, and out of sight. The incident was perhaps fitting for this enigmatic bird, its outward passivity belying an underlying vigour and tenacity.

Given the rate at which many bird populations are unravelling, you wouldn't bet against the collared dove being among our last wild bird companions in this life. So maybe it's time we appreciated it a bit more for the way it has adapted in response to a rapidly changing world. And for its own sake. Let's hope it is here to stay.

AWAY WITH THE FAIRIES

These are two extracts adapted from the web diary I kept during a year working for conservation in the Seychelles. The first is a real-life fairy tale with an unexpected ending.

As a conservationist, I'm not, as a rule, in the business of raising orphaned birds. Saving a planet on finite resources, and with limited time, it isn't sensible. Quite apart from the sustainability issues. Baby birds tend not to be 'just for Christmas'. But I recently found myself forced to make an exception.

I'm working in the Seychelles for a year (well, someone has to) as part of the RSPB's international programme to 'build capacity' in our partner non-governmental organisations (NGOs) in BirdLife International. Helping them to fly, and keep flying, you might call it. There's a boy at the door of the office. From my desk I can see he has a bird perched on his finger. He comes in and I can see he's got a fairy tern. 'I found this by the beach at Baie Lazare,' he explains.

Fairy terns are, by any standards, bewitching birds, light as paper in the blue sea air, translucent in sunlight, glowing like angels in the clear tropical light. You may be familiar with the species, if not from direct experience then from the media. If, like William Blake, you fancy you can see heaven in a wild flower, you will also see it in these birds, the angel pose adding to the effect.

Conversely, they are indolent when at rest. It amuses me that they don't build a nest. Why bother? It's hot. They take tropical torpor to its logical extreme, simply laying their single egg directly on a branch, or similar. You have to admire the economy of this approach. The fairy tern (or *Golan blan*, in Creole) is so laid back and approachable on seabird islands, like Cousin Island, managed by Nature Seychelles and free of rats and other dangers. But the species' low-input nesting strategy sometimes ends in tragedy. The one in front of me has now been abandoned by its parents, having fallen from its perch.

It is intact, and maybe a week old. I know from experience that adopting birds in this sort of situation usually ends in disappointment. Only a few days ago a lost hobby was brought to us from a tuna boat, on which it had flopped, exhausted, somewhere out on the Indian Ocean. Despite my efforts to save it, it died after a day or so. But I decide to give the tern a go. I'll try feeding it sushi and maybe it will get airborne and independent. Provided of course it wants to eat. At least it doesn't appear stressed.

At my house Dylan (as I've called him/her) eats greedily between naps. He looks the part, perched on our BirdLife International telescope. The logo of BirdLife is a tern, maybe an arctic tern, a related species that circumnavigates the globe on migration, and symbolises the boundlessness of wild birds.

Dylan takes to his new home in an old chicken coop in the blink of an inky eye. Not that he'd ever do anything as energetic as try to escape. Within a week he has lost his dumpy, downy look and grown into a sleek, streamlined and slightly irritable adolescent. This is a good thing all round, as he happily eats the raw fish I offer with tweezers, but appears not too attached to me. When it is time for him to leave, I figure, he is unlikely to go and land on the nearest human being. I am hoping he will fall in with some adult tern company.

Mid-month. The time comes for Dylan to graduate to the halfway house of the porch. He sits nonchalantly on his perch, occasionally shuffling along it to demonstrate his independence, occasionally exercising his wings or preening, between siestas.

A week or so on, one Sunday morning Dylan launches forth. He lands on the lawn. Pongo, our adoptive dog, goes to have a closer look. Dylan moves to the guttering. Rejecting my advances with more fish, and enjoying this new 'flying around' thing, he moves on to the television aerial for the afternoon. Later, I am able to provide him with supper by attaching the tweezers to the end of a home-made bargepole, fashioned from an invasive sapling. He dozes off up there, in a halo of moonlight.

After work, Dylan is awaiting the bargepole treatment. I don't know what this looks like to the neighbours, come feeding time, but if anyone asks I may tell them it's a hygiene measure.

Days pass. He appears quite blasé. I'm wondering if he'll ever find the inclination to fly off, as long as these morsels of bonito fish keep appearing on the end of the pole. Sitting pretty, like a weather vane, he can survey half of the Indian Ocean from up there but is still not showing much interest in exploring it.

Saturday morning, late in December 2005. While we are break-fasting on the porch a fairy tern flies over, heading ocean-ward. Surely it can't be Dylan. I try to keep my eye on the dwindling shape while making my way outside to check the TV aerial. No Dylan there. Hurray!

Dylan's maiden flight makes a mockery of his earlier torpor, as he spirals high into the sky, disappearing against a pile of cloud, then reappearing against the blue, until he is finally out of sight. This is a great feeling. I have a hint of what an early aviator might have felt like when an early prototype contraption took off, and stayed up. I watch the bird circling high overhead, imagining I have some little control box in my hand that can ease him down to the tern pad. But this of course he does of his own accord, in his own sweet time, as they say here. He comes shimmying and shivering his wings, dropping a few dozen feet at a time, and then taxiing in to land on half-folded wings, back on the aerial.

December arrives. I get home and Dylan won't feed. He shuns the tweezer pole, flies off and does a few laps of the sky. My neigh-bour reports that he's been missing for most of the day. I wonder if maybe, just maybe, he's been out fishing.

The next day, there is no sign of Dylan at dawn. Not on the tele-graph pole, nor the aerial. And then… now, you're going to think maybe I've been watching too many Disney films when I tell you what happens next. Dylan appears from the sky. And there are two of him. Synchronised flying.

'Dylan's back, with company!' I shout to Lynn, and she leaves her laptop to come and witness the event. Dylan hovers over the aerial, but his partner seems not at all convinced of the wisdom of this. So they dance off along the forested slopes of Beau Vallon, to explore other options.

I realise the cynics among you may be thinking, You don't fool us, Conor. We bet that Pongo ate the tern on day 3. Whatever. Let's hope Dylan's companion has shown him how to fish and they've found their way to Cousin Island, an altogether much more sensible place for fairy terns to settle down. If you ever make it there, you'll be helping them all – birds and bird-saving people – to fly, and to keep flying.

CASTAWAY

I've washed up on a desert island, dropped here in a boat, on a carefully-chosen breaker. The island is two miles across, a kinked hoop of bleached sand separating ocean from forest. It's part of an archipelago, a thousand miles from India and from Africa. A wavelet of ghost crabs parts as I make my way across hot sand to the top of the beach.

Seychelles. The very word conjures instant images of purity, as though it were selected for its echo of sea breeze, shell-sand, surf. In fact, 'Seychelles' was a sailor. It is perhaps fortunate that Captain Pugwash didn't get here first.

I reach the trees and find that none are the palms of myth. The one-time coconut plantation has been replaced by native species like *Pisonia*, and the birds that long depended on this tropical island are now restored to them too. Welcome to Cousin Island.

This is my chance to see beyond the colour-supplement image of paradise. What these can't show is the slow-cooker, sometimes stewing, mind-melting heat and humidity of the tropics. Onshore breezes bring scant relief. The air is even thicker amid the greenish tints of the forest interior. The aroma is physical, taste-able, like a pet shop: part-sweat, part-dung, part-pheromone. The sounds are like those of a pet shop too, oscillating at the edge of my vision. The ground around my sandals converges, as hermit crabs and skinks tiptoe and sashay towards me.

A giant tortoise staggers forward, a living link between geology and biology: an animate boulder, time-smoothed, sun-dried lump of the granite mountain top beneath us, with sprouted tanned leather neck and limb. It peers weepily, mouthing noiselessly, like the toothless, mummified ghost of the succession of human forms it has encountered here in the last couple of centuries: navigators, pirates, castaways, smugglers, plantation workers, conservation volunteers, ecotourists... While the tortoise moves in slow motion, the nesting fairy terns and tropicbirds just look knackered.

I stumble on a scattered party of turnstones poking around in the flaky leaf-litter – the very same scurrying, plover-like birds that feed and breed on the brutal, rugged coastlines of north-west Europe. Who knew? It's like I've rumbled them, on a crafty holiday, on the skive. I'll bet they haven't turned a stone since they got here.

I meet the fabled magpie-robin, the nearly-dodo, one of the great success stories of conservation, of extinction averted. It's a species that was reduced to almost single figures on just one island in the Seychelles. A few were moved here, the restored Cousin Island, and have thrived. Restoration also involved the removal of anything mammalian – rats and cats, mainly – against which these docile, trusting natives have no chance.

Like its fellow islanders, *Pi santez* – as it's known in Creole – comes to check me out. Perched here in black and white, it is all too easy to imagine it as a museum exhibit, in this dingy, stuffy archive of a place. But then life ignites: the robin angles its head, riffles its tail, and arrows down to my feet, snatches an insect, then back to its perch.

But the best, most Alice-in-Wonderland moment, is yet to come. I step over a tree trunk and an animal – by this I mean a hairy animal – bolts from under me and slaloms off through the trees. What the...? It's the only furred, fast and running-away thing I've encountered. Surely not a rat? Not that big? That would be a disastrous development. No, if I had to stick my neck out on this, I'd say it was, of all things, a hare.

I replay the befuddling image of the streaking beast in my head as I walk back to the volunteer hut. I wonder whether I should even mention this to anyone. They might think I've got the fever, the *grippe*. I can just hear them. 'You think you saw a *hare*? On a *desert island*?'

Choosing my moment, I have a quiet word with Catherina, who leads ecotours. 'Ah yes!' she laughs. 'There are some castaway hares still out there. We don't talk much about them. You were lucky – not many people have ever seen one!'

Alice in Wonderland did say that, of all her tea party guests, 'The March hare will be much the most interesting. And perhaps, as this is May, it won't be raving mad – at least, not so mad as it was in March...' Or as mad I might add – as it looks in paradise. Hares, I learn, were imported decades ago as a source of food for plantation workers.

I still smile to recall that Robinson Crusoe hare. You'd think by now, in paradise restored, it might have learned to relax a little.

SEASONS TO BE CHEERFUL

If you think about it, the seasonality of our planet is astonishing. To give a sense of how much this is so, I've borrowed from the writings of celebrated Victorian novelist and historian H.G. Wells. 'If we represent our Earth as a little ball of one-inch diameter,' H.G. proposed, 'the sun would be a big globe nine feet across and 323 yards away; that is, about a fifth of a mile, four or five minutes' walking.' Wow. 'The moon,' he added, 'would be a small pea two feet and a half feet from the world.'

So Earth is like a golf ball, spinning and tilting slowly on an unvarying yearly elliptical orbit around a burning ball roughly the size of a haystack, nearly 300 metres away, while the small pea orbits us. If you can get your head around that, then the overall precision and variety of our seasons, year in, year out, around the golf ball – I mean globe – are mind-boggling.

It is intriguing too that our seasons in the UK are generally so consistent and, if not exactly the same each year, at least consistently different to the seasons felt and experienced just a short distance away in continental Europe, or in Africa, say. They are different, too, if you go just a few hundred feet uphill, or a few tens of miles closer to the coast.

It seems reasonable to call on H.G. Wells' 'smaller yet bigger picture' because many of our birds seem to do that, as do lots of other creatures that make light of planetary distance, and treat the globe as their home, and the galaxy as their satnav.

Each year, the Earth 'breathes in' from the autumn equinox to the spring equinox and 'breathes out' from the spring to the autumn. Time-lapsed footage of this really does make the planet look as though it is breathing. Imagine, then, the world's birds moving in response to that inhalation; that sheet of ice, snow and cold air easing them south in autumn, and drawing them back north again in the spring – at an estimated five miles per hour – as it retreats.

Here in the UK we look forward to and take heart from sighting the first swallow of summer, and the first cuckoo, although we fear for the future of the latter. But how much do our friends in Africa celebrate them on their return journey?

'The arrival of small birds like swallows is hardly noticed by local people,' Dr Chipangura Chirara of BirdLife Zimbabwe told me. 'Mainly because we have resident birds in the same group, and so there are identification challenges.'

As you might expect, other birds have more seasonal and cultural significance in Zimbabwe, and other African countries. Dr Chirara explained:

> One group of birds that is used to mark the beginning of our summer is the storks – the white stork and the Abdim's stork. The local Shona people have one name for both birds – Shuramurove, literally meaning 'omen for rain'. Normally farmers start preparing their fields once the storks arrive. Where I grew up, on my father's farm, we were not allowed to chase the birds from the field as it was feared this would 'chase the rain away'.

The RSPB and others are now carrying out more urgent research in central Africa to find more of these migrants of European birth. Whinchats, nightingales, spotted flycatchers and wheatears are all in decline. We are trying to understand why this is so. How much of the problem lies at each end of their north–south world? Are illegal trapping, netting and shooting factors that they must navigate along the way?

It's been fascinating to ask people about their favourite seasons and seasonal highlights. I'd call myself a spring person, if pushed. But I am learning to love winter. A few things have helped me in this, not least taking a global perspective on seasonality. I lived and worked in the tropics for a while. I missed our seasons in fundamental ways, although I loved the experience of a different annual cycle, and enjoyed experiencing the world from a different angle.

A northern winter has much to cherish. Without it, there would be no fieldfares and redwings arriving in squadrons from Scandinavia, no geese from Greenland descending on our western shores, nor whooper swans arriving on our eastern fields, magically, overnight. There would be many fewer robins and blackbirds visiting our back gardens to see what we've got for them in our temperate, ocean-insulated island group. I've even learned to love rain. I've lived in western Scotland: eastern England can feel semi-arid by comparison, which in fact it often is.

I especially like frozen rain. One of the highlights of my year was the sudden duvet of snow laid upon us one dark December night. I can barely recall ever having serious snow before Christmas in the lowlands of the UK, and waking up to blue skies and a foot of pristine, sparkling snow, and yomping to work through it, was a day that glitters in my memory. I sensed Mother Earth gently reasserting her power, and her beauty; dazzling us with ice-crystal jewels, both to disrupt our comfort zones (and certainly our reliance on road transport) and any complacency we might have about who, ultimately, is in charge round here.

It was a resounding restatement of Nature's capacity to surprise, to send us a serious winter day in an age when climate change has neutralised so many of our recent winters. Days like these are so rare that when they come they are *de facto* national holidays, giving children and families an unexpected chance to embrace the outdoors. It's hard to believe that an average school day offers so much formative benefit. Perhaps we should think of snow days as a chance to celebrate the Earth, the weather, the season, again.

Without a proper winter, there can be no magical days like this, and perhaps no proper spring. I'm taking the long view here. If it's not currently your favourite season, wait a while. It'll be along soon enough, and with any luck its birds – and maybe its butterflies too – will be with it, or ahead of it.

POSTSCRIPT

Finally, to quote Henry David Thoreau, I hope that with this compilation of 'Nature File' journal entries I have conveyed some sense of 'where I lived, and what I lived for'.

And, if I may borrow once again from Mr J. Steele-Elliott, 'let me hope that in making these notes public they may promote a further interest in the study of Natural History within the county [and beyond], and if possible to kindle the flame of such knowledge...'.

A century ago the finiteness and fragility of nature were only just beginning to dawn on us. A combination of that pioneering knowledge, concerted conservation action, clean technologies and individual action will ensure that a hundred years from now there will still be much to celebrate and inspire in this extraordinary world of ours.

Sing the new year in under the blue.
Last year you sang it as gladly.
'New, new, new, new'! Is it then so new
That you should carol so madly?

Alfred, Lord Tennyson, *The Throstle*

Organisations mentioned in this book

Audubon Society (www.audubon.org)
The Audubon Society's mission is to conserve and restore natural ecosystems for the benefit of humanity and biological diversity.

BBC Natural History Unit (www.bbc.co.uk)
The department of the BBC which produces television, radio and online content with a natural history or wildlife theme.

Bedfordshire Natural History Society (www.bnhs.co.uk)
The BNHS's main function to record the fauna and flora of Bedfordshire, to help, encourage and support those with an interest in wildlife.

BirdLife Cyprus (www.birdlifecyprus.org)
Works to conserve wild birds, their habitats and wider biodiversity in Cyprus, through research, monitoring, lobbying, conservation and awareness-raising actions.

BirdLife International (www.birdlife.org)
The world's largest nature conservation partnership, with over 120 partners world-wide – one per country – and growing.

BirdLife Zimbabwe (www.birdlifezimbabwe.org)
To promote the survival of birdlife in Zimbabwe and elsewhere for its intrinsic value and the enjoyment of future generations.

British Birds (www.britishbirds.co.uk)
The journal of record, in print and online.

British Trust for Ornithology (www.bto.org)
An independent charitable research institute combining professional and citizen science to inform the public and decision-makers.

Centre for Ecology and Hydrology (www.ceh.ac.uk)
UK centre of excellence for integrated research in terrestrial and freshwater eco-systems and their interaction with the atmosphere.

Earthwatch (http://eu.earthwatch.org/)
People from around the world take part in expeditions, protecting species and habitats.

Forest and Bird (www.forestandbird.org.nz)
Works to preserve New Zealand's natural heritage and native species.

Organisations mentioned in this book

Gulbenkian Foundation (www.gulbenkian.org.uk)
An international charitable foundation with cultural, educational, social and scientific interests, based in Lisbon with offices in London and Paris.

Joint Nature Conservation Committee (www.jncc.defra.gov.uk)
The public body that advises UK government and devolved administrations on UK-wide and international nature conservation.

Lega Italiana Protezione Uccelli (www.lipu.it)
BirdLife International partner in Italy. Associazione per la conservazione e la tutela della natura.

Ligue pour le Protection des Oiseaux (www.lpo.fr)
BirdLife International partner in France. Est aujourd'hui l'une des premières associations de protection de la nature en *France*.

Mammal Society (www.mammal.org.uk)
A charity advocating science-led mammal conservation, leading efforts to collect and share information on mammals.

National Trust (www.nationaltrust.org.uk)
Protects historic places and green spaces, and opens them up for ever, for everyone.

National Trust for Scotland (www.nts.org.uk)
Cares for Scotland's heritage.

Nature Seychelles (www.natureseychelles.org)
Nature Seychelles is an independent environmental NGO involved in a wide range of conservation activities.

New Zealand Department of Conservation (www.doc.govt.nz)
Protects natural and historic heritage.

Royal Society for the Prevention of Cruelty to Animals (www.rspca.org.uk)
The UK animal welfare charity that specialises in rescue, animal welfare and preventing animal cruelty.

RSPB (www.rspb.org.uk)
Saves nature in the UK and abroad through practical conservation, working with others, education and campaigning.

The Rufford Foundation (www.rufford.org)
A UK-based charity that gives grants for nature conservation.

The Tubney Charitable Trust (www.tubney.org.uk)
A former UK-based charity that gave grants for nature conservation and other causes.

Vincent Wildlife Trust (www.vwt.org.uk)
An independently funded charity that carries out pioneering research, undertakes surveys to assess how well our mammals are doing, and offers expert advice.

Vulture Conservation Foundation (www.4vultures.org)
Is committed to the conservation, restoration and protection of vultures in their natural habitats throughout Europe.

Bibliography

Avery, M. and Leslie, R. (1990) *Birds and Forestry*. Poyser, London.

Baker, J.A. (1967) *The Peregrine*. New York Review Books, New York.

Bannerman, D. A. (1953–1963) *The Birds of the British Isles*. Oliver and Boyd, Edinburgh.

Bate, J. (2003) *John Clare – A Biography*. Picador, London.

Baxter, E. V. and Rintoul, L. J. (1953) *The Birds of Scotland*. Oliver and Boyd, Edinburgh.

Birkhead, T. (2012) *Bird Sense*. Bloomsbury, London.

Brown, L. (1976) *British Birds of Prey*. Collins New Naturalist Series, London.

Cairns, P. and Hamblin, M. (2007) *Tooth and Claw – Living Alongside Britain's Predators*. Whittles Publishing, Dunbeath.

Carson, R. (1962) *Silent Spring*. Houghton Mifflin, Cambridge, MA.

Chinery, M. (1977) *The Natural History of the Garden*. Collins, London.

Cocker, M. and Fanshawe, J. (eds) (2011) *The Peregrine, The Hill of Summer & Diaries: The Complete Works of J. A. Baker*. Collins, London.

Cocker, M. and Mabey, R. (2005) *Birds Britannica*. Chatto & Windus, London.

Cotter, G. (1988) *Natural History Verse – An Anthology*. Christopher Helm, London.

Crofts, R. and Boyd, I. (eds) (2005) *Conserving Nature: Scotland and the Wider World*. John Donald, Edinburgh.

Crossland, J. R. and Parrish, J. M. (eds) (1934) *Britain's Wonderland of Nature*. Odhams Press Ltd, London.

D'Arcy, G. (1999) *Ireland's Lost Birds*. Four Courts Press, Dublin.

Dazley, R. A. and Trodd, P. (1994) *The Breeding Birds of Bedfordshire 1988–92*. Bedfordshire Natural History Society, Bedford.

Dick, D. (2012) *Wildlife Crime*. Whittles, Dunbeath.

Dutt, W.A. (1906) *Wild Life in East Anglia*. Methuen, London.

Elphick, J. (2014) *Birds – the Art of Ornithology*. Natural History Museum, London.

Gardiner, L. (1923) *Rare, Vanishing and Lost Birds* – Compiled from Notes by W.H. Hudson, J.M. Dent & Sons Ltd, London.

Gibbons, D.W., Reid, J.B., Chapman, R.A. (1993) *The New Atlas of Breeding Birds in Britain and Ireland: 1988–91*. T. & A.D. Poyser.

Flegg, J. (1981) *A Notebook of Birds, 1907–1980*. Macmillan, London.

Foulds, A. (2009) *The Quickening Maze*. Jonathan Cape, London.

Gibson, G. (2005) *The Bedside Book of Birds*. Bloomsbury, London.

Greenoak, F.G. (1979) *All the Birds of the Air*. Andre Deutsch, London.

Griffiths, J. (2008) *Wild – An Elemental Journey*. Penguin, London.

Hart-Davis, D. (2002) *Fauna Britannica*. Angus Books Ltd, London.

Bibliography

Hinde, T. (1985) *Forests of Britain*. Victor Gollancz, London.

Hines, B. (1968) *A Kestrel for a Knave*. Penguin, London.

Hudson, W.H. (1915) *Birds and Man*. Duckworth & Co, London.

Hudson, W.H. (1919) *The Book of a Naturalist*. Hodder & Stoughton, London.

Hudson, W.H. (1924) *Birds in London*. J.M. Dent & Sons Ltd, London.

Hudson, W.H. (1927) *The Illustrated Shepherd's Life*. Guild Publishing, London.

Jones, G.L. and Mabey, R. (1993) *The Wildwood*. Aurum Press, London.

Kenward, R. (2005) *The Goshawk*. T. & A.D. Poyser, London.

Leopold, A. (1968) *A Sand County Almanac, and Sketches Here and There*. Oxford University Press, Oxford.

Lever, C. (2005) *The Naturalised Birds of the World*. T. & A.D. Poyser, London.

Lever, C. (2009) *The Naturalised Animals of Britain*. New Holland, London.

Lever, C. (2013) *The Mandarin Duck*. T. & A.D. Poyser, London.

Lovegrove, R. (2007) *Silent Fields: The Long Decline of a Nation's Wildlife*. Oxford University Press, Oxford.

Mabey, R. (1996) *Flora Britannica*. Chatto & Windus, London.

Mabey, R. (2010) *Weeds*. Profile, London.

Maclean, M. (2006) *Hedges and Hedgelaying*. The Crowood Press, Marlborough.

Martin, F. (2008) *The Life of John Clare*. Tutis Digital Publishing Private Ltd.

McKelvie, C. (1994) *Beloved Land – A Richard Jefferies Anthology*. Swan Hill Press, Shrewsbury.

Newton, I. (1986) *The Sparrowhawk*. T. & A.D. Poyser, London.

Newton, I. (2010) *Population Ecology of Raptors*. T. & A.D. Poyser, London.

Nicholson, E.M. (1926) *Birds in England*. Chapman & Hall, London.

Nicholson, E.M. (1927) *How Birds Live*. Williams & Norgate Ltd, London.

Orton, D.A. (1989) *The Hawkwatcher*. Collins, London.

Parker, R. (1976) *The Common Stream*. Paladin, London.

Parkin, D.T. and Knox, A.G. (2010) *The Status of Birds in Britain and Ireland*. Christopher Helm, London.

Petersen, R., Mountfort, G. and Hollom, P.A.D. (1965) *A Field Guide to the Birds of Britain and Europe*. Collins, London.

Rackham, O. (1993) *The History of the Countryside*. J.M. Dent, London.

Rackham, O. (2004) *Trees and Woodland in the British Landscape*. Phoenix, London.

Samstag, T. (1988) *For the Love of Birds – The Story of the RSPB*. RSPB, Bedfordshire, England.

Sharrock, J.T.R. (1976) *The Atlas of Breeding Birds in Britain and Ireland*. BTO/IWC, Tring, Great Britain.

Smout, T.C. (ed.) (2000) *Nature, Landscape and People Since the Second World War*. Tuckwell Press, East Linton.

Spindler, K. (1993) *The Man in the Ice*. Weidenfeld & Nicolson, London.

Steele-Elliot, J. (1901) *The Vertebrate Fauna of Bedfordshire*. Printed for private circulation, Birmingham.

Summerfield, G. (ed.) (2000) *John Clare – Selected Poems*. Penguin, London.

Taylor, M. (2010) *RSPB British Birds of Prey*. Christopher Helm, London.

Ussher, R.J. and Warren, R. (1900) *The Birds of Ireland*. Gurney and Jackson, London.

White, T.H. (1951) *The Goshawk*. New York Review Books, New York.

Wilkinson, G. (1979) *Epitaph for the Elm*. Arrow Books, London.

Winn, M. (1999) *Red-tails in Love*. Pantheon, New York.

Yalden, D. and Albarella, U. (2009) *The History of British Birds*. Oxford University Press, Oxford.

Index

Index

Index

Index

Index

Index